LOOKING *into* LANGUAGE

CLASSROOM APPROACHES TO KNOWLEDGE ABOUT LANGUAGE

LOOKING *into* LANGUAGE

CLASSROOM APPROACHES TO KNOWLEDGE ABOUT LANGUAGE

EDITED BY

Richard Bain
Bernadette Fitzgerald
and Mike Taylor

Hodder & Stoughton
LONDON   SYDNEY   AUCKLAND

British Library Cataloguing in Publication Data

Bain, Richard
  Looking into language.
  I. Title   II. Fitzgerald, Bernadette
  III. Taylor, Mike
  420.7

  ISBN 0-340-57326-0

First published 1992
Second impression 1992

Typeset by Multiplex Techniques Ltd, Orpington.
Printed in Great Britain for the educational publishing division of Hodder & Stoughton Ltd, Mill Road, Dunton Green, Sevenoaks, Kent by Clays Ltd, St Ives plc.

Contributors

'Knowledge about language in an infant classroom' © Pat Baldry 1992. 'Knowledge about language through literature' © Karen Hill 1992. '"You taught me language": language and power in *The Tempest*' © Kate Hirom 1992. 'Changes in English since the time of the Plague' © Deborah Shepherd 1992. 'Using books to develop children's knowledge about language' © Lorraine Dawes 1992. 'Language in the environment' © Ros Bartlett and Diana Fogg 1992. 'Language and gender' © Jacqueline Barnfield 1992. 'The Dazzler's Dictionary' © Alison Sealey 1992. 'Language acquisition' © Paula Hearle 1992. 'Talk words' © Nora Prince and George Keith 1992. 'Exploring register through role play' © Mary Fowler 1992. 'Drama and knowledge about language' © Carole Bingham 1992. 'Watch with mother, or view with Mum?' © Frances Smith 1992. 'Writing newspaper stories' © Liz Slater 1992. 'The language of argument in the writing of young children' © Jenny Monk 1992. 'Writing recipes' © Gill Clarkson and Hazel Stansfield 1992. 'Writing stories for a younger audience' © Gill Clarkson and Julie Young 1992. 'Dr Xargle's guide to Earthlet knowledge about language' © Holly Anderson 1992. 'The Newham Press' © Lynn Newton 1992. 'Karen's poems' © Peter Nightingale 1992. 'Written and spoken versions of the same situation' © Elaine Hines 1992. 'Getting the message across' © Kim Wilkinson 1992. 'Differentiation in the knowledge about language curriculum' © Nigel Kent 1992. 'Children describe their own experience as language users' © Carolyn Boyd 1992. 'Home and away' © Gaik See Chew 1992. 'The two worlds of language' © Shabanah Waheed 1992. 'Many voices' © Angela Jensen 1992. 'Researching accent and dialect' © Kate Parkes 1992. 'The language of Miguel Street' © Linda Croft 1992. 'Primary Planning 1' © Marilyn Cain 1992. 'Primary Planning 2' © Nick Jefferson. 'Primary Planning 3' © Jim Crinson and Tom Noble 1992. 'Secondary Planning 1' © Jim Porteous 1992. 'Secondary Planning 2' © Nigel Kent 1992. 'Secondary Planning 3' © Nick Batchelar 1992. 'A whole school issue' © Margaret Cook 1992.

Acknowledgements

The Publishers would like to thank the following for permission to reproduce material in this volume:

Tressell Publications for the plague statistics on page 35, taken from *Contemporary Accounts of the Great Plague* by G. A. Alton; Jeanne Willis for the letter included on page 126; Young Lions and the Collins Publishing Group for the illustration from *Ging Gang Goolie, It's An Alien* by Bob Wilson which appears on page 176.

Contents

Foreword

This is a collection of classroom evidence which illustrates the many different ways in which teachers are encouraging the development of children's knowledge about language across the curriculum and across the age range 5–16. The examples and case studies included here are a small but representative proportion of the activity and endeavour which has found a focus through the Language in the National Curriculum (LINC) project. Most schools in England and Wales have had close association with the LINC project since it began in 1989, through attendance at INSET sessions, through a wide network of national and regional professional resources, newsletters and journals, or through action research projects in which they have reflected upon this aspect of their classroom practice in English.

The whole domain of knowledge about language has not been extensively considered by teachers until the last three years, and there is necessarily still much to be learned. Editorial constraints have restricted the range and number of examples which are included in this volume. The examples should be read, however, against a background of innovative practice, planning and reflection involving literally thousands of teachers. They are also to be read as an acknowledgement of the huge amount of time, energy and goodwill which teachers have invested in their endeavour to foster children's understandings about language within the framework of the National Curriculum.

The book is organised in order to provide more than an illustration of knowledge about language in classrooms. The case studies are related to a broader set of possible contexts and activities, and there are also guidelines for planning and teaching the curriculum in this area. In this sense, it is hoped that the book will act both as a practical handbook for individual teachers, schools and departments and as an exemplification of good practice.

The LINC project has embraced the preparation of materials for practising teachers, the integration of linguistics with theories of language learning and the development of good INSET practice. These developments have been significant, but all associated with the project believe that the heart of LINC is in the classroom and that this book represents a natural culmination of the project's work.

Professor Ronald Carter
Professor of Modern English Language
Department of English Studies
University of Nottingham
National Coordinator of the LINC project 1989–1992.

Introduction

We begin this book with a brief glimpse into four classrooms. In the first, in Essex, a small group of primary children are gathered with their teacher around the draft of a book they are composing. It is a book about hamsters written in the same idiom as Jeanne Willis's *Dr Xargle* books and they are busily refining the text.

Pupil 1	(reading from the text) They live in cages.
Pupil 2	He's put 'prisons'.
Teacher	So we've already chosen a word to represent cage, haven't we?
Pupil 3	We could have 'live', sort of...'they live in'.
Pupil 1	No I don't think...I don't think we'd better change too many...words...like if we go around changing words like 'live'...
Pupil 2	They won't know what it means.
Pupil 1	They won't be able to understand it because we can't show 'lives' in the pictures.
Teacher	Right, do you want to use 'they', though? Do you want to use the pronoun 'they'?
Pupil 3	Umm...Why don't you just put 'the Nibblers'?
Pupil 1	No, 'they'.
Pupil 2	I've got four 'theys'.
Pupil 3	Yeah. 'Nibblers', that's what I'd use.

In another classroom, in Birmingham, children of a similar age have been making dictionaries of some of the words from their own street language. In their search for authenticity they have discovered what abbreviations such as *n* and *vt* in dictionaries mean. As one girl puts it:

You just look at them and you think, 'Ooh what does that mean?' And now we know — like, nouns, Miss, and things like that...you need to know things like parts of speech and the way things are set out...we looked up 'batter' and that just had 'batter' and not 'battered'...you need to know all that to make your dictionary look proper, Miss.

Meanwhile, in Bradford, a secondary class of Asian girls has prepared paired interpretative readings of Edwin Morgan's poem 'The First Men on Mercury'. In the readings the students have explored the role of gestures, body language and intonation, and have speculated about the switch in power relations that occurs half way through the poem. Some of the students have made an instinctive link between 'Mercurian' and their 'home' languages as a result of identifying the colonial aspects of language (English) in the poem. As Jabeena reflects:

I really enjoyed 'The First Men on Mercury'. It's like when I go home, I have to change the way I speak to my mum.

In Gloucestershire, another secondary pupil has followed a module of work based on autobiography and diary and has looked at the ways in which Valerie Avery creates distinctive voices for the characters in *London Morning*. He now takes the four central characters and projects them into new invented situations of his own, writing the scenes in dramatised form. In his evaluation he writes:

I have captured the different personalities by using slang and different accents, e.g. the grandad is always moaning so I used stage directions saying 'he moaned', 'he shouted', 'he yelled'. For grandad I have also used a cockney accent which misses out some sounds...Val's personality has been captured by sentences running into one another and the speech going on and on. Yet the grandad speaks in short sharp sentences...I've used hesitations and pauses because of the situations some of the characters get themselves into.

These snapshots have something in common. Each of them illustrates pupils revealing something about what they already know or have recently been helped to understand about the nature, structure and variety of language. In terms of the National Curriculum for English these are illustrations of 'knowledge about language' at work in the classroom.

WHERE HAS THE TERM 'KNOWLEDGE ABOUT LANGUAGE' COME FROM?

Few if any teachers would have used this term to describe aspects of children's competence (or their own professional practices) before the advent of the National Curriculum. Many still have difficulty with it, perhaps because of its association with 'knowledge' in the sense of rote-learned banks of fact. Perhaps 'Knowing about language', or 'understanding language' (as the NCC non-statutory guidance puts it) places the emphasis more clearly where it was intended – upon a capacity for informed reflection rather than the reproduction of transmitted fact. What the term does clearly signal, however, is that there are many useful things to know about language – its functions, structures, variations, and so on. This is a step forward from the rather narrow preoccupations with 'sentence grammar' which were typical of some language teaching in the past.

Of course, previous initiatives have highlighted the importance of knowledge about language in children's learning. As long ago as 1971, the Schools Council published *Language in Use*, pioneering investigative classroom approaches to language study. The Bullock Report, *A Language for Life*, stressed the pervasiveness of language in children's learning and recommended that responsibility for language development be shared 'across the curriculum'. More recently, the

'Language Awareness' movement has laid joint foundations for understanding language variation and structure between English and Modern Languages departments.

A detailed account of the debate surrounding English teaching over the past decade or more, and the emergence of the concept of 'knowledge about language' from within that debate, is included in John Richmond's article, 'What do we mean by Knowledge about Language' (in *Knowledge About Language and the Curriculum: the LINC Reader*, 1990). It may be helpful to reproduce a schematic version here.

1976   As a result of a government committee of enquiry into literacy, the Bullock Report is published. Its scope and recommendations for English and language development are comprehensive and wide ranging. The report stresses the interdependence of talking, listening, reading and writing in literacy experience and in children's learning, and places English teaching and language development firmly within the context of purposeful and varied uses of language across the curriculum.

1984   HMI publish *English 5–16*. This discussion document re-affirms that the teaching of English should support children's development as speakers, listeners, readers and writers; as well as this, however, teachers should 'teach pupils about language, so that they achieve a working knowledge of its structure and of the variety of ways meaning is made, so that they have a vocabulary for discussing it, so that they can use it with greater awareness, and because it is interesting.' The document also proposes age-related objectives for pupils at 7, 11 and 16.

1984–5   Most professional responses to the document raise fears that it might herald a return to discredited teaching methods involving grammar drills and formal exercises.

1986   HMI publish *English 5–16: Responses to Curriculum Matters 1*. This acknowledges a wide ranging dissent from the position outlined on age-related objectives and teaching pupils about language, and recommends an enquiry into the area.

1988   A government-appointed committee of enquiry (chaired by Professor Kingman) reports. It proposes a model of language to guide discussion and implementation of the English Curriculum and outlines attainment targets for pupils in knowledge about language. It recommends the dissemination of the model to teachers through funded inservice provision and initial teacher education.

1989   The LINC Project is established through an Educational Support Grant to disseminate the Kingman model to teachers in all schools in England and Wales.

1989   Building on Kingman, the recommendations of the Cox Report lay the foundations for the National Curriculum in English. The report has specific chapters on Standard English and Knowledge about Language.

1990   The Statutory Orders for the National Curriculum in English include Knowledge about Language in the statements of attainment and programmes of study. As a guide to practice, non-statutory guidance includes a related section on 'Understanding Language'.

WHAT KNOWLEDGE ABOUT LANGUAGE IS

When thinking about children's school experience of language it is helpful to bear in mind the three ways in which language forms part of their learning.

During the course of their education children are learning:

- *through* language;
- *to use* language;
- and *about* language.

Nearly all teaching and learning is mediated through language. Efforts to ensure that pupils are properly supported in this aspect of their learning are often reflected in 'whole-school' language policies and initiatives associated with 'language across the curriculum'.

In the context of pupils' use of language, we are concerned with their developing competencies as speakers, listeners, readers, and writers. Much of the National Curriculum for English is devoted to this end, and the programmes of study describe the varied and purposeful language situations that children need to experience to develop and extend their repertoires as proficient users and receivers of language. (While the particular focus here is on pupils' learning of English, or other languages, there are clear cross-curricular implications too.) Of course, this development involves a huge amount of linguistic knowledge, but it is knowledge largely of an *implicit* kind.

Learning *about* language describes those moments (or more sustained interludes) when language users step back from composing, communicating or comprehending language, and reflect upon these competencies and how they work. For instance, returning to the first page of this introduction, it is clear that such insights can emerge through the exchanges and compromises of collaboration. The young writers of *Dr Xargle's Book of Earth Nibblers* found their discussion turning on such issues as 'What is the difference between a story and an information book?' or 'When do you use a pronoun?' At other times, as in the Birmingham dictionary project, an investigative task provides the context for explicit language enquiry and explanation, or, as in the literature work from Gloucestershire, a written self-evaluation task provides an opportunity for reflecting on learning. All of these opportunities build upon what pupils already know about language, but shift the status of such understanding from the *implicit* to the *explicit*. Such explicit knowledge can then become a further powerful resource for shaping and controlling pupils' language production and response.

In terms of the National Curriculum, 'knowledge about language' describes those opportunities provided within the curriculum to develop pupils' thinking and reflection about language – its purposes, variation, and systematic patterning. Such opportunities are built into the programmes of study for English at all key stages, and assessment of knowledge about language is represented in the attainment targets from level 5 onwards.

WHAT KNOWLEDGE ABOUT LANGUAGE ISN'T

Despite constant calls in the media and elsewhere for a return to traditional grammar teaching, all professional opinion and empirical evidence indicate that such an approach to grammar is *not* appropriate. The Kingman Committee, established with the specific brief to provide a model of English Language for the classroom, had this to say:

Many people believe that standards in our use of English would rise dramatically if we returned to the formal teaching of grammar which was normal practice in most classrooms before 1960...Research evidence suggests that old-fashioned formal teaching of grammar had a negligible, or, because it replaced some instruction and practice in composition, even a harmful effect on the development of original writing. We do not recommend a return to that kind of grammar teaching. It was based on a model of language derived from Latin rather than English.

The Kingman Report, para 27 (HMSO, 1988)

The kind of grammar exercise described here (and described in similar terms in the Cox Report) failed to represent the wide ranging varieties of language in most users' repertoires; it took no account of the patterns of spoken language, only analysed decontextualised extracts of formal prose, and was generally restricted to the identification of parts of speech within sentences. And just as there is no call in the National Curriculum for a return to grammar teaching of this kind, there is no endorsement within it either of other artificial language activities such as arbitrary dictionary work or comprehension exercises.

None of this means, however, a retreat from grammar. As we shall see from the contents of this reader, children are being encouraged through the National Curriculum to look closely at the structures of the English language and to identify and discuss its rules and patterns. The difference is that they are doing this by reflecting upon examples of speaking and writing which have some meaning in their lives, and which have purpose and relevance in their own learning.

REASONS FOR TEACHING AND LEARNING ABOUT LANGUAGE

The imperatives of the National Curriculum apart, there are a number of good reasons for teaching knowledge about language. These were highlighted in the Cox Report:

Language is an essential part of our cultural environment.

(*The Cox Report*, 5.20)

The physical and cultural environment features prominently in the curriculum we offer our pupils: we teach about trees, towns, the weather, our shared history and so on. This is because we consider it important that pupils understand and appreciate the world in which they live. By the same token, we need to explore and identify aspects of our linguistic environment. Indeed, there is a case for saying this is even more important, since language is not just a neutral feature of the environment but is also a medium through which we experience that environment, and a medium through which we interact with it. And, as pupils catalogue and explore the functions of aspects of their language environment, it is a natural development of their exploration that we should teach them means of describing that environment more precisely. Children who pond-dip and identify minibeasts are ready to begin classifying some of the patterns and distinctions which typify linguistic phenomena.

The world would be a better place if people could talk coherently about the many language problems which arise in contemporary society.

(*The Cox Report*, 5.20).

As a topic for discussion, language generates strong feelings. This is hardly surprising, since people's sense of personal and social identity is strongly bound up with their ways of speaking and writing. Similarly, many people see language competence as a key to personal advancement and social mobility. Unfortunately, however, strong feelings sometimes cloud clear thinking. For instance, some idealised notions about what language *should* be like pay no attention to what it really *is* like. Other views assume that certain varieties of spoken English (Received Pronunciation, for instance) are intrinsically superior to other varieties; and others that the language of formal writing (Standard English) is the yardstick against which to judge all language use, spoken or written. What all these views about standards of 'correctness' fail to account for is the fact that skilled speakers and writers have access to a range of 'Englishes' which they select from, as appropriate, to meet the needs of different situations and audiences.

Standard English is a particularly powerful variety, and all children deserve access to it. Nevertheless, the study of language should allow opinions based upon ignorance or prejudice to be considered against the evidence, and can make an important contribution towards the creation of a more tolerant society.

Language performance is helped by the systematic discussion of language in use.

(The Cox Report, 5.19)

While there has been some research into the effectiveness of formal grammar teaching (largely concluding that it was more likely to have an impairing than an enhancing effect on children's spoken and written language) there has so far been insufficient research into the link between reflection on language and competence. *The Cox Report* claims that it is 'very plausible' that other aspects of knowledge about language taught in context will support pupils' language competence. This is probably true, for there is evidence already to suggest that 'process' approaches to writing, for instance, build in reflective opportunities for writers to adjust their content to meet the requirements of purpose, audience or generic structure. The contents of this volume also provide powerful evidence to endorse Cox's hypothesis, although persuasive proof can only come about through longitudinal studies beyond the immediate timescale of projects like LINC.

Reflection can also be particularly fruitful in generating knowledge about language when pupils use one mode of language to explore another. Some examples of this are spoken comments on writing, readers' logs or transcribing the spoken word. When opportunities for transforming one mode into another (a chapter of a novel into a radio play; alternative versions of well known stories; an encyclopaedia entry into a lively magazine article) are added to these, the comparative insights generated become particularly rich.

Of course, reflecting on language not only improves speaking and writing (our competence in *using* language); more importantly, perhaps, is the potential such knowledge provides to help us to see when and how language is using *us*. Grammatical description can be invaluable here in pinpointing precisely the mechanisms through which speakers and writers shape and manipulate our thoughts and feelings.

The articles in this reader illustrate all of these complementary processes at work. They come to no watertight conclusions: these are classroom cases studies, not rigorously controlled, scientific research papers. However, they do provide pointers for ways in which others might explore the same issues and ask similar questions in their own classrooms.

Three central questions emerge:

- What does evidence of improved competence look like?
- How do you measure it?
- How can you identify which specific teaching has led to improved competence?

The case studies suggest that competence is made apparent in real communicative contexts, and not in examinations or tests. Pupils reveal their knowledge about language in the choices and decisions they make in such processes as drafting and collaborative discussion, and any measurement of competence must involve an assessment of the appropriateness of those choices. The case studies also suggest that it is not enough to 'teach' knowledge about language on a single occasion. Children's understanding of language develops in a supportive, collaborative classroom environment where language is continually discussed, relished, twisted, prodded, trimmed, polished and held up to the light. In such circumstances, it is rarely possible to say that *this* moment of teaching led to *that* manifestation of competence.

HOW THIS BOOK IS ORGANISED

The chapters following this introduction all include accounts by teachers and advisory teachers which document the classroom teaching and learning of aspects of knowledge about language.

Contexts for learning provides nine illustrations of ways in which teachers are incorporating reflection about language into broader learning experiences and contexts.

The four chapters following this offer a wide range of case studies grouped under the following headings: **Ways of talking; Kinds of writing; Spoken and written language; Language diversity**. Each chapter starts with an introduction locating the studies within a shared framework of knowledge about language ; at the end of each case study, there is a summary of those aspects of the programmes of study which have been most prominent in the pupils' learning. The aspects selected in these summaries relate specifically to developing children's understanding of language.

Alternative ways of systematically mapping knowledge about language into the curriculum are described in the final chapter, **Making Changes**. In this chapter, further case studies exemplify approaches taken to the management of change in a number of primary and secondary schools and, generalising from this evidence, we offer some guidelines for curriculum planning and review.

Within most chapters we have included examples from a number of key stages and from both the primary and secondary phases. It is our belief that all of these case studies can be read with interest by teachers of all age ranges. As with other aspects of the English curriculum, knowledge about language is recursive, similar issues being revisited as children grow older, within new contexts, and at increasing levels of explicitness and intellectual sophistication. In this sense, teachers of all key stages can glean ideas from each other and can be reminded of those features which characterise progression and continuity in this key area.

Note: There are many examples of pupils' written work in this book, a large number of them in draft form. Similarly, there are many transcripts of pupils' talk. All these examples have been transcribed without corrections or alterations, even when non-Standard forms of language have been used.

Contexts for Learning

The National Curriculum for English emphasises strongly that learning about language should take place in real contexts, rather than through exercises. The challenge for the teacher is to integrate knowledge about language into a crowded curriculum in such a way that it enhances and illuminates existing contexts for learning. Such integration might take place in three ways:

- through *incidental reflection* on language;
- through knowledge about language as a *contributory focus* within a topic or unit of work;
- through knowledge about language as the *main focus* for a topic or unit of work.

These complementary approaches will merge and overlap, but nonetheless they provide a useful characterisation for a range of classroom strategies. None of these approaches is adequate in itself: a combination of all three is needed to provide a balanced knowledge about language curriculum.

KNOWLEDGE ABOUT LANGUAGE THROUGH INCIDENTAL REFLECTION

If a move from spontaneous practice to considered reflection is sensitively handled by the teacher, it becomes quite natural to talk about language in classrooms.

(*The Kingman Report*, §29)

In any classroom there will be children reading, writing, listening and talking, using language as the principal medium of learning. Giving children opportunities to reflect on the language they are using is to develop their learning about language. This type of learning about language, which we might call incidental reflection, is absolutely pervasive. It might as easily arise from the language of a science lesson as from the language of an English lesson. Children are naturally curious about language, and if they feel that their curiosity is encouraged, they will extend their questioning of language to all parts of the school learning environment and even to their homes. Certain practices in the classroom are particularly likely to encourage incidental reflection:

- the drafting and refining of written work;
- group problem solving and discussion;

- collaborative, responsive and critical reading of fiction and other texts;
- taking risks, experimenting, being willing to make mistakes and to learn from them.

Such opportunities will help children to reflect on the central theme of the English National Curriculum: how the forms of language vary according to purpose, audience, and topic.

Incidental reflection is particularly important because it is so pervasive. Knowledge about language can be integrated into every part of the curriculum, and it can be developed at the point of need – in relation to the pupil's own reading or writing, in response to the pupil's own questions, at the moment of relevance and interest. But incidental reflection is not enough: it is too haphazard; some pupils may not ask questions; some language issues may not arise naturally and spontaneously. A more systematic approach is also required to ensure that all pupils experience the full range of language opportunities to which they are entitled.

KNOWLEDGE ABOUT LANGUAGE AS A CONTRIBUTORY FOCUS

Many teachers, in the course of planning a topic or unit of work, run through a National Curriculum checklist in their minds: 'I've chosen to work on "Changes" as my main focus: where are there opportunities for writing, for reading, for speaking and listening, for drama, for media, for IT?' They might not choose to develop all of these constituents in the course of any one topic or unit of work, but they would expect to consider the possibilities at the planning stage, and to achieve a balance over several topics or units.

Knowledge about language needs to be part of that checklist, to be considered as a potential contributory focus at the planning stage of every topic or unit of work and to be integrated where appropriate. For example, children studying *The Tempest* might explore how power relationships are expressed through language, alongside a range of other activities; children working on a theme, such as 'the family', might explore the functions of spoken Standard English through a role play sequence; children studying electricity might explore the origins and purposes of scientific vocabulary. It is difficult to conceive of a topic or unit of work where there would not be the potential to include knowledge about language as a significant contributory focus.

KNOWLEDGE ABOUT LANGUAGE AS A MAIN FOCUS

If knowledge about language is developed every day through incidental reflection, and within most schemes of work as a contributory focus, teachers will be able to address most of the requirements of the programmes of study. On some occasions, however, teachers will want to take an aspect of knowledge about language as the main focus for their work. Their starting point may be 'Communication' or 'Language acquisition', but they will plan in the usual way, scanning their checklist to find opportunities for writing, reading, speaking and listening, drama, media and information technology within their exploration of knowledge about language. Although this is the most direct and intensive way of approaching knowledge about language, it is likely to be the least frequent.

THE CASE STUDIES

The case studies in this chapter have been chosen to illustrate the variety of classroom activities which might be described under the three approaches described above.

Knowledge about language through incidental reflection

In 'Knowledge about language in an infant classroom', Pat Baldry explores the knowledge about language work that has arisen incidentally out of the class topic on trees. We see how the teacher's enthusiasm for language has been communicated to the children, so that language concerns permeate all their work. The case study illustrates:

- an emphasis on word-play, through puns;
- writing in a wide variety of formats;
- the discussion in context of punctuation and writing conventions;
- sensitive teacher intervention to make terminology explicit;
- children writing for real purposes and real audiences.

Knowledge about language as a contributory focus

In 'Knowledge about language through literature', Karen Hill explores how knowledge about language can arise from the class study of literature texts with year 9 pupils. They explore literary language and are introduced to terminology in relation to poetry. They also explore accent and dialect, gender stereotyping and language acquisition.

Drama is a very powerful means of developing an understanding of language. Voice machines make clear the power of alliteration, freeze frames bring imagery to life, and all aspects of context, purpose and status can be explored through movement and role play. In '"You taught me language…"', Kate Hirom develops issues of language and power in *The Tempest.*

In 'Changes in English since the time of the Plague', Deborah Shepherd describes a class project undertaken by year 7 pupils who were studying the Tudors and Stuarts in History. The historical interest of the material gives a clear context for the language study, while the exploration of language change gives a concrete focus to their study of history.

Knowledge about language as a main focus

Lorraine Dawes takes a topic approach in 'Using books to develop children's knowledge about language', with books as the language focus for the whole topic. Throughout the work there is a strong emphasis on reflection, on learning appropriate terms in context, on writing for real audiences, and on careful planning.

In 'Knowledge about language in the environment', Ros Bartlett and Diana Fogg investigate the language of the immediate local environment with a class of year 6 children. The article shows the excitement and potential of exploring the local environment, and the variety of types of language work that can be integrated into a knowledge about language focus.

Gender is an issue that teachers will want to deal with throughout their English work. In 'Language and gender', Jacqueline Barnfield shows how gender issues might be raised through looking at language. Her workshop approach with year 10 pupils is aimed at giving abstract ideas a tangible form as a starting point for longer term investigations.

In 'The Dazzlers' Dictionary', Alison Sealey sets a year 6 group the task of producing dictionaries of words and phrases from their own slang. She shows the tremendous motivation that can be harnessed by involving pupils in a language investigation that relates to their own experience. The article shows how to give a purpose and context to the teaching of parts of speech, and a purpose to the exploration of dictionaries.

In the final article, 'Language acquisition', Paula Hearle describes a half-term project with a year 7 group. She shows a variety of ways in which children can analyse and re-present their own research. The children are involved in reading, writing, viewing, close listening, speaking and research. They explore their own backgrounds, their perceptions of a baby's thoughts, the role of parents, differences between speech and writing, the process of reading, and the structure and content of children's books, as well as grammar and linguistic terminology.

KNOWLEDGE ABOUT LANGUAGE IN AN INFANT CLASSROOM

PAT BALDRY

I was on my way to a local school's annual fete when I took a short cut through the classrooms. My 'short cut' proved something of a misnomer, as I became side-tracked by the classroom settings. I made an arrangement to return during a school session, and the following account describes a morning spent with a class of 27 year 1 and 2 children and their class teacher, Elizabeth Osborn, at Ashingdon Primary School.

Class 4/O and Elizabeth are involved in tasks based on their topic of 'trees'. Work is planned to spread over three terms [see opposite]. I sense, and see evidence of, the teacher's and children's enthusiasm for words, which is reflected in the classroom environment. Puns abound: 'Branch Out and Discover your Roots' heads children's work on their family trees; 'Knotty Problems' presents a working mathematical display with problems to be solved; 'Open the Door to Gore' invites you to read the children's Dracula stories. I laugh at the collection of Class 4/O's favourite jokes, and read their 'owl' poems signposted with the metaphor 'On Silent Wings'. These were written after Mrs Wayne came to visit, bringing in George, the barn owl. Elizabeth's own interest for words is much in evidence:

I like using phrases that make a play on words, and these are often thought up in discussions at home and at school. Let me tell you about 'Open the Door to Gore'. The children came up with the word 'gorey'; I elaborated on this and gave them the word 'gore'. We then scribbled related words all over the board, and came to a jont decision that 'Open the Door to Gore' had a nice 'ring' to it. I had to restrain myself, as I was getting quite out of hand. 'Open the Door to Gore and find yourself in a Jamb (Jam)' is probably stretching it a bit!

The children are writing for many different purposes and, to suit the writing tasks, are producing a variety of formats. Two children, helped by Michelle's grandad, and Elizabeth's right-hand man, are painting a slogan on their T-shirts urging people to

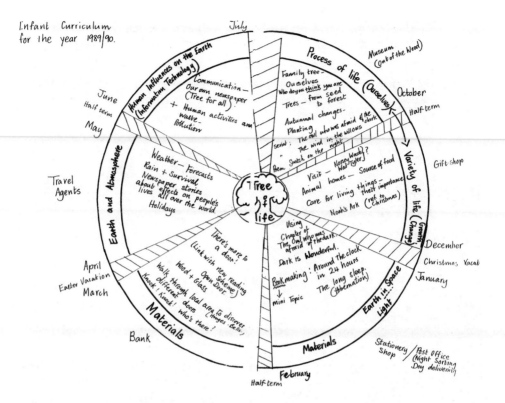

Infant Curriculum for the year 1989/90.

save trees. Another group of children are writing 'Knock, Knock' books, basing them on the format of the Ahlbergs' *The Jolly Postman*. They are sticking them in envelopes and writing letters to people of their choice, who range from the fictional Tom and Jerry to their pop idol, Michael Jackson. They freely read their letters to each other and anyone else who happens to be around, to find out if it 'sounds right'. Tanya is busy with a dedication to her mum and dad on her book about 'Beauty and the Beast' [see page 22]. I am invited to read it; in answer to my enquiry, she tells me confidently, pointing to some inverted commas, that she puts these marks when she makes her people 'say something'. I am impressed by this six year old's understanding of writing conventions.

More children are working on the theme of 'Family Trees'. Harry is busy pasting up labels to accompany his drawings that are going into his family album. Another little girl illustrates her 'family acrostic'. Glen is working out an 'annual rings' chart. He knows that you age a tree by counting its rings and he is making a chart that goes from 0–7 years, showing a skill he has acquired for each year of his life. Another group is making up an 'alphabet of trees'. This involves discussion and access to reference books as they track down trees for some of the more obscure letters. Stephen shows me the

Beauty and the Beast.

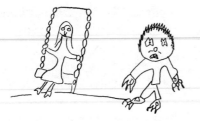

To MUM and DaD
Jodie and Carla also
rest of the family.

by
Tanya

Index

Chapters	Contents.

Chapter 5

The man loked very Sad Beauty Said "Ho! father is eveything all right" Beauty's father Said "No Beauty it is not all right" Beauty asked Why. this is what he Said.

information book he is writing about owls. I note that he has produced pieces of non-chronological writing, in contrast with Alison who is writing a book called 'Around the Clock' which is a chronological account of one day in her life. Both children carefully compile a list of contents and indices to signpost readers through their books. The morning session comes to an end, and the children get ready for dinner.

What are the implications of these observations? I have seen a powerful demonstration of both the teacher's and children's knowledge about language. The teacher has shown this in the provision of appropriate contexts which have enabled her learners' own language competence to develop. As a skilled language user with a delight in and an enthusiasm for words, she has provided a model for her pupils. This has been an interactive process; she made her own knowledge explicit (e.g. in the discussion on puns) and so developed and extended children's knowledge about language. (Note the title of Stephen's book on owls: 'Who Gives a Hoot'.) It was a classroom where the children's 'literacy acts' were given a high profile and status. Their implicit and explicit understanding of language was demonstrated by the broad range of writing produced which gave evidence of an ability to use different kinds of writing for different purposes. Many of the writing tasks were (as in the 'real' world) written for social purposes and reached a real audience. Their books became part of the classroom's reading resources, where children received genuine feedback on their writing. Appropriate words were used in their discussion of book parts ('dedication', 'publisher', 'contents', 'index') which revealed thoughtful and appropriate teacher intervention with terminology made explicit at the moment when pupils were ready.

To conclude, I saw firm evidence of what Yetta Goodman has described in her own classroom observations:

Language concepts grow and develop depending on the settings in which they occur, the experience that children have in those settings, and the interaction of the people in those settings.

(Goodman, Y (1985))

Grateful acknowledgements to Elizabeth Osborn, Class 4/O and Ashingdon Primary School, Essex.

This article shows children:
- making their own books about particular experiences (§6, Reading);
- talking about the ways in which language is written down, in shared reading or writing sessions or in discussion with the teacher (§6, Reading);
- having frequent opportunities to write in different contexts and for a variety of purposes and audiences;
- playing with language (§9, Writing);
- discussing their writing frequently, talking about the varied types and purposes of writing, and meeting terms such as punctuation, letter, capital letter, full stop, question mark (§12, Writing).

KNOWLEDGE ABOUT LANGUAGE THROUGH LITERATURE

KAREN HILL

When I read the National Curriculum document, I was reassured by its emphasis on teaching and assessing children's knowledge about language within the context of a whole range of language experiences, building on pupils' own expertise. However, I was still left with a niggling doubt: I was not sure that my practice lived up to my rhetoric, because I had never been specifically required to monitor and assess children's acquisition of knowledge about language. I knew my attitude had been somewhat ambiguous: while I was quite happy to introduce metalanguage when exploring literature, I was unhappy about going through the parts of speech (which colleagues in the Modern Languages Department felt I should do). And while I was keen that we should explore register/usage/purpose/style, I have to acknowledge that I *hoped* that such knowledge was being acquired, but that I never questioned the effectiveness of this 'rub off' style of language teaching.

This work offered me the opportunity to focus on knowledge about language, considering approaches to its teaching and assessment in a more rigorous way than I might otherwise have achieved. At the end of my study, I feel much more cheerful about both.

Planning the work

I chose to focus my study on my class of year 9 pupils. 3Y are a mixed ability group: there is no withdrawal or in-class support for those with learning difficulties. The work I do with them (as with my other classes) tends to be literature-based, and so I decided to monitor what knowledge about language was apparent, developed or acquired, within the scope of my normal literature teaching over a period of time. During this period we read and discussed a range of poems which might be loosely linked under a heading of 'Maladjusted Children'. (During the same period, we also worked on Mary Rodgers' *Freaky Friday*, Rony Robinson's *Frankly Frankie* and Michelle Magorian's *Goodnight, Mr Tom*.)

For the purpose of this study I chose to focus particularly on the work of two children, Barry and Claire. They are both articulate but, being of differing levels of attainment, they provided opportunities for comparison.

Discussing poetry

In approaching the poetry which we were to study that term, I decided to try to begin by looking at the words less in terms of their poetic connotations, or a traditionally literary style, and more as a vehicle of language study. From the selection, we chose three to look at as a whole class. The first was Vernon Scannell's 'The Incendiary'.

I realised, when preparing the work on this poem, that the whole poem revolved around the contrast between the descriptions of the boy and the fire. I therefore chose to focus specifically on the adjectives in the poem.

We first checked that everyone understood what an adjective was. Only one pupil, Claire, was certain what the word meant, but all seemed to understand the concept of 'describing words'. I asked them to label objects and people in the room with appropriate adjectives as imaginatively as possible. I discovered immediately that some of my pupils could not grasp the distinction between an adjective and a noun and felt that names described their objects. When we had resolved this problem (one girl remained adamant that the best word she could think of to describe a desk was 'desk'), we read the poem and talked about it briefly so that they'd all 'got the gist'. Then I divided them into small groups and asked them simply to make two lists: one of words used to describe the boy, and another of adjectives relating to the fire.

They took to this with relish because they thought it was an easy task. Some of the discussion which followed made fascinating listening:

Claire	'pallid cheese' is one.
Sally	It can't be. It's two words.
Claire	Well, you can't just put 'pallid' or 'cheese' because that doesn't make sense. It says 'a face like pallid cheese'. It's a thingy...er...
Sally	But she (*teacher*) said a list of words, didn't she, Susan?
Susan	Mmm.
Trevor	Miss, can we have phrases?
Me	Yes, of course you can. Sometimes adjectives come in phrases. We call them adjectival phrases. Sorry, I should have said. (*Calling to the class*) Everbody! Some of the describing words are just one word, but some of them are two or three word phrases.
Claire	'like pallid cheese' is a simile, isn't it, Miss?
Me	Yes.
Trevor	What's a simile?
Claire	It's when you say something is like something else, like he's as cool as a cucumber.
Trevor	I think that's stupid. Whoever heard of a cucumber in shades? I can just see a cucumber in shades.

I was interested to hear Claire's input. She obviously understands explicitly the concept of the simile, but also had an instinctive awareness of compound adjectives.

In Barry's group the discussion focused more on the meaning of this simile.

Barry	The boy's got 'a face like pallid cheese'.
Mike	What's 'pallid' mean?
Barry	Sort of pale and ...er...well, pale...Dull, I suppose. I suppose pallid cheese is a bit mouldy.
Anthony	You mean he's got bad skin.
Barry	Yeah, I suppose.
Mike	Ugh.
Hink	He isn't very healthy then, if he looks like cheese.
Barry	He can't be very healthy, because it keeps saying he's small and pale.

I was pleased to hear them trying to find ways of exploring and articulating their understanding of what the poet was saying. Although they were trying to come to a literal understanding of what it is like to have 'a face like pallid cheese', they were echoing the poet's implied condemnation of the boy's state. It is difficult to determine whether this is evidence of their sensitivity or of the poem's effectiveness, but Barry was already making connections which underlined the poet's voice.

In all the groups it was interesting to hear pupils dealing with quite complex ideas. You need to do quite a lot of deconstruction to check whether an adjective refers to the boy, the fire or something else, and to fulfil what appears a simple task: making a list of words. As Barry commented, 'It got more difficult than it sounded'. When they had finished the lists, all pupils seemed to have a thorough knowledge of the events described in the poem.

I then asked them to look at the lists to see if they could see any connections between the words and phrases in them. Although such was not my intention, this became a whole group discussion which was led by Claire and Barry.

Claire	Miss, all the words describing the fire, 'roaring tigers', 'red', 'gold', they're all...big words...you know...sort of big...They're big and...bright.
Barry	They're violent.
Claire	Yeah.
Trevor	Yeah. The fire's choking the stars.
Claire	Yeah...And it's sort of the opposite of the boy, cos he's little and pale.
Hink	He's got bad skin and he's cold. He isn't well looked after, and I think he's only about eight.
Barry	It's strange, because the words used to describe the fire make it seem powerful, but the boy started it and it just keeps saying how little he is.

It was Claire who made the 'connection in meaning' for all of the class.

Claire	Yeah, it says he just wanted to be warm, but, like, inside. He wanted to be warm...er...loved.
Trevor	So he started a fire.
Claire	But it got out of control. But the poet's saying that, if he'd been loved...you know...'the warm kiss'...he wouldn't have started the fire.

Following this discussion, the written task which most of the pupils chose to do was a newspaper report of the fire. What was interesting was that almost noone was able to remain detached from the emotional power of the poem, so that even those who tried to write objectively included a sympathetic editorial line, such as: 'Something must be done to make parents take better care of their children' or 'This wouldn't have happened if his parents had stayed in more often'.

The next poem we studied as a class was Stephen Spender's 'My Parents Kept Me'. For this I adopted an approach I have used before and found successful, and which seems to give even the weakest children a feeling of success.

I began only by telling the class the first line of the poem: 'My parents kept me from children who were rough'. I then asked them to jot down, individually, anything they thought might be true about the type of person the poet was, his or her family and background, anything at all they thought after hearing that line. When they had done this I asked them to compare notes with a partner before being ready to report back to the class. Every time I do this there is almost universal unanimity of response, and pupils seem able to respond not only to the narrator's voice, but also to the implied voices of the parents.

They 'know' that the boy is lonely, that he probably is afraid of the 'children who were rough' and that these children probably pick on him because his parents won't let him mix. They are convinced that he is probably a 'wimp' and that his parents are snobs, who think that they are better than everyone else and so won't mix with their neighbours. And they know that the narrator is a boy.

Once we have discussed our speculations we read the poem together, and the class leap with glee on the concrete evidence that they were right. They will spend some time trying to prove that their speculations which went beyond the scope of the poem are nonetheless supported by it.

With 3Y I found this approach successful once again: they responded to the register of the narrator's voice and to the cultural loading of the opening line, and constructed a scenario similar to that of the poem. However, I was particularly interested to discover that the activity produced animated discussion, for the first time, about the narrator's gender and about the definition of a snob.

Sally was insistent that a girl was far more likely to be told to stay away from rough children 'nowadays', because parents liked their sons to be 'a bit on the rough side', whereas they wanted their daughters to be 'nice'. Most of the class agreed with the basic principle but still felt that the narrator was more likely to be a boy. Only Claire managed to frame an argument in support of the general feeling:

I think it's more of a boy who...er...would be told to stay away from rough kids...because girls from...er...mm...families like that...er...stay away from rough kids anyway. They don't like them, do they?

The discussion about snobs was very heated, and it soon became apparent that its meaning was different for different children. While the class was agreed that the parents were snobs who felt themselves to be superior to other people, the judgmental phrasing of 'children who were rough' was never expressly identified but was obviously felt by everyone; some felt that it meant that the parents were well off and 'talked posh'.

Barry argued that this was not necessarily true:

They can't be well off, because if they were much better off than the rough kids' families they wouldn't live in the same area, would they? And they...er...wouldn't have to tell their own kid to stay away from the other kids, the rough kids, would they, eh?

He persuaded some, but not all, and for many 'snob' still equated with money, and vice versa. However, it also became apparent during a heated interchange that snob is a derogatory term applied to anyone who appears to be actively ambitious. Thus Claire was called a snob because she tried to do well in school. This seemed the appropriate moment to end the discussion.

In the following lesson we did a role play based on the poem. The situation was a moment of confrontation between the 'children who were rough' and the young Spender. Much of this proceeded predictably: the 'boys' issued threats and insults with gusto, and Spender tried not to look at them, shrank away and was firmly stigmatised a 'wimp' when he threatened to get his dad. In his group Barry took the Spender role and, to my surprise, immediately adopted a 'plummy' voice. This seemed to me to contradict the argument he had previously made about snobs not having to be circumstantially different from their neighbours. He, however, could see no paradox when I raised the issue with him.

As I have said, I always find this approach to the poem successful, and 3Y evinced all the signs of enjoyment. I must, however, admit that there are, as far as I can see, two intrinsic weaknesses in it as a basis for literary study: it can reinforce the pupils' firm conviction that, whatever I say to the contrary, there must be a 'right answer' and, on a subtler lever, it does not allow for the fact that the narrator's voice is not necessarily identical to the poet's. The process also seems to reinforce stereotypes of sensitive boys as wimps and rough lads as adventurers. On the whole, while trying to tackle this last issue in discussion, I am prepared to overlook the others in this instance because of the number of children who say, 'I enjoyed that, Miss'.

The third poem we looked at together was 'Dumb Insolence'. As we read it, someone asked a question about the boy, and Sally once again challenged the assumption that the speaker was male. Refusing to respond as a way of winding up her parents was a technique she had often used. This inspired the group to re-read the poem carefully; they had to admit that there were no gender-specific references in the poem, if one discounted the poet's name, which Sally felt we should because 'writers didn't always mean themselves when they say "I"'!

I asked all the class to write a social worker's report on the speaker in the poem, collating evidence from the various sources mentioned in the poem. These were disappointingly short for the most part, and I think I should perhaps have had more talking in role before writing, instead of just general discussion. However, many did show an understanding of register and consciously tried to adopt the more formal phrasing found in reports. There was also an awareness, among the more able, of the need to use indirect speech when reporting conversations with teachers and parents. Interestingly, all pupils, including Sally, identified the poem's subject as a boy in this report.

We have yet to do more detailed reflective writing on these texts, but already I am aware of the rich resource that any piece of literature can provide for study of knowledge about language. More importantly, I have achieved a greater awareness of what is going on in my own classroom. I am now less concerned about the potential hazards of the still political debate on knowledge about language.

Thanks to staff and pupils (especially 3Y) at Dyke House School, Hartlepool, County Cleveland.

This article shows pupils:
- discussing literary language and how it conveys meanings (§19, Reading);
- discussing themes, settings and characters, and making a personal response (§20, Reading);
- discussing different types of sound patterning, and figures of speech (§24, Reading).

'YOU TAUGHT ME LANGUAGE...'
LANGUAGE AND POWER IN *THE TEMPEST*

KATE HIROM

8R was a mixed ability group in a girls' comprehensive school in Richmond and the latest of several classes in Hounslow and Richmond with whom I had been studying *The Tempest*. This was their first encounter with Shakespeare.

Power and language

That the central theme of *The Tempest* is power is not a new idea. Within this it is also worth exploring the way in which the text interweaves the political aspects of this theme with quite explicit consideration of the power of language itself. As the power of liquor liberates lies and nonsense in the comic sub-plot, Prospero uses his command of language not only to frame the play in the telling of his story but also as a very large part of his control system during the course of it.

In my first lesson I decided to explore the way in which Prospero manages to prevail over an initially reluctant Ariel in Act 1 Scene 2. I wanted to show also that words never operate out of context but are given meaning by the relative status of the participants and through intonation and body language.

'Bring me the chair!' I yelled to a startled child, who sprang up to do as she was told. I repeated the words several times with different intonations and body language, cajoling, pleading, suggesting. We discussed what was different about each and what effect it had on the listener. We moved on to a discussion of teacher talk – Are you chewing? – and came to the conclusion that while the same grammatical structure can be both command and question according to intonation and context, the teacher's question was very definitely a command rather than an expression of polite interest. We considered the imperative, when it can be used, and by whom, and the way in which status is conveyed. We also talked about pupil resistances and which style of speech produces the most resistance.

As always, when I talk about language with a class, I was amazed both at what the children knew and at the degree of their interest. When I remember the old style language exercises on the imperative, where you were invited to put an exclamation mark at the end of simple sentences, I was aware of how much more the pupils were learning now about the way in which language really works.

What are the ways in which we can get others to do our bidding? I handed out an abbreviated version of Prospero and Ariel's encounter under the heading 'Prospero and Ariel have a quarrel'. With a previously prepared, experienced reader I gave a little performance in front of the class in a couple of different ways, first with Ariel slouching against a wall and Propsero bearing down arms akimbo, and then with Prospero looking out of the window and Ariel approaching with hesitation. The pupils then went off to work in pairs.

Of the most memorable were a seated Ariel with Prospero darting at him from all sides, and another quite unexpected and moving pair. Elizabeth is a very able pupil, and Tracy has learning and emotional difficulties. Elizabeth, with her arm round Tracy, reminded her very slowly and quietly of her debt of gratitude. 'Thou liest, malignant thing' was said more in disappointment than anger. You could have heard a pin drop. While it might be said that this was confirming Tracy's position in the class as 'special needs', her concentration, commitment and faultless delivery had the effect of enhancing her status within the class. Her portion of text as Ariel was well within her capabilities, and she had, while working on the text earlier, asked for an explanation of 'bate' so we were able to talk a bit about 'rebates' and what the word could mean in context. She had also had a chance to reverse roles; the longer speech of Prospero had, however, presented more difficulty, and they did not perform this version to the class.

When, as a class, we discussed our responses to the text and various presentations of it, we decided that blackmail and reinforcement of obligation go a long way in persuading someone to do something. 'Just like my mum. "After all I've done for you and you won't even wash up! Well, no pocket money unless you do it."' We were all very surprised by the number of variations and different interpretations which were produced.

I was also aware that I had given too much text at one go. So much discussion was generated by quite small variations in positioning. Suggestions were made about each presentation:

She should get closer there and look straight in Ariel's face.

Ariel should sort of crouch down at the end to show Prospero has won.

Because of the length of the text we had to skate rather quickly over the subtle changes in the relationship between the two characters at this point and therefore lost some impact. However, the class had certainly been made aware of the implications of status and power and how these can be conveyed through the body as well as through the language.

Caliban

When thou didst not, savage,
Know thine own meaning, but wouldst gabble like
A thing most brutish, I endow'd thy purposes
With words that made them known.

You taught me language, and my profit on't
Is I know how to curse.

Caliban made his first appearance in the following lesson. We began with trust games and then, developing this, role played Caliban showing Prospero around the island without speaking. At a given signal, the Prosperos turned on the Calibans and drove them into the centre of the room. We progressed to master/slave commands and discussed how these felt, before moving onto the abridged text in which Miranda and Prospero go to visit Caliban. The class was divided into groups of three.

It quickly became apparent why Prospero's attitude towards Caliban had changed.

But why, apart from the obvious, should Caliban wish to violate Miranda?

Katy showed that she was well aware of the power struggle going on here.

He saw that Miranda would inherit the island and he wanted to take it back for himself through his children.

I thought Caliban couldn't speak.

He could, but noone could understand him?

Ah, but could Caliban understand himself? How can you not know your own meaning?

There are indeed puzzling questions here about language. But we are hearing Caliban's speech, of course, through Prospero's ears. Ownership of language and ownership of land would seem to be connected.

I told the story of the Kenyan writer Ngugi, in whose English-speaking school anyone who was found speaking the tribal language of Gikuyu was forced to carry a metal plaque on which was inscribed 'I am a Donkey'. How did it happen that English became the dominant language in so many countries? Why do some languages have higher status than others? What about the position of Welsh in the British Isles? What is it like to have your own speech and experience interpreted as 'brutish'? The BBC *Language File* slotted in very nicely here, as we began to discuss the idea that some languages have higher status than others. The children found it fascinating, and a confident, multicultural class may well have considerable experience to contribute.

It is interesting also to collect cuttings from the press to examine the language used about other cultures. Robert Maxwell wrote of Ayatollah Khomeini during the Rushdie crisis:

We need waste no words on this barbarian...Let us deal with the barbarian in his own coin, the only coin that so diseased and underdeveloped a mind can understand.   (*The Bookseller*, 24 February 1989)

Of course, Shakespeare is no slouch when it comes to invective. Caliban has some wonderful curses:

All the infections that the sun sucks up
From bogs, fens, flats, on Prospero fall, and make him
By inch-meal a disease.

Such curses can be voiced and adapted with evident, if somewhat malicious, pleasure and contrasted with words of acceptance or blessing from the text.

The beauty and pathos of Caliban's descriptions of his island and suffering can ask us to question whether he did, in fact, learn only how to curse.

Other topics for discussion

The other aspect of *The Tempest* which can be fruitfully explored is the position of Miranda. After building up the meeting of Ferdinand and Miranda under the heading 'The Love Story', we paused later and considered Prospero's strange words to Ferdinand:

Then as my gift and thy rich acquisition worthily purchased, take my daughter.

It did not take long in a girls' school for them to see the point. Who's selling whom?

As we go on to *Romeo and Juliet* in year 9, the position of women in the Elizabethan hierarchy will be further explored.

Alongside the textual reading, we worked on creative pieces: storm poetry, magical islands, Ferdinand or Miranda's account of their first meeting written years later, Caliban poetry, and film/stage sets and costumes. One of the most rewarding aspects is the quality of the written work produced. The children's language borrows from Shakespeare's and the vigour and force of the children's writing demonstrates the power of the encounter:

Caliban speaks:
'I remember now, that night, when the sea roared like thunder and the wind blew the clouds so that the stars showed through...I remember him approaching, him with the child. Only a child then. She could not have known what he was planning and, even if I could have seen through his eyes, I could not have protested. Those eyes, like nothing I'd seen, swirling pools of darkness, and the voice, although in words unfamiliar to me, it was mesmerising...all I knew was to obey. That was when I misunderstood his interest.'   (Louise)

I do not aim with twelve year old children for a thorough and complete understanding of the play. I abridged shamelessly and did not finish the play, but story-told huge sections. I felt, however, that I had carried out my intention, which was to convey something of the rich variety of language uses and the way in which so many factors contribute to meaning. Certainly 'language' as an issue had been thrown up in the air and kicked about, reflected on and, above all, used.

Thanks to pupils and staff at Waldegrave School for Girls, Twickenham.

This article shows pupils:
- discriminating between fact and opinion and recognising bias (§6, Speaking & Listening);
- reflecting on their own effectiveness in the use of the spoken word (§6, Speaking & Listening);
- discussing the range of purposes which spoken language serves (§9, Speaking & Listening);
- discussing the forms and functions of spoken Standard English (§9, Speaking & Listening);
- being encouraged to respect the languages and dialects of others (§11, Speaking & Listening);
- discussing how language can be a bond between members of a group, a symbol of national pride, a barrier and a source of misunderstandings, and can be used to alienate, insult, wound, offend, praise or flatter, be polite or rude (§21, Speaking & Listening)

- exploring literary language and how it creates meaning (§9, Reading);
- discussing ways in which English is constantly changing (§19, Reading);
- discussing the possibility of multiple meanings in texts (§28, Reading).

CHANGES IN ENGLISH SINCE THE TIME OF THE PLAGUE

DEBORAH SHEPHERD

During the spring term, year 7 at Elm Tree Middle School were studying the Tudors and Stuarts. It was decided that each half of the year group should take an aspect of the period to study as a class project. One half chose the Great Fire of London, the other the Great Plague. In addition the children, individually or in pairs, were to present some aspect of the period of their own choosing.

My own group was to study the Plague. We were fortunate in having materials which enabled the children to look at some contemporary documents. I decided that there was considerable scope for looking at the way our language has changed. I sorted out the materials into three groups. There was a wide range of attainment in the class and the intention was that everyone should do as many tasks as possible, but that not everyone should have to do them all.

We began with a whole-class activity with the children working in pairs at tables of four. Everyone had a copy of a contemporary document which showed the causes of death in a single week in London during the Plague of 1966 [see opposite]. Having established what the document was about, the class was asked to find the most common causes of death. This led to instant discussion as to what some of the diseases actually were in the first place. What were 'rickets' and 'flux'? There were one or two guesses and then a suggestion that the dictionary might help.

At the discovery that 'flux' was a watery diarrhoea the children's interest deepened! We then encountered another problem in the form of a letter which we did not recognise: the mysterious long 's', which looks like an 'f'. It was easy to work out that this was a form of 's', but only in the middle of words. Many other words instantly became accesible, with demands to know what 'kingsevil' was, along with 'dropsie' and 'rising of the lights'. A good dictionary answered most of our questions. We talked about familiar diseases like 'cancer' and 'jaundice', laughed at 'frighted' and 'wormes'. We discovered that we could substitute 'u' for 'w' and we were amazed at the sheer number of deaths from the Plague.

I then distributed other materials. One was a handwritten copy of a letter from a pupil to his teacher, where we were again to find the alternative 's'. The letter was difficult to read; fortunately there was a typed version [see page 36] which retained all the original spellings as well as the word order. The children were encouraged to talk

The Diseases and Casualties this Week.

Abortive	6	Kingsevil	10
Aged	54	Lethargy	1
Apoplexie	1	Murthered at Stepney	1
Bedridden	1	Palsie	2
Cancer	2	Plague	3880
Childbed	23	Plurisie	1
Chrisomes	15	Quinsie	6
Collick	1	Rickets	23
Consumption	174	Rising of the Lights	19
Convulsion	88	Rupture	2
Dropsie	40	Sciatica	1
Drownd two, one at St.Kath. Tower, and one at Lambeth	2	Scowring	13
		Scurvy	1
Feaver	353	Sore legge	1
Fistula	1	Spotted Feaver and Purples	190
Flox and Small-pox	10	Starved at Nurse	1
Flux	2	Stilborn	8
Found dead in the Street at St.Bartholomew the Less	1	Stone	2
		Stopping of the stomach	16
Frighted	1	Strangury	1
Gangrene	1	Suddenly	1
Gowt	1	Surfeit	87
Grief	1	Teeth	113
Griping in the Guts	74	Thrush	3
Jaundies	3	Tissick	6
Imposthume	18	Ulcer	2
Infants	21	Vomiting	7
Killed by a fall down stairs at St. Thomas Apostle	1	Winde	8
		Wormes	18

Christned { Males — 83 / Females — 83 / In all — 166 }

Buried { Males — 2656 / Females — 2663 / In all — 5319 } Plague — 3880

Increased in the Burials this Week ——— 1289

Parishes clear of the Plague ——— 34 Parishes Infected ——— 96

about the differences which they found and were also directed towards certain details. They were asked to find the words whose spelling had changed and to make a list of the old and the new spellings of these words. I also asked them if they thought that any of the old spellings were easier than the versions which we have today; 'Wensday' was instantly chosen as preferable to 'Wednesday', as it sounds the way it is said. The letter 'y' seemed to be used instead of 'i'. I asked the children if there were any rules for this. Some suggestions were that it appeared to be used before an 'e' and also to replace 'ie'. The children also discovered that an 'e' was added to the ends of many words, and we decided that we could not proceed much further without the language to talk about language, since many of the words to which an 'e' was added appeared to be verbs. A suggestion was made that English might once have been like French, with different forms of the verb. We were making progress. I also asked the children to look at word order, another area where their study of a foreign language was to pay dividends.

London July the 18 1665

Honoured Sir

Blessed be the lord I got to London safe on Wenesday by eleven of the clock and there is but very little notice tooke of the sicknesse here in London though the bills are very great. There dyd threescore and 18 in St Giles in the feild scince the bill, and 5 in one hour in our parish scince. It spreads very much. I went by many houses in London that were shut up – all over the city almost. Nobody that is in London feares to goe anywhere but in St Giles's. They have a bellman there with a cart. There dye so many that the bell would hardly ever leave ringing and so they ring not at all. The citizens begin to shut up apace; nothing hinders them from it but fear of the houses breaking open. My fathers has beene shut up about a weeke, but theyr is hardly an house open in the Strand, nor the Exchange.

Thus with my humble service to you and Mr Blith Junior

      I rest your obedient pupill

        Samuel Herne

Another group was asked to read a seventeenth century illustrated story which contained many unfamiliar words. They were also given a partly illustrated glossary of words of the period. Their task was to rewrite the story in modern English and then to make up a story of their own using as many of the old words as they could, including some from the glossary which were not in the original story. These stories were to be illustrated and shared with other members of their group before being displayed. Some interesting points arose from this too.

One of the old words was 'lip-clap', which in the glossary was translated as 'kissing'. When the children came to use this in their own writing there was considerable discussion as to whether the form should be 'lip-clapping'. I also asked them to try to illustrate some of the old words from the glossary which had not already been illustrated. There were no problems with words like 'malshave' (a caterpillar) and 'nabcheat' (a hat or cap), but it was very hard to draw 'carked' (fretfully anxious) or 'thirp' (finger snap). We talked about the fact that feelings are much more difficult to illustrate than things. Some of the children, in doing this task, were able to talk about nouns, verbs and adjectives.

The last task concerned the clothing of the period. The children were given labelled pictures of the people of those times in the costumes of the day. Their job was to put the modern equivalents of words for items of costume beside the originals; this involved them again in the use of the dictionary. Some of the old words were unfamiliar; some were familiar but in a different context. For example, the word 'tabby' was associated in our minds with cats and not with silk. There followed some fun with a 'tabby in a tabby vest'. Someone who had spent some time in America knew that 'vest' still meant 'waistcoat' there, and we were able to talk about the way language travels.

Perhaps one of the most rewarding moments came in the following term during a field study trip to Pakefield. One of the pupils was examining a grave stone with another boy, who was wondering about the word 'alfo'. 'It says "Edwin and *alfo* Elizabeth"', he said. 'I wonder what that means?'

His companion replied, 'It's 'also', don't you remember? Those things which look like 'f 's are an 's' in the middle of a word. What's the date of this grave? 1886. That's two hundred years after the Plague. I wonder when it changed to be like it is now?'

With thanks to the pupils and staff at Kirkley Middle School, Lowestoft, Suffolk.

This article shows children:
- discussing ways in which English is constantly changing (§19, Reading);
- discussing the reasons why vocabulary changes over time (§23, Reading);
- identifying changes in English grammar over the centuries (§26, Reading);
- developing their understanding of the range of purposes which written language serves (§22, Writing);

USING BOOKS TO DEVELOP CHILDREN'S KNOWLEDGE ABOUT LANGUAGE

LORRAINE DAWES

This sequence of activities to develop children's knowledge about books was done during the summer term, when the children had been in year 1 for two terms. They already saw themselves as readers and knew what books had to offer. I wanted to give them the chance consciously to think about books, hold and express opinions about them, understand a little of what goes into making a book and develop the language to discuss all these things (see curriculum plan opposite).

Story telling: 'The Beast with a Thousand Teeth'

I told this story, from Terry Jones's *Fairy Tales* (Puffin), with a few modifications – the beast's six feet were rather smelly, so people had warning of him. One of the advantages of telling a story like this is that when it all becomes too scary for the listeners, you are immediately aware and can inject some humour (such as smelly feet) to relieve the tension.

I probably wouldn't *read* this story to year 1 children, but telling it is safe enough. After a discussion about what a good story it is, the children drew posters that people might have put up to warn children about the Beast. They then requested a reading of *Avocado Baby* by John Burningham and drew pictures of him.

The experience of hearing a story told and hearing one read was something I wanted the children to think about. So a few days later, when all the pictures had been collected, we all sat round and looked at them and considered: What is the difference between a story that is read and a story that is told? Here are some of the children's ideas:

When you read a story to someone it is from a book, and when you tell a story you make it up.

You just think of a story as you tell it.

When a story is read you can look at the pictures and you know what it looks like.

When a story is told, you see it in your head, you can imagine what it looks like.

We could see the Beast with a Thousand Teeth in our heads!

It was interesting to see the range of images of the Beast that the children had produced. Most had lots of teeth and six feet, but no two were similar: proof that each child had made her or his own meaning from the story telling. In contrast, and instantly noticed by the children, were the very similar depictions of *Avocado Baby*. 'We read this book, so we knew what he looked like!'

This process of reflection was valuable to introduce the idea of thinking about stories and books, as the children had something concrete (the pictures) on which to base their thinking. It also signposted for them the abstract concept of their own interaction with texts, giving an inkling of the idea that the characters in a story are created anew in a reader's or listener's head.

We used the pictures and the comments to make the first few pages of our big book about books. I made a very large spirally-bound card book to contain the outcomes of our activities. All through the term I thought of this book as 'Class 6's Big Book About Books', but when the children came to decide on the title (as all authors should) they chose 'The Words and Pictures Book that Class Six Made'.

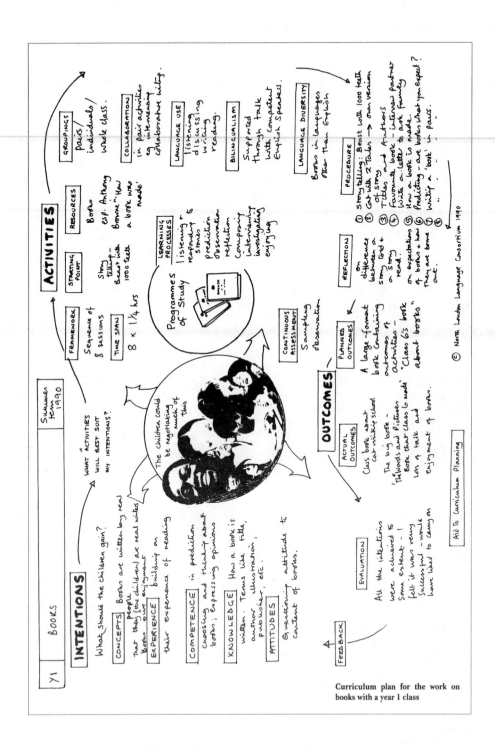

Curriculum plan for the work on books with a year 1 class

Writing a class version of a story

This activity was to ensure that all the children could know what it felt like to be an author. Many children had already made books on their own or with others, but I wanted them all to have the experience as a class. I read them the story *The Cat with Two Tales* by Alix Nathan and Sarah Hedley (MacDonald), and we talked about what would happen if Tiger, the cat in the story, moved to our school. The class arranged itself in pairs and I gave each pair a prompt card to talk about and then draw a picture together. The prompt cards asked a question such as 'If Tiger moved to our school, what would she think of painting?' Each pair had a different aspect of the classroom to talk about: the book corner, the sand, PE, dinnertime, assembly, the register, etc. As they talked and drew their picture together, I went round asking each pair about it and noted down what they said was going on. Using my word-processor, I wrote the text of their version of the story. Each picture went on one page, along with a text based on what the children had said and including their names. Here is an example of one page's text:

Nicola and Alexis were doing some painting. Tiger looked at it and thought about how she could paint a picture. She painted it by footprints — she put her foot in the paint and walked on the paper. She had to wash it off after.

Because I used the children's own words, they recognised it as their writing, feeling themselves to be the authors and me the typist. For some, the picture came first and the text was a result of describing it to me:

Katie and Victoria were in the home corner when Tiger came along. Tiger dressed up as a king. She put on a crown made out of gold paper, with diamonds on and a cape and some nice shoes.

With others, prediction and hypothesis about what might happen resulted in an interesting text where the illustration was of secondary importance:

Bhakti and Gina were playing with the sand. Tiger came out to have a look and when she saw the sand she tried to eat it. It made her feel ill and she was sick. Miss Malyon gave her some medicine, and Mrs Darvell cleaned up the mess.

The resulting book was popular with the children. Their ideas and names were in it, and they enjoyed having it read and reading it themselves. Having the text typed helps bridge the gap between class-made books and commercial books and enables the children to feel they are real authors, even when they have not physically done the writing themselves.

Titles and authors

Looking at the class's own version of *A Cat with Two Tales* provided the starting point for this activity. I had brought in a selection of books that the class had not seen before, and we compared our front cover with some of these books. As we talked about them, words such as 'title', 'illustrator' and 'author' arose naturally, and speculation about what the other words on the cover might mean led to my explaining a little about publishers. Our own class book provided an analogy for this.

I gave the children a selection of books each and a simple chart to fill in, working in pairs. They had to choose one of the books and copy its title and the name of the author on to the chart. The value of this simple copying activity lay in the talk that accompanied it, as the children used the appropriate language to discuss what they were doing. They were pleased to discover that the author of *Avocado Baby* had written other familiar books and, when they had completed their chart, went off to the book corner armed with important knowledge about authorship.

Favourite books

The children thought about which book they considered to be their favourite and then told everyone. As they named their book or story, I noted them down; later this became a typewritten page in the big book. I suggested we might try to find out what other people's favourites might be, and it was decided to write to people they knew to ask them. The children discussed the wording of the letter and came up with a simple text: 'What book did you like best when you were six? Please write and tell us in Class 6'.

We were all rather pleased with this, and each child decided who to write to. Some chose a parent, grandparent, sibling or cousin; some chose a friend or neighbour. We happily anticipated replies full of interesting opinions. Who could fail to respond to such a letter? The outcome was very disappointing. Only a few letters were received, even though we had asked for written replies. Some people told the child orally, and she or he relayed this to the class. But many read the letter, put it down (according to the children), and it was forgotten. We made use of the oral reports by having a 'lift the flap' page. Readers were invited to lift the flap to find out the favourite books of the person named on the outside of the flap. The children liked this page in their big book. When they were familiar with all the choices, they played guessing games with each other over who liked what book. One knowledge about language point that the children were interested to realise was that grandparents and parents were fond of the old timeless stories that they enjoy so much themselves. This kind of understanding also helps children's developing sense of history.

How a book is made

The resources for this activity were *Piggybook* by Anthony Browne (Magnet, 1986) and *Making a Book* by Thompson and Fairclough (Franklin Watts, 1988). In *Making a Book* the production of Anthony Browne's *Piggybook* is described, from first idea to distribution of the finished book. The book is probably aimed at junior age, as there is much interesting detail about publishing, but it is also accessible to infants because of the photographs, and it is possible to tell the story of *Piggybook's* publication by talking through the pictures page by page. The children were highly entertained by *Making a Book* , to see the book they held in their hands featured in another book. (I provided a set of six of each book, as I was doing this activity with the whole class at once.)

During the telling of *Making a Book* I focused especially on certain pictures that were to figure in the worksheet to follow. Then, in pairs, the children put line drawing representations of these significant pictures in the right order and stuck them in the appropriate place on the worksheet. To do this they had to recall the order (this involved a lot of talk), refer to the book (page references were on the sheet), stick them down and colour them in. I had to insist that noone reached for a coloured pencil until the work was finished – line drawings just ask to be coloured in.

I felt the knowledge about language gained in this activity was far more implicit than explicit. The children could refer to printing and binding etc., but most of the learning was probably difficult to express: just a fuller understanding of what a book is, a deeper concept of authorship, an inkling of the huge machinery of publishing. However implicit, I'm sure it will be of value in helping them make sense of the world of books and inform their future experience.

Are books what you expect?

Prediction is a necessary skill in choosing books, but practice in predicting story content was not the only purpose in this activity. Young readers, especially when they are reading for themselves alone, are liable to accept what they read as true; not only the overt message of the text but the hidden opinions are absorbed. Older children can readily appreciate that every text is the product of a point of view when it is pointed out to them, but this is quite an abstract concept for young children. Yet they, perhaps more so than children with years of experience, need the ability to say 'Does that match up with my view? Are people really like that?' Readers need to know they have the right to compare the author's views with their own, be aware of any difference and still enjoy the book.

I told the class I would read them a story about a grandmother and asked them to think what she might be like. They were to draw her and say what she looks like, things she does and things she says. They volunteered ideas and I wrote them on the board and we read them back. The ideas obviously came from experience of real life as well as stories:

She would say, 'You are a nice boy, you are'.

Grandmothers spoil you.

We think she is old. And she has lovely and curly grey hair.

She is old and she has lots of wrinkles and she has curly and grey hair and she has ironing to do.

Then I read *My Grandmother has Black Hair* by Hoffman and Burrows. Spontaneous discussion followed:

She's more like a big girl, really!

Like a teenager.

She didn't have wrinkles!

And she drove a fast, noisy car.

We followed the same procedure with *Crusher is Coming!* The children thought that he would crash into things and be rude and naughty – but in the story he was 'good and nice', he didn't cause any trouble and he was very polite. The talk that ensued as the children drew pictures was full of expressions of opinion about the two books. Prediction had enhanced their enjoyment of the stories, but more important was how they felt as readers who could hold views on how the characters were portrayed.

Writing a book with a partner

For this activity each pair of children was provided with a 'story plan' to help them plan the outline of their story. In the story they were to go to a place with books, look at a particular book and meet character(s), maybe have an adventure and then return to normality again. I was ambitious in expecting the children to complete a story plan together, but the activity was successful in terms of supporting their talk about what might happen in their story. The example by Dean and John [see page 44] shows how difficult the completion of the story plan was for them, but the drawings indicate the movement of the story, and they were able to tell me how Dean became *Avocado Baby* and gave John (Burglar Bill) a shock. Bhakti and Priya, two of the most able pupils, could make use of all the story plan and they shaped a story on it very clearly [see page 44]. But by the time they came to write the story, interest had palled, and their story is a very brief summary! Later, we reflected on how difficult it was to plan out a story and how working with someone could help with ideas. On the whole the children felt storyplan   Names. Dean + John.

1. BULSCARBill   2. Baby AVOCaA   3.   4.   5.

Dean   Burglar Bill   John is Bill
John   gave Avocado Baby   Dean is Avocado
                                    a shock.   Baby

Who is in   Where does   Which books   What happens?   How does it
the story?   it begin?   do you look at?   end?

storyplan   Names. Bhakti . PriyA . . .

1. teddy   2. at home   3. how do   4. the teedy   5. they all
   girl   at Priyas   you I Put   fell over   had a
   boy   home   it on.   and he got   Party
   man   better and
   dolly   a girl got
   pig   it the teedy
   teedy   home

Who is in   Where does   Which book   What happens?   How does it
the story?   it begin?   do you look at?   end?

that planning a story with someone else was fun, but writing it down was more difficult – a typical response of year 1 infants. The solution would have been to tell the story on to tape for transcribing (more work!), but by then it was the end of the term. This final discussion about being an author provided a natural conclusion to the project. We all read through the big book again and admired everyone's contributions and concluded that investigating books was interesting and fun.

I thank Derek Hoddy and Gill Dalley and their pupils at Redbridge Junior School and the children of Class 6 at Parkhill Infants School, London Borough of Redbridge.

This article shows children:

- engaging in prediction, speculation and hypothesis (§6, Speaking & Listening);
- asking and answering questions about what has been heard or read (§6, Speaking & Listening);
- talking about the ways in which language is written down (§6, Speaking & Listening);
- talking to the teacher and each other about the books and stories they have been reading (§6, Reading);
- discussing their favourite reading (§16, Reading);
- talking about varied types and purposes of writing (§12, Writing);
- recognising that writing involves decision making, planning, and drafting (§14, Writing);
- writing personal letters to known recipients (18, Writing);
- considering some of the ways in which writing contributes to the organisation of society, the transmission of knowledge, the sharing of experiences, and the capturing of imagination (§20, Writing).

LANGUAGE IN THE ENVIRONMENT

ROS BARTLETT AND DIANA FOGG

This project began with the idea that the language to be found in children's immediate environment would yield sufficient variety, and provide enough interest, for a class of mixed ability year 6 children to engage in different types of investigation which would extend their knowledge about language.

A walk to the shops

We first organised a walk from the school to a nearby shopping precinct. The children had paper, pencils and a few cameras and were asked to record as many different examples of the different printed or written language they saw along the way and at the precinct. This proved very successful, in spite of the fact that at first glance the area around the school appeared to have very little to offer. The children were sharp-eyed and really enjoyed the activity.

The next task was to sort and classify the examples of language into categories, e.g. advertisements, directions, warnings, etc. Then, using these categories, the children engaged in a number of activities.

Street names

One of these activities focused on street names. A group of children worked in pairs with a number of local street names. Their task was to come up with an agreed reason for the name of each road. The groups were so arranged that two pairs had the same street names to discuss. After the pair work, the pairs came together and were asked to share their ideas as a four and come up with a reason for each street name. The children enjoyed this work and co-operated well. They used enlarged maps of the area to support their explanations (e.g. Parklands was near a park), and they used dictionaries to investigate words like 'loke', 'croft', etc. The children were able to check some of their ideas with extracts from a series of articles in the parish magazine on the history of local street names. The children wrote out their street names and explanations attractively and worked together to produce a wall display.

Arnfield Lane
Children's initial ideas: There was a man called Arnold and he owned a field.
Later research: The name 'Arnfield' comes from the Norfolk pronunciation of Earlham Fields. Two housing estates were later built on these fields. Norwich Road used to be known as Earlham Fields Lane.

Longwater Lane
Children's initial ideas: We think that Longwater Lane was called that because there might have been a river running under the road. Does it exist?
Later research: The name Longwater appeared in the Manorial records of Costessey for hundreds of years. It could refer to the river Tud which was widened to form a lake of three acres complete with two islands, then in the ground of Costessey Hall. Over the years the lake has silted up and been filled in. It was often referred to locally as 'The Long Water'.

The children's talk during this activity gave us a good opportunity to see what background and language experience children brought to their investigation.

Shop names

Another group of children categorised all the shop names. They decided on these categories:

- owners' names, e.g. Sainsbury's;
- names to do with what was being sold, e.g. Fish and Chip Shop, Chemist;
- 'funny' names.

The children were particularly interested in this last group. The ensuing discussion centred on regrouping them according to their language properties:

- rhyme, e.g. Paws and Claws:
- alliteration, e.g. Bubbles and Bobs;
- metaphor, e.g. Shoe Mine.

The terms 'metaphor' and 'alliteration' were introduced at this time. The children reported back to the other groups and went on to invent their own appropriate names for shops. They made three-dimensional shop fronts for a wall display.

This work caught the attention of other children who also wanted to make shop fronts. The *Yellow Pages* was introduced, and the children looked up shops and firms with interesting names and discussed reasons for them before inventing their own. Aspects of language such as play on words (kitchen-range), word association ('Petals' for a flower shop) and deliberate misspellings were discussed.

Fur, Feather and Fin: I think it is called Fur, Feather and Fin because it has everything that animals with Fur, Feather and Fins need. The name also sounds good because all the first letters in the name are the same.

Pro Foto: I think Pro Foto is called that because of Pro meaning professional and Foto meaning photograph. They have changed the spelling of photo deliberately to make you look.

Barnets: On the outskirts of London there used to be a fair called Barnet Fair and it became part of cockney rhyming slang, Barnet Fair – Hair.

House names

This was another category which produced some very interesting work. The children had collected a number of these names during their walk and also from the streets around their own homes. It was decided to write letters to the occupants of these houses asking for an explanation of the name. The response was excellent. Many residents replied, and the children were thrilled to receive real letters in response to their own. The reasons for the naming of homes were roughly categorised and the letters kept for reference. Interesting aspects of knowledge about language came from this too: foreign words with exotic meanings, syllables of people's names joined together, etc.

Many interesting replies were received:

Dear R.,
Our house name 'Jeanteca' is derived from the first two letters of all of our names who live in the house:
JE — Jessie, our dog, who was with us when we moved here; AN — Angie; TE — Terry; CA — Casey.
I hope this helps you with your project.

Dear M.,
Thank you for your letter.
Our family like the 'Pink Panther', so we decided to paint our house pink all over and call our bungalow 'The
Panthers'. You can see a pink panther on the sign. We have many pink panther ornaments and pink panther
teddies. We hope you enjoy doing your project.

Dear Sir or Madam,
Please could you tell me why your house is called Adelboden. It is a very interesting name for a house. We are
doing a project about language in the environment at school.
    Thank you.
Yours sincerely ... C.

Dear C.
Thank you for your letter enquiring about the name Adelboden.
    We thought of a few names like 'Windy Corner' or 'Bowthorpe View', but they didn't seem right.
    In 1980 we went to Switzerland and stayed at a lovely place called 'Adelboden', which is a German name
which means 'homestead'. We were told a story of a boy who came over the mountains and came across the
place which he called 'Adelboden'. He had found the place where he wanted his home to be. It seemed a good
idea at the time to call our house by that name.
    My youngest daughter's second name is French — Adèle, the first four letters matching the first four letters
of 'Adelboden'! This also seemed a good reason for the name.
    I hope you find this information useful and I wish you well with your project.
Yours sincerely ...

It was particularly interesting for the children to see which parts of people's names had
been used in order to make the house name sound right, e.g. Darmalie, from Darren,
Mark and Julie, the occupants' children. An unexpected spin-off from this work was
that two elderly residents made direct contact with the school and were able to come
in and talk to the children. One of these people brought in a beautiful example of a
family scrapbook album containing photographs, artwork, poems, etc. which had
been collected over many years.

Interview

Another session of the project was devoted to compiling questionnaires to use when interviewing the school caretaker, who is in his sixties and has lived locally all his life. The children worked in small groups. We encouraged them to think about how life and language might have changed since the caretaker's boyhood, and devise questions to ask him.

Personal names

During the project, the children were introduced to a number of reference books, i.e. *The Guinness Book of Names*, *A Dictionary of Historical Slang* and *The Oxford Book of Place Names*. These books interested some children, who borrowed them to browse through and talk about.

This led to some unplanned work on the children's own first names. The children were so interested in the history and meaning of their own names that I provided a reference book of these names. The children then brought in photographs of themselves as babies, and these were used on posters designed by the children to show the history and meaning of their own names.

BEN

Means: Peak of Mountain
History: The old Scottish word to describe a mountain. 'Ben' means 'son' in Hebrew language and 'Ben' is short for 'Benjamin' sometimes.

They also asked their parents why they had been so named. This gave some insight into a personal aspect on language. For example, several parents mentioned that they'd considered a particular name 'pretty for a girl', or that the child had been named after a relative.

Final display

The project ended with all the class involved in presenting their findings and investigations as a display within the classroom. Three boys with severe literacy problems worked with some of the photographs taken of other children during the walk. They stuck these into a book and captioned them with the teacher's help.

Another group also used photographs and classified the types of language in a display entitled 'Language is …'

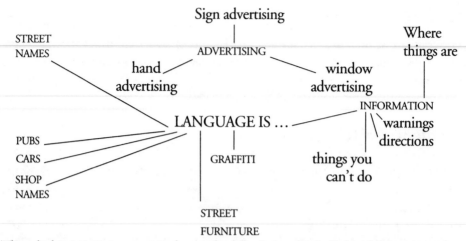

The whole project was extremely worthwhile. It involved all the children in a great variety of interesting language activities, and encouraged them to look closely at some of the language around them. It also highlighted other areas which could have been covered if time had been available, such as advertising. We realised that we had not exhausted the full potential of this work for knowledge about language in the environment.

Thanks to pupils and staff at Costessey School, Norwich.

This article shows children:

- discussing vocabulary that is specific to local communities (§14, Speaking & Listening);
- discussing texts which make imaginative use of English in order to bring out the way the choice of words affects the impression given by the text (§13, Reading);
- considering the way word meanings can be played with (§13, Reading);
- discussing ways in which English is constantly changing (§19, Reading);
- discussing the reasons why vocabulary changes over time (§23, Reading);
- evaluating material and drawing it together coherently (§26, Reading);
- considering features of layout in the materials they read (§18, Writing);
- discussing ways in which writing contributes to the organisation of society (§18, Writing).

Language and gender

JACQUELINE BARNFIELD

Language and gender is not an issue that can be tackled on its own and without preparation; it needs to be part of an ongoing discussion in which pupils are encouraged to be sensitive to other people's feelings and ideas, and to value people on their merits. Looking at language and gender is, however, a very powerful way of raising gender issues while at the same time showing children how deeply the values and ideas of society are embedded in our language.

This case study describes a workshop I have run a number of times with students of fifteen and over. The objectives of the workshop are to demonstrate the power of language and to show that the words we use can exclude a large proportion of the population. A 60–90 minute workshop can only raise the issues, of course, but it can be a starting point for more detailed and extended work. For example, students may wish to examine the reading books of 3–6 year olds. This may provide ideas for a unit of research in several curriculum areas. School text books, curriculum topics, posters around school ... all provide excellent available resources for students to do their own research. I know of one group who monitored their sociology teacher's language for a week and presented the teacher with their findings. I have asked senior students to listen to the radio or TV news and current affairs programmes for one week and to note how many times the language of the presenters is exclusive. The results are surprising. I silently cheer if I hear a report that refers to a 'fire-fighter' or a 'police officer'.

Stage 1: 'Put down' words

I begin the workshop by asking the students to walk round a cleared floor space. While they are walking, they are to think of all the 'put-down' words for women; they have to keep moving until the words dry up. Meanwhile, I keep a note of the time the students spend moving around the room. When all students have stopped, I ask them to repeat the procedure, this time thinking of 'put-down' words for men. Students, particularly girls, will walk around for 60–90 seconds for female 'put-down' words; for male 'put-downs', some girls don't even move – those who do will walk for about 30 seconds, if that, and usually in stops and starts. Students have commented like this:

I've never thought about it like that before.

I couldn't even get started.

Incredible. It's not fair.

That was hard.

After gathering comments from the participants I share these two points with them:

- There are 220 words for sexually promiscuous women.
- There are 20 words for sexually promiscuous men.

I have found this to be a powerful but non-threatening means of raising the issue of language and gender. The activity draws on the pupils' existing knowledge and experience, and the physical movement provides an almost tangible demonstration of the gender bias within that experience.

Stage 2: Generic 'man'

For this activity I divide the students into groups of three or four, and give each group a sheet of A3 paper and felt tip pens. I then give each group an envelope containing one word or phrase from the following selection:

primitive man	mankind
man conquers space	businessman
the man in the street	the best man for the job
policeman	

I ask each group to prepare a collage/cartoon/diagram to depict the word or phrase in their envelope. Once the task seems to be completed, I bring the groups together and ask a spokesperson from each group to discuss their picture. I have managed this in different ways according to the confidence of the groups. Sometimes I have drawn out interesting comments or explored stereotypes as they enter into the presentations, but I have often found it more effective to allow the groups to question each other. Either way, what quickly emerges is the 'maleness' of the diagrams, despite the fact that many people would claim that, in those words and phrases, 'man' is used in a generic sense to include both men and women.

Drawings of a 'policeman', for example, bring out the aggressive side of the job: the truncheon and cosh, handcuffs, fast car, police motor-bike, blue light, and the expression 'you're nicked' always appear somewhere in the drawing. One of the best drawings of a 'businessman', drawn by a group of 16 year old girls, showed a man in a suit taking up the whole of the left side of the sugar paper. Arrows led round the page to: his briefcase, very important papers, his lunchbox packed (by his little wife at home) with healthy foods, tall office building, (male) chauffeur-driven car, aeroplane, flight tickets booked by his (female) secretary, a large clock to indicate a busy schedule. Lots of stereotypes here! 'Primitive man' involved lots of 'cavemen' and a female being dragged by her hair by a male holding a club.

Once again this activity draws on the students' existing knowledge and experience, re-presenting the inequality of the language in a more tangible form.

Stage 3: Exclusive language

The purpose of this activity is to give students some examples of exclusive language so that they can consider its possible effects. Each group is given a selection of cuttings from letters or notices within a school, all of which use exclusive language. The groups are asked to comment on each cutting:

- Why might it be exclusive?
- What could be wrong with the message it is purveying?

I usually ask the whole class to provide feedback, and they do this orally. I may also invite each group to give a version of one of the letters that might make it more inclusive. This leads to an activity where students can consider the alternatives to a wide variety of exclusive expressions. Working in groups, they take a list of words and phrases and consider whether or not each phrase is exclusive, and what the effect of phrasing it differently might be. I usually use the following lists:

Group A
early man
mother earth
motherland
mankind
she has mastered the art of
I'll have my girl check that
lady doctor
camera man
businessman
dinner ladies

Group B
man-made
man power
mother tongue
mastercopy
the men and their wives
she corners well
male nurse
fireman
salesgirl
chairman

Group C
Peter listened patiently to the ladies' chatter.
The pioneers moved west taking their wives with them.
Mr Jones owns a travel agency with his wife, a striking blonde who mans the telephone.
The history of mankind.
To survive, man needs food, water, shelter and female companionship.
Man sometimes had difficulties giving birth.
Mr Wilson runs a garage in partnership with his wife.

Group D
Man being a mammal breastfed his young.
The man in the street.
God bless her and all who sail in her.
The telephones were manned at lunchtime.
Marie Curie did what few men and women could do.

Mary Wells is a highly successful woman advertising executive.
Masterpiece.
Man-sized tissues.
The history of mankind.

At the end of the discussion I ask each group to report to the whole class so that all students can comment on the phrases they have considered and can have the opportunity to question and challenge the ideas of other groups.

Conclusion

As anyone who has tried working with language and gender – or any gender issue – will verify, such work can be difficult and sensitive. On several occasions students have been quite hostile to the idea of discussing the issue, and such hostility is as likely to come from girls as from boys. A general comment has been that it is trivial and that there are larger issues to address. My argument is that our language is something we should *all* have control over. I would like people to realise that language can be exclusive and that its exclusivity can be a barrier to a large section of the population.

For example, if children's books show *firemen* at work, and not *fire-fighters*, then girls quickly come to see that a fire-fighting job is not for them. At the same time are we not reinforcing attitudes among boys that fire-fighting is a man's job and not a woman's career?

It is during the primary years of schooling that girls begin the process of 'learning to lose', not simply from the explicit curriculum but from the messages they receive from the hidden curriculum.

(Janet White, (1983))

As individuals we can use language that is inclusive. For me, the workshop I have described represents one of the first steps on a long journey. If we want to remove some of the barriers that exist, the language we use is a powerful tool.

With thanks to pupils and staff at Thorncliffe School, Barrow-in-Furness.

This article shows students:

- expressing and justifying feelings, opinions and viewpoints (§6, Speaking & Listening);
- reflecting on their own effectiveness in the use of the spoken word (§6, Speaking & Listening);
- discussing the use of language (§18, Speaking & Listening);

- learning that language can be a bond between members of a group, a barrier and a source of misunderstandings (§21, Speaking & Listening);
- analysing documents critically (§28, Reading);
- being made aware of the subtler uses of language (§28, Reading);

THE DAZZLERS' DICTIONARY

ALISON SEALEY

The starting points

As in many schools, the children at Osborne Primary School used a number of words and expressions among themselves which were not used with adults. Obviously, this vocabulary included some taboo words, but the range was much wider than that: words like 'Quality!' used as an exclamation to express admiration, for instance, and a number of expressions associated with the situations children find themselves in at school. One of the teachers, Jill Hoad, who often works with small groups of children from different classes, found the children very willing to respond to her interest in these words. For example, they explained how it was fashionable for one child to react to another being told off, or found not to have been telling the truth, by taunting them with the expression 'Blaze', contracted to 'Blam' and sometimes used in the phrase 'Blam you down'. This expression was related to the exclamation 'Shame', used in the same circumstances, by which children conveyed the idea that the friend who was in trouble was 'burning up' with shame and embarrassment.

As we planned the work, the assumption – which was indeed borne out – that the children would find it interesting and motivating was an important consideration. In addition, Anne Bright, class teacher of the year 6 children involved, felt that the work might make a contribution to the positive ethos which she aims to develop in her classroom. Anne felt that it would be appropriate for the children, who would soon be leaving their primary school, to explore some aspects of the role of language in personal relationships.

The project

The central task which we set the children was to produce dictionaries of some of the words and phrases from 'their language'. This language was defined as 'words which you and your friends know and use but which you think adults would not use'. We believed that by taking on the role of lexicographers themselves, the children would learn a lot about dictionaries and about language (including many aspects of the programmes of study for English), and this was indeed the case. The audience for the children's work was identified as: Jill, who they knew was interested in the topic but who could not attend the lessons; other children in the school; teachers in other schools who might want to undertake a similar project with their pupils. The children worked in four groups, each of which was required to produce a dictionary, which meant that focused collaboration was essential.

The work fell into five phases:

- preparatory work about dictionaries of all kinds, their function, organisation and uses;
- compiling the list of words and discussing definitions;
- planning and designing the dictionaries;
- redrafting and completing fair copies of the dictionaries;
- an evaluative discussion between myself and six children representing various groups, in which they reflected on what they had learned in the whole project.

The work spanned a period of five weeks, with two or three hourly sessions each week spent on the project.

Some aspects of the teaching methodology

We tried throughout to maintain a balance between encouraging the children to recognise, reflect on and extend their own knowledge and expertise, and introducing new information for them to use actively in the context of their writing task.

Models

We could not expect the children to compose authentic dictionaries of their own without providing a range of opportunities for them to assimilate various features of published dictionaries. In an early session, therefore, the children listened to some definitions read aloud from different dictionaries and attempted to guess the word being defined. In pairs and fours they compared the different definitions given for the same word in a range of dictionaries, from those of the 'first school dictionary' type to large adult editions. They were presented with single words on pieces of card and given the task, in pairs, of writing definitions which would enable another pair to guess the word. These activities were complemented by free browsing through a wide variety of dictionaries, some brought in by the children themselves. The range included different 'levels' of school dictionaries, dictionaries for translating between languages, dictionaries of shorthand and speedwriting, a dictionary of slang, and so on.

In the course of this part of the work, several children revealed that they had until then thought that the sole function of a dictionary was to check spellings. Some also mentioned pronunciation, but many said that they did not know what a 'definition' was and had never used a dictionary to seek the meaning of an unfamiliar word. This was particularly interesting as Anne knew that many of the children had in fact worked their way individually through dictionary exercises at various points in their school careers. That the children had indeed encountered dictionary work before was borne out by a comment made by one girl at the end of the project, with which several others agreed:

I must admit, like at the ... when we heard that you was going to come, I thought 'Oh no, not another thing about how to use the dictionary', but it turned out really good.

Acquiring new information

The browsing and small-group activities generated lots of questions which the children put to the teachers as they arose: 'What does "adj" mean?' 'Why does it say "1", "2" and "3" by the definitions for this word?' 'What does "colloq." mean?' Some of these points of interest formed the basis of short teaching sessions, when we gave the children the information they needed at that time.

For example, as they looked at the more sophisticated dictionaries, some children were intrigued by the abbreviations denoting parts of speech, while another task presented this concept from a different angle. When the children had produced, as a class, the list of words which were to be defined in their own dictionaries, we asked them to search the published dictionaries to see if the words were included and, if so, what definitions were given. Some children failed to notice that, while there was no entry for a word such as 'battered' (which they used to mean 'beaten up'), the word 'batter' *was* to be found in the dictionary, and was related to the word they were looking for. This led to a whole-class lesson on parts of speech – a teaching method which was by no means wholly satisfactory, but which was an attempt to supply 'information' which the children needed to put to immediate use in their writing task. As the project progressed and the groups drafted the various entries for their dictionaries, the teachers were frequently asked to confirm that the children's classification of a word as a particular part of speech was correct. Not surprisingly, they often made mistakes in their classifications. However, what was noticeable was that, for many children, while they were sometimes mistaken about individual instances, they seemed nevertheless to be coming to grips with the general concept of regarding words in this way.

Some children also acted as transmitters of information as it gradually became clear that, while there were few children to whom any of the words on the list were unfamiliar, many were not sure what they all meant. Two boys in particular, who had not often perceived themselves as 'star pupils', became 'teachers' who were consulted about definitions for many of the words.

Information about the history of dictionaries and the processes involved in their compilation was given to the children both by the teachers and via other resources. I showed them a short article about the compilation of dictionaries from *The Guardian* education supplement, and an edition of *The Gentleman's and London Magazine* of 1755, which includes 'Some account of Mr Johnson's dictionary'. The fascination of the latter was partly due to its age and antique typeface, and both this and *The Guardian* article seemed to lend further authenticity to the children's own investigations. Some children borrowed the magazine article and struggled with the text, which includes the following explanation about Johnson's orthographic decisions:

As to Orthography ... that practice is preferred which preserves the greatest number of radical letters ...

'Radical' was in fact one of the words on the children's list, used by them (following the popular American children's programme, *Turtles*) to mean something like 'exceedingly good/impressive', and I had a lengthy discussion with one of the children about the common ground between the children's usage, Johnson's usage and the 'literal' derivation of the word. Several of these issues were reviewed in the evaluative discussion:

Z.   Miss, Samuel Johnson making his dictionary, and it said in that article that ... what was that newspaper – The Telegraph?
AS. The Guardian.
Z.   The Guardian, that if Samuel Johnson heard some of the words that we use today, he looked them up in the dictionary and they've got totally different meanings, he'd be horrified for what we use them for.
M.   One word as an example, Miss, which I couldn't help laughing about, it said 'radical' in it and it never meant what we mean.
AS. (*to S.*) Although in fact we talked about 'radical', didn't we? It's nearer to the meaning than we realise.

Organisation of groups

The dictionary-making groups were quite large (eight children in each), partly because there was a lot of work involved in producing one complete book, and each group included a mixture of strengths and personalities. It was clear to the children that as individuals they were each required to make a contribution to the work of their group, and we discussed the skills needed to do this successfully. Despite this, there was one group (who were, interestingly, predominantly boys) who took longer than the others and produced a less satisfactory result, an experience which we can only hope provided an object lesson for them on the importance of collaborating throughout the process rather than operating as individuals. The other three groups were more successful in sharing out the various tasks: choosing a common format for each entry, together with a page design; allocating words from the list, sometimes by assigning sections of the alphabet, sometimes by choosing people according to their confidence in writing about particular words; deciding on fair shares of graphics and writing, and so on.

At other times, the children worked in pairs, while we monitored some aspects of the work by occasionally setting individual writing assignments. These were also a means for the children of consolidating particular things they had been asked to learn, such as the general principle of classifying words as parts of speech.

Differentiation

There was a wide range of academic attainment within the class, and we tried to structure the work so that all the children would be able to participate throughout and to make significant progress during the project. For some children, the organisation of the words they were dealing with into accurate alphabetical order, and the composition of several precise definitions, proved an absorbing challenge. Others were quite prepared to grapple with most of the components of the entries found in sophisticated dictionaries, and some children absorbed into their own working vocabulary such terminology as 'etymology', 'derivation' and 'derogatory'. This last was a word I suggested to a pair of girls who asked me to help them redraft their definition of the word 'biddy'. They knew that it meant an old woman in a less than complimentary sense and needed the word to convey that concept.

The knowledge about language

Semantics

The most obvious kind of knowledge about language generated in this project was semantic knowledge; the children had to stop and think about the exact meanings of some of the words they use readily every day. A more overarching concept which was developed right from the first comparative activities with published dictionaries, however, was that words cannot really be given static, absolute meanings. Some of the children reflected on this in the final discussion:

K.   I didn't think ... I didn't realise that everybody had a different sort of definition about all the words. It sort of ... I thought it was just one definition for a word ...

Some children articulated the sense of power they experienced when deciding on definitions to include in their own books:

G.   Miss, and you had the choice of your own definitions, Miss, like putting your own definition and not other people saying 'Well you have to put this', but you just ... not like ... you didn't have an adult standing by saying 'Oh "cool" don't mean that; that just means some'at what's not hot ...'

M.   Not having to look up the dictionary to find out what it is but your meaning, not the dictionary's.

Changes in word meanings over time

Developments in the children's awareness of change in word meanings over time were evident as the project progressed. Some found examples of expressions which amused them because they sounded old-fashioned (such as 'courting' and 'walking out'). They speculated about where the words on their list originated, citing television programmes, records and children from other schools. Again, some children showed that they were capable of generalising about changes in words over time:

S.   Miss, cos Miss, if you thought about it, Miss, if you chose a word, Miss, you could do like a family tree on it, Miss, like when it (*stumbled a bit*) one before that it come from and then where it come from before that.

Z.   It's like its family history.

They also thought about the future fate of their currently fashionable words. While most of the children thought that their words would become dated and that their own children would find them old-fashioned, one boy suggested the alternative possibility that what was slang today might be standard tomorrow:

Miss, I think when, if we have children, Miss, when they come to be our age, Miss, they'd look at them words, Miss, and they'd know them properly, Miss. I reckon, Miss, like they'd know them better, Miss, and people … but adults would know them, adults would probably use them.

Parts of speech

The principal motivation for the children to come to grips with the classification of words into different parts of speech was to add authenticity to their own dictionaries. One girl put this into her own words as she reflected on what she had learned:

Z.   Parts of speech, Miss, like the little 'n's and the 'adj's and things like that and the 'v's.
AS.   Are you clear about those now?
(*Several reply at once*)

M.   Cos usually …
K.   I didn't know anything about them before.
Z.   You just look at them and you think 'Ooh, what does that mean?', and now we know like nouns, Miss, and things like that.
(*later*)

Z.   Miss, and you need to know like things like parts of speech and the way things are set out, like we looked up 'batter' and that just had 'batter', not 'battered' and things like that, you need to know all that, Miss, to make your dictionary look proper, Miss, real like.

AS.   Well, you have managed to do that, haven't you? They do look good.

Z.   Yes, Miss. We tried to work out what parts of speech matched up to which words and we put those in.

Of course, the children will need to encounter the concept and its application in a range of contexts before it is fully assimilated, but their experience in this project undoubtedly contributed to their understanding of this aspect of word grammar.

Genre

The dictionaries investigated by the children shared some basic generic features, such as alphabetical organisation. As we discussed how they might write definitions, we pointed out the importance of not using the word itself in a definition, and the distinction between a *definition* and an *example* of the word used in context. Most groups decided that they would find it useful to include both in their own entries, following the format of many of the dictionaries they had looked at. We did not, however, discuss explicitly the 'genre' of the dictionary entry, and some of the entries retained a rather immature style:

Quality: when somebody is smart and in the fashion.

Blam: If you do something wrong people say 'blam you down'.
e.g. Blam you down, Michael.

Other groups, however, demonstrated that they were able to adopt the concise phraseology characteristic of dictionary entries. A particularly noticeable feature of the children's definition of verbs was the use of the infinitive:

Dazzle: To beat a team in netball, rounders, etc.
The word was made up by boys in the rest of our school.

Dob: v.
To tell of someone, to get them into trouble
e.g. Sebastian stole a Mars bar, and Wayne dobbed to his mother.

Sociolinguistic knowledge

At first sight, a project about dictionaries, whose focus is on individual words considered in isolation, might not appear to involve much knowledge of a sociolinguistic kind. However, it was this sort of knowledge which was explored in much of the children's talk during the work. The category of words which they were asked to list, of course, required the children to distinguish between language as used by different social groups, and they had little difficulty identifying words which they thought they would use but adults would not. An additional constraint was that words which were hurtful or offensive should not be included.

Despite this, the original list included some words which the children decided to omit when it came to writing them down and supplying definitions. Several children reflected on the ways in which writing about words affected their perceptions. They observed that they had sometimes used words casually, without being sure of their meaning, but writing a definition 'makes you realise':

G.   Miss, and what makes you feel even bad, Miss, is when you write the example ... something like 'Jim saw an old lady so he called her a "biddy"'...

Z.   And say if you went out and called an old woman 'an old biddy' you think when you get older you wouldn't like to be called 'an old biddy', but you think that you've used it to other people.

Some of the children insisted that the work itself had made a difference to the kind of language they used among themselves:

M.   I think we've learned, like, if we was to go to senior school now and say all these words we was going to say at this school we'd get in really big trouble, so really, one of the things you've learned us is learned us to control our mouth — to control it before we say it.

I was a little sceptical about this, but Anne assured me some time after the project was over that she too had noticed a lessening in the incidence of name-calling and 'bad language' among the class.

The work also led to discussion about why many of the words used exclusively among children might be offensive, and the children suggested that they were a means of saying rude things in adult company without being understood.

Another reason for knowing the current slang, they explained, was to stay in the fashion, something which became important to children as they moved up through the school. This line of thought led on to discussion about how young children 'pick up' words and repeat them, without knowing what they mean, including racist expressions, and about the role of older children in setting an example to younger siblings.

Conclusion

In documenting the project for others to read, it is impossible to be unaware of the perspectives from which the LINC project has been attacked, and of the current fashion for denigrating indiscriminately all 'child-centred' or 'discovery' learning. Language could, of course, be manipulated, for political reasons, to misrepresent a project like this by exaggerating the connection with taboo words – Anne, Jill and I could imagine the headlines!

What was actually revealed as the project progressed were some possibilities for teaching about such matters as alphabetical order, parts of speech and inflexions, at the same time as extending children's implicit knowledge about appropriate social registers. Indeed, the two strands of knowledge about word grammar and knowledge about language in social contexts were almost inextricable in this particular project. Furthermore, the children could be seen to engage with the concepts with which they were presented in the context of a writing task which had a clearly defined form, purpose and audience:

S.   ... it sort of was the experience of how a proper dictionary writer would feel, like thinking ... like taking ages just choosing one word and thinking how to spell it and whether it's offensive or not and what it means ...

Z.   Miss, you felt important, like you was writing an important book, you was writing a dictionary.

Perhaps it would be appropriate to conclude with this question, which arose during a class discussion about the evolution of dictionaries. It rather took us aback in the implicit sociolinguistic knowledge that it revealed:

Miss, did Samuel Johnson have to get permission from the government to publish his dictionary?

Thanks to Anne Bright and the year 6 class at Osborne Primary School.

This article shows children:
- discussing vocabulary that is specific to local communities, local usages, and particular age groups (§14, Speaking & Listening);
- handling and using dictionaries (§17, Reading);
- considering some of the ways in which English is constantly changing between generations and over the centuries (§19, Reading);
- responding to the way information is structured and presented in reference books (§23, Reading);
- discussing examples of words which tend to undergo very rapid change in use or meaning (§23, Reading);
- discussing differences in the use and meanings of words used by pupils, their parents and grandparents (§23, Reading);
- discussing the reasons why vocabulary changes over time (§23, Reading);
- increasing their awareness of what is suitable according to purpose and context (§21, Writing).

LANGUAGE ACQUISITION

PAULA HEARLE

The sequence of work described below invited pupils to reflect on their own early language development, through considering examples of early speech as well as books offered to early readers. The topic of language acquisition seemed particularly appropriate for year 7 classes: their work in English would give them regular opportunities to reflect on their development as talkers, listeners, readers and writers, and this study would provide both a valuable starting point and a broader prospective.

I chose to begin the work at the start of the academic year. Sharing childhood memories about early language development proved a good ice-breaker for groups of children who were just getting to know each other and beginning to learn to work together. The activities allowed a combination of individual, pair and group work and encouraged children to think about working collaboratively as well as doing it. It was important that the children were actively and personally involved in the learning. I hoped to ensure this by encouraging them, in a modest way, to be their own researchers. I was also aware that the planned unit of work would provide opportunities to introduce linguistic terms in a context where these would be useful and make sense. During the course of our discussions about language, I kept a large sheet of sugar paper to hand in order to record these as they arose.

Starting with the children's experiences

A memo circulated among form tutors ensured that pupils arrived at their very first English lesson clutching half a dozen snapshots of themselves from birth to four years old. Pupils were grouped in fours or fives from different primary schools. I gave them time to share their photographs by way of an introduction to the group. As I mingled, I quickly realised that the discussions were becoming anecdotal. The groups chatted enthusiastically, and even those pupils who have since shown themselves to be a little reticent in some oral situations confidently talked about their former selves:

This was taken when I'd just swallowed the key to our holiday caravan in Borth.

My mum knitted that dress for me from her favourite jumper.

Consequently, rather than moving straight onto putting the photos in order, as I had originally intended, I asked groups to choose one anecdote to share with the class. I pointed out that it need not be the funniest: it could equally well be the most extraordinary or terrible tale. Groups had to advise their storyteller on the best way to tell it to the rest of us: what information was essential, which bits might need cutting or developing, or when it would be most appropriate to show the photographs. We then gathered round as a class for the last twenty minutes of the lesson and listened to the selection of anecdotes. The subsequent discussion took us down the road of childhood memories:

My mum said when I was three ...

This led naturally into writing family tales. The initial drafts were written at home, and pupils were encouraged to share them, where possible, with the people – parents, grandparents or friends – who had first told them the stories, asking them for comments on the written version.

At the start of the second session, the same groups swiftly put the photographs in chronological order. I then asked them to look at themselves as they had been at around three months and at three years old. On a large sheet of sugar paper, they had to generate and assemble ideas about how they had changed over this time. Among the comments about shoe size and potty training, I was relieved that all groups identified a considerable difference in language ability!

We pursued this as a class with some general questions, such as: 'When did you say your first words?' 'What age were you when your mum could first understand you?' It quickly became clear that, although there were slight variations in personal development, we were able to make some generalisations about language development in young children.

Investigating the stages in speech development

Next, we watched a short extract from the television programme, 'The Hardest Thing You'll Ever Do', the second in the BBC Schools Television *Language File* series, which focuses on language development from birth to approximately four years old. I asked pupils to watch carefully and to jot down what they could discover about the stages in speech development. Subsequent discussion was accompanied by sorting their photographs into the age bands defined by the video. These were mounted on separate sheets of sugar paper and displayed with corresponding age labels, such as 0–2 months, 2–4 months and so on.

Pupils were then asked to share notes in groups, and each group was asked to produce a series of brief statements about language ability in each age band. One group came up with the following:

0–3 months	– crying
3–9 months	– gurgling and giggling
9–18 months	– words like 'dadda'
18–30 months	– putting words together
30 months – 4 years	– talking in sentences

Each group's conclusions were reported back to the class and discussed; if necessary, the conclusions were altered, at times with reference again to the video, before being added to the display.

The pupils had thus had an opportunity to research for themselves the question of how young children learn to talk.

The display they produced to communicate their findings was very similar to the one I found in the *Language File* book (BBC/Longman, 1990, page 19). However, I felt the pupils' understanding was much greater than it would have been if they had simply been presented with the book, because they had explored the stages in an active way.

I found it useful to make these statements about language development detachable. Pupils began the next session trying to match the statements to the appropriate age band.

Researching babies' first words

At this point, we started to think specifically about a child's first words. Pupils were sent away to research what their own first words, or the words of their brothers and sisters, had been. They then listened to a recorded conversation between one of the school PE teachers and his 18 month old son, James, during bath and bed time. This gave them an opportunity to add other first words to their personal lists.

I chose to say nothing at this point about the child's words, turning attention instead to the way the father spoke to his son. Pupils were quick to recognise how differently Mr Brett spoke to them at school, but they had more difficulty describing his manner. We were better able to explore the differences after a role play exercise in pairs:

You meet your teacher coming along the corridor. Your teacher is very upset because he or she has just been shouted at by the Head. Speak to him or her as if you were talking to a two year old.

(*The Languages Book*, English and Media Centre)

The next hour session was devoted to the child's first words. I wanted pupils to consider the kinds of words a child first learns, and why. However, having led the discussions quite firmly up to this point, I intended to stand back and let pupils draw their own conclusions about the words they'd collected.

I restructured the groups, trying to achieve more of a mixture of attainment than the initial grouping of 'strangers' had achieved. Each group of four was simply given a task card, several sheets of sugar paper and marker pens. This was the task card:

FIRST WORDS

1 Working in groups, make one list of all the words you have collected so far.
2 Now divide them into groups such as food, family names, activities, feelings and needs and nursery rhymes. (You will probably need to add more groups.)
3 Look at your groups of words. What kinds of words are most common? Can you think of any reason for this? Do children seem to learn similar kinds of words?
4 Make a list of all the words you have learned in French in the last two weeks. How are these different from the kinds of words babies first learn?

The range of responses was encouraging. To the group headings suggested on the task card, ingenious additions were made including *animals, toys* and *bodily functions.*

Feedback from the groups gave an opportunity to compare the classifications. The technical terms 'noun' and 'verb' arose quite naturally in the course of the discussion. Groups were also asked to report back on how they had shared the tasks and how successfully they had collaborated. Hard lessons were learned in some groups about organisation and co-operation. A helpful coincidence was that some suggestions for effective group talk, compiled by year 9 pupils, were on display at the time.

From a baby's first words we took an imaginative leap to a baby's thoughts. Pupils had to imagine what might go through a baby's head when being washed or fed, for example, writing down a series of adult equivalents to baby thoughts. This provided an opportunity for quiet individual written work as a respite from the collaborative talk of previous sessions. The responses ranged from fairly mundane routine activities to more adventurous thoughts on being born or being christened.

Telegraphic talk

We then tackled what we'd identified as the next stage in a child's language development: two-word utterances. I gave pupils a series of telex/telegram-style messages on diverse topics and asked them to tell me what the messages had in common. The pupils were easily able to tell me and then experimented with writing similarly economical messages to friends in the group. The recipients of these sometimes colourful missives then wrote out the full version, underlining the words that had been left out in the original.

Working as a class, we listed the words; pupils were quick to recognise the way the words fell into separate groups. Thus it became necessary to introduce some linguistic terminology as we gathered together articles ('the', 'a') prepositions ('in', 'at', 'to') auxiliary verbs ('have lost', 'is gone') on sheets of paper.

The similarities between such 'telegraphic talk' and the speech development of a typical two year old were now explored. We listened again to the recording of James, confirming our ideas. We were also able to identify other characteristics of a young child's language from the tape: the omission of word endings, for example, for both plurals and verb endings. These ideas were consolidated in a five-minute activity to end the lesson. From a list of two- and three-word phrases, pupils had to identify which ones a two year old might use:

Here are some two- and three-word phrases. Which ones might a toddler use?

was running	eat apple	car go
that doggie	because I	Mummy sit chair
go fast to	Did you go?	my teddy
Daddy run	is sitting on	Dally play ball
some flies	ball go	allgone milk
I play with	the dog jumped	

Although children use very simple language at the two- and three-word stage, they express many ideas.

Making a transcript of a two year old's talk

This two-word stage was further explored in the next session as we watched a video of Rob Hubbleday, a Shropshire primary headteacher, talking with his two year old daughter, Anna. A group of three pupils volunteered to make a transcript of the conversation. The class offered them some advice about layout and how to proceed. By the next lesson I had made multiple copies of the transcript.

Transcript of Anna's story about her finger

Anna	Got poorly hand … finger.
Daddy	Oh dear. Have you got a poorly finger?
Anna	Give it medicine?
Daddy	No. Shall I kiss it better?
Anna	No … Yes, I kiss it better.
Daddy	You kiss it better.
Anna	Better.
Daddy	Better now. That's better then, is it?
Anna	Poorly.
Daddy	Oh … never mind.
Anna	Bump the stairs.
Daddy	You bumped it on the stairs?
Anna	Yes.
Daddy	How did you do that?
Anna	Crying.

Daddy	You were crying, were you?
Anna	Yes.
Daddy	Oh dear. Did mummy look after you then?
Anna	No.
Daddy	Did she give you a cuddle?
Anna	No ... That one's poorly now.

We watched the video of the conversation again, following closely and making the odd correction to the transcript. Group analysis of the conversation was directed by a series of questions:

What's the difference between the way Anna talks and the way her father talks?

How is Anna's father helping her to communicate?

Write out the full version of what Anna might say. Underline the words you've added and see if you can gather them into groups of words. Can you find a term to describe each group of words?

This activity worked particularly well. I was pleasantly surprised by the children's attention to the ways Rob helped Anna learn language. Reference was made to the initial video extract from *Language File*, in which we had seen how the mother treated her baby's noise and smiles as 'turns' in a conversation. Subsequently pupils in pairs composed 'Advice to Parents'. One example is given below:

Advice to parents for helping their children to talk

1 Talk to your child as you do things together.
2 Never tell them off for saying a word strangely. Just say it to them again clearly.
3 Ask them questions to get them to talk and say it for them if they can't answer.
4 When you introduce new words, repeat them to them clearly, showing them what you are talking about.

How children discover the rules of adult grammar

And so to our next stage, 30 months to 4 years, in which the child begins to sound more and more like a fluent speaker, two- and three-word phrases giving way to real sentences. During the research of their own first words, several lessons previously, one pupil had returned with a list of larger phrases, and her group had enjoyed a good chuckle over her 'mistakes' – 'I wetted the bed' was one that particularly stays with me! I was now able to refer to her examples, as we began to explore how children discover the rules of adult grammar and syntax; how these kinds of 'mistakes' show that children are really very clever.

I presented pairs with a series of 'mistakes' made by a fictitious three year old, Matthew.

I runned down the road.	See my tooths?	I eated the apple.
I bringed the shoe.		I maded this yesterday.

Matthew discovers the rules

I catched the ball.		We saw sheeps.
I wented to the shops.		I got two foots.
My feets are wet.	The doggie goed outside	The mens are running.

Pairs of pupils were asked to read Matthew's sentences, underline his 'mistakes' and then explain why he was making them. This led to fruitful discussion of the different ways plurals are made in English and the different ways in which the past tense is formed. More linguistic terminology was added to the sheet on display. Having identified from Matthew's 'mistakes' several language rules and their exceptions, the pairs combined into groups of four and transcribed them onto posters. Here is a copy of one group's work on singulars and plurals:

Singular		Plural		Singular		Plural
2 x dog	=	dogs		2 x tooth	=	teeth
2 x apple	=	apples	BUT	2 x foot	=	feet
2 x road	=	roads		2 x man	=	men
				2 x sheep	=	sheep

From looking at how we learn to talk, a natural progression would be to consider children's development as both readers and writers. However, I found time galloping by and so brought this sequence of work to a close by considering learning to read.

Thinking about learning to read

Pupils went home to try to discover how they had learned to read and to collect together books that were favourites when they were very young. I borrowed a range of picture books from a neighbouring primary school. We spent a lesson sitting in groups swapping stories about early experiences of learning to read, sharing books and talking about favourites. For some, the memories of learning to read were painful. Others could only recall just knowing one day that they could do it.

For the next lesson, pupils were given a variety of books and asked to classify them into groups. I said the classification was to be of their own making and pupils offered groupings according to types of stories, styles of illustrations, quantity of text, use of rhyme or repetition, to name a few.

I asked them to think about Mr Brett and his young son, James. What kind of books would they recommend he get for his child? I advised them to think about:

- language:
- presentation: print size, layout, page design;
- illustration;
- story and plot;
- central characters.

After sharing the suggestions, one group turned to composing a letter of advice to Mr Brett for selecting books. Another group compared the kinds of books chosen with those that would appeal to an 11 year old. Meanwhile, the other groups prepared to read a book to the rest of us as if we were three years old. They had to take care in their selection of the book and think about how they should read it to us. Groups finishing more swiftly than others were asked to jot down reasons for their choice of book and what they were trying to do to make their reading appeal to three year olds.

The reading of the books, followed by justifying their choices and styles of reading aloud, provided an enjoyable, lively hour. Finally, pupils considered what advice to give to parents about helping a child to learn to read. To do this, they used the following extract from the *Language File* book:

In pairs, discuss this list of things that a parent or guardian could do to help a child to learn to read. Rearrange the list into an order of importance, missing out any you think would not help at all. Note down your order and compare it with another pair's order:

(a) buy lots of interesting books
(b) read out loud to the child
(c) point out writing for the child to read, e.g. signs, labels
(d) join the local library
(e) encourage the child to ask questions about what is read
(f) pick books with good pictures
(g) choose funny books
(h) read the same books lots of times
(i) let the child choose the books to be read
(j) ask the child to retell the story using the book.

An obvious progression at this point would be to have groups making books for young children with an accompanying log reflecting the pupils' own learning. Visits to local nursery/primary schools would guarantee a real audience as well as enabling them to evaluate the success of their books. Pupils could extend their observations to young children as talkers and writers too.

I was pleased at the way this unit of work enabled pupils to explore language acquisition by drawing on their own experiences. Further use could be made of this rich resource, drawing together the ideas into a language autobiography. The *Language File* book offers a possible structure for this writing about language development.

With thanks to pupils and staff at Ludlow Church of England School, Ludlow, Shropshire.

This article shows pupils:
- reflecting on their own effectiveness in the use of the spoken word (§6, Speaking & Listening);
- focusing on the range of purposes which spoken language serves (§9, Speaking & Listening);
- considering language appropriate to situation, topic and purpose, and how inappropriate language can be a source of humour (§18, Speaking & Listening);
- focusing on some of the main characteristics of literary language (§19, Reading);
- widening their knowledge of some of the main differences between speech and writing (§22, Writing);
- becoming familiar with some word-building processes and spelling patterns (§25, Writing);
- learning that speech typically takes place in a situation where the speaker and listener are present and learning about some of the characteristics of speech which derive from this fact (§28, Writing);
- coming to understand that, at its most characteristic, speech is interactive, spontaneous and informal (§30, Writing).

Ways of Talking

As adults we have experience of speaking and listening in a wide range of contexts and for a variety of purposes. We use this repertoire so freely that unless we are in an unusual or threatening context – being interviewed, for instance – we are hardly aware of the adaptations we make.

The four case studies that follow show how pupils can be encouraged to think about the purposes and contexts for talk and the ways in which spoken language can vary according to purpose, audience and setting. There is a particular focus on register in these articles – on the ways in which speakers switch and slide in their styles of speech as they modify (often unconsciously) their ways of speaking according to the expectations of fellow speakers or listeners and the settings they share. Register also involves questions of accent, dialect and identity, of course; these are specifically dealt with in the section on 'Language Diversity' later in this volume.

During such shifts of register, choices are made at all levels of the linguistic system – choices of voice quality, intonation and pronunciation (as in our 'telephone voice'); choices of syntax and words (as in talking technically to an expert, or chatting to a baby); and choices within larger structures (as in the uses and abuses of such shared conversational features as turn-taking moves, ritualised exchanges, politeness and cooperation strategies, and so on). The classroom activities which are described in this section have provided children with the opportunity to make such choices and to reflect upon them.

In the first article, 'Talk words', Nora Prince's year 1 children are exploring the language of talk by collecting all the words to describe talk they can think of and discovering which relate to their own experience of speaking and listening. The invention by the teacher of an ogre who eats words provides the imaginative stimulus for widespread enthusiasm and collection. The discussion which the project provokes touches on wide-ranging issues like turn-taking, politeness, differences between speech and writing and an experiment to see what it feels like to spend a day not talking at all!

Mary Fowler's 'Exploring register through role play' describes work with year 3 children which starts with a consideration of their experience of and attitudes to accent and dialect. The teacher then moves beyond this into role play based upon the children's shared experience of a Margaret Mahy story. The role plays they develop around the story, the comments other children make about these role plays, and the children's own reflections on their performances reveal the beginnings of a sophisticated understanding of those features which define a language repertoire.

In 'Drama and knowledge about language' Carole Bingham reflects on the kinds of knowledge about language which are intrinsic to good drama education, and on those aspects of the spoken language repertoire which can be extended and enriched through drama. These involve students in developing and talking about two kinds of register: the ways of talking which they experience 'in character', through being engaged in dramatised role play and reaching for ways of talking beyond their everyday experience; and the ways of talking they use among themselves for sharing and reflecting upon such experiences.

Finally, in 'Watch with mother, or view with mum?', Frances Smith describes a media-based activity where years 5 and 6 children focus closely on features of spoken language and attitudes to spoken variation by comparing children's television presenters recorded thirty years apart. Responding through role play, writing, and discussion, they explore the issue of appropriateness, commenting on body language, accent, slang, and language change over time.

TALK WORDS

GEORGE KEITH AND NORA PRINCE

This small project took place at Bryn Gates Infant School, Wigan, where the teacher's initial interests lay in talking and listening, and in developing in her year 1 pupils their natural curiosity about words. They began to collect words for different kinds of talk, although other kinds of vocalisation were not excluded, e.g. 'singing', 'snoring', 'grunting', 'hissing', 'sneezing'. Each time a new word was discovered, it was written on a card and added to a collage on the wall. One morning, for example, while reading her story to the others, a child used the word 'cackle', and somebody immediately called out, 'That's a talk word', and added it to the ever-growing list.

Here are some examples of words and phrases discovered by the pupils:

natter, whisper, mumble, yell, giving a talk, read aloud, being silly, talk quietly, chatterbox, talk the hind legs off a donkey, tell, listen, swearing, being rude, shouting, singing hymns, arguing, telling off, being cheeky, telling a story, asking, speaking up, burble, huffing and puffing, crying, laughing, telling jokes, playing 'I spy', calling out, wittering on, not listening, calling names (in two senses, the register and insults), cheering, jeering, I'm not talking to you, reading the news, giving the weather forecast, being in a play, putting your hand up (a curious one this, yet it makes sense!), said, say, enquired, rabbiting on, earwigging, tongue-twister, a scary voice, belt up, shut up, spit it out, let me hear you say it.

There is already a fascinating web of meanings to be played with here. We can see what an agglomeration the list is, with purposes for talk ('to ask', 'to tell', 'to swear') mixed in with different ways in which people talk ('whispering', 'shouting', 'mumbling'). Listening and talking are inseparable. 'Putting your hand up' and 'not listening', for example, are lively starting points for a discussion on ways in which we talk and listen to each other. Some of the words are clearly derived from reading, others from everyday conversation. Some examples are not only found in talk (e.g. 'being silly'), but nevertheless identify familiar forms of speech behaviour such as putting on a silly voice and making up silly or nonsense words.

The important thing for the teacher at this stage is to recognise just how many possibilities a collection of this kind opens up, but not to try and investigate all of them at once. For example, from such a starting point a class could:

- collect rhyming pairs and turn them into poems, e.g. 'natter' and 'chatter', 'huff' and 'puff', 'cheer' and 'jeer', 'tell' and 'yell';
- collect contrasted meanings, e.g. 'whisper' and 'shout', 'natter' and 'give a talk', 'tell jokes' and 'sing hymns';
- devise fantastic drawings or tales to illustrate or explain figures of speech, e.g. 'talk the hind legs off a donkey', 'belt up', 'rabbiting on', 'earwigging';
- dramatise different ways of talking, e.g. 'whispering', 'cackling', 'giving a talk', 'reading the weather forecast';
- make a dictionary (with or without the aid of IT) of talk words;
- investigate how speech is produced by the use of breath, vocal cords, lips, tongue, teeth (use tongue twisters as examples);
- listen to different tones of voice and identify how they communicate meanings;
- look at pictures of people talking and decide what they might be saying.

The class teacher in this particular case believed that observation and reflection would develop confidence in the children's powers of speech; she wanted her class to continue investigating different purposes and different ways of talking. In order to sustain their collection of talk words, she invented an ogre: the class had to feed the ogre talk words in order to stop it feeding on children. All the words they found were fed into the ogre's mouth, and it was not very long before they began to ask what would happen when there were no talk words left. The ogre, which was a fun element in the activity, led the children to become sufficiently interested in the topic itself to want to try an experiment. They asked the teacher if they could have a whole day in which nobody talked at all, just to see what it would be like. Not only was this a heaven-sent gift to the teacher, it also proved an effective way of enabling pupils to test the power and function of talk in their school lives. They enjoyed the day immensely. One girl, reflecting on how we would manage without talk, remarked: 'We could tell the weather, but we wouldn't be able to understand the news'. She was referring to television, where the weather forecast can be read from the symbols without the need to hear the announcer's words, whereas newsreel pictures cannot be fully understood without the newsreader's commentary. This example of knowledge about language and media education provides an opportunity for discussing a wide range of signals, symbols and sign systems in modern society.

In the course of the rest of the project, the class thought about listening, turn-taking and rules of politeness among different groups of people (children together, children and parents, children and teachers), describing this behaviour in pictures and stories.

They looked at examples of talk and writing, in order to understand some of the significant ways that speech differs from writing. They compiled talk autobiographies, starting from questions like 'How did I learn to talk?', 'What were the first things I said?', 'What kinds of talk do I find easy or difficult', 'What kinds of talk do I like or not like?'. This naturally involved some enquiries at home. Lastly, they learned something about the use of dialogue in narrative. For example, they began to add speech bubbles to their drawings and acted out dialogues with a lively understanding of some of the features of that kind of talk – repetition, interrogation, changes of tone of voice.

With grateful thanks to the children and teachers at Bryn Gates Infant School, Wigan.

> This article shows children:
> * reflecting on and evaluating their uses of spoken language (§4, Speaking & Listening);
> * discussing the range of purposes which spoken language serves (§9, Speaking & Listening);
> * talking about the ways in which language is written down (§6, Reading);
> * playing with language (§9, Writing).

EXPLORING REGISTER THROUGH ROLE PLAY

MARY FOWLER

A class of year 3 children at St. Edmund's R.C. Primary School explored the question 'Do we speak in different ways to different people?' The work began in the spring term 1990 and spread into the first few weeks of the summer term.

Many of the children in the class speak with an Irish accent, and a few have a parent or grandparent who speaks Gaelic. Others come from homes where Italian, Spanish, Greek, Filipino, Tamil and French Creole are spoken. To begin with, the children talked about accent and dialect. The discussions covered questions such as 'Are some accents better than others?' and 'Can you tell how clever someone is by the way they speak?'

From this they moved on to looking at their own spoken language repertoire. They were surprised to find that they spoke in different ways in the playground, the classroom, at home, at a friend's house. When they looked closely at some of their own classroom and playground talk, they also discovered differences between boys' and girls' talk.

Throughout, the quality of the discussion was high. The children had positive attitudes towards the collaborative work, and so we looked for ways to develop this aspect further. We wanted to make explicit some of the understandings they had about why different styles, accents and vocabularies may be selected by someone talking in a particular situation.

We made a list of possible role plays which were within the children's own experience. They chose one which interested them and worked on it in pairs. The children slipped easily into such roles as a parent refusing more pocket money or a headteacher being stern.

Developing role play from story

In order to broaden the scope of the role plays and of the language we used in them, we introduced the story 'Frightening the Monster in Wizard's Hole' by Margaret Mahy from her collection *Non-stop Nonsense* (Magnet 1986, Mammoth 1990). It tells the story of a village which has, on its outskirts, a wizard's hole. This has been the home of a monster for 100 years: a monster that has not bothered the villagers or been visited by them within living memory. Two boys find some bricks, and this gives one of them an idea. He decides that the monster has been with them for too long and rallies other villagers to the cause. Despite a few dissenting voices, they arrive at the wizard's hole ready to throw bricks at the monster. The monster looks out and speaks to them. He is delighted to have visitors, but his monster language cannot be understood by the villagers, who drop their bricks and run.

After listening to the story, the children discussed the morality of the villagers' actions and thought about some of the consequences. Working in pairs, they developed role play situations around the story. When they were ready, they showed their role play to another pair. We suggested that the observing pair should find something they liked and something that they thought could be improved. The children spent time working on their situations. A few pairs changed what they were doing completely. Some situations which were popular at the beginning had completely disappeared by the end of the work; an example of this was a courtroom scene. The children found this difficult to develop and abandoned it for a television interview.

Throughout, the girls followed the initial instruction to work in pairs, but the boys soon merged into larger groups. While the girls selected domestic, personal role plays, most of the boys chose television interviews and outside broadcasts which had a wider perspective, or the action-packed scene outside the wizard's hole.

Girls' role plays
Mother and child
Two old ladies
Cafe owner and customer
Mother and teacher
Headteacher and teacher
Monster and monster's relation
(All these role plays were done in pairs.)

Boys' role plays
Television interviews
Television outside broadcast
Group outside the wizard's hole
(These role plays were done in larger groups.)

Two villagers
(This was the one paired role play done by the boys.)

The language used by the children

We made transcripts from five of the developed role plays. Two were news broadcasts by groups of boys, and three were paired conversations by girls: a headteacher and teacher, two old villagers and a mother and child.

All the transcripts showed a knowledge of the kind of language appropriate to the situation and the speaker. The status of the characters was established through the choice of language and the progression of the conversations. The news broadcasts showed an understanding of television and other media news conventions.

The role play between the mother and child brought out the mother's concerns for the child. She was angry about the teacher's irresponsibility in taking the class to the wizard's hole:

I'll be down that school first thing tomorrow morning without fail, and if your teacher doesn't give me a simple explanation for this, I'm going to see the Headmaster.

The child, in contrast, conveyed her excitement as she told her mother the story. When reflecting on her role as the child, Frederica said, 'I spoke excitedly because I was an adventurous girl'.

The transcript of the headteacher and teacher brought out the difference in status between the two. The teacher is made to justify her actions and is then reprimanded:

I heard from a certain member of staff that you stopped in the middle of class to throw bricks. Is that right? Well, would you mind explaining to me what happened?

Throughout this role play the headteacher is interrogating the class teacher, demanding explanations. Her language is formal: 'May I interrupt here?' and 'Why did it seem all right to steal bricks from a building site?' This role play ends with the headteacher dismissing the teacher:

I'm very disappointed. You can have two weeks without your wages. And remember, I don't pay you to go gallivanting around wizards' holes: I pay you to teach children. You may leave.

The two old ladies from the village show the children's understanding of the lack of status of many old people and how they feel out of tune with the modern world. The girls start this role play with 'What is the world coming to these days?' They don't think it was right to threaten the monster: '… but who would want to harm that monster? He hasn't bothered us for 100 years'. They decide to complain to the council, although they don't expect much success. 'But they wouldn't listen to a pair of old villagers, would they?'

When asked to reflect on the language they had used, Gemma said that the council would not take notice of the old ladies. 'They wouldn't, because they aren't very special and could be telling lies.'

Both the outside broadcasts demonstrated the boys' knowledge of media news conventions and the kind of language heard in news reports. They introduced their role plays in similar ways:

Big story tonight. Townspeople drop their bricks and run for their lives. I'll be talking to the Lord Mayor himself and Harry from the village. 'Lord Mayor, do you think the dragon should be killed and why?'

The boys present different points of view in their interviews and bring in experts to give their opinions: 'I heard you've got an expert on language next to you'. People who had witnessed the event were asked to express their feelings. 'I'd like to ask Paul, how did he feel when the dragon stuck his head out of the wizard's hole?'

Later, in describing his part in one of the role plays, Paul explains his challenge to the mayor in the following way:

I spoke in that way because I disagreed with the mayor, and I decided to speak how I did because we decided [in the group] that I would come from a posh part of the village.

Letters in role

Alongside the role plays the children wrote letters in role.

1. Parent to headteacher

Dear Mrs Ross,

I heard from my son that in the middle of class Mr Sullivan said to pick up a brick and go to Wizards Hole. He also said that the monster has not bothered anybody for hundreds of years. I would like to see you about this when ever you can. I would not like this to happen again.

Yours sincerely,

Mrs Green.

2. Headteacher to parent

Dear Mrs Green,

I am very sorry about this misunderstanding I'm sure that won't happen again I hope you will forgive Mrs O'Dea for taking your child and the rest of the children in the class to go and throw bricks at the monster in the wizard's hole once again I'm very sorry.

Yours faithfully,

Mrs Ross.

3. Police inspector to parent

Dear Mrs Puddenytame,

I understand that you did not listen to your eldest son on the 25th June. He complained that you and your partners were disturbing the monsters peace.

The county agree with your son so do I. I am therefore taking you to court for disturbing the Monsters peace.

Yours sincerely,

The police inspector.

4. Building company to boy

Dear Tom Tom,

I am writing to you about the bricks you will have to pay a lot of money. The amount will be £85.15p. I was not pleased at all when I heard about how all the people took the bricks off our lorry. The man that was driving the lorry was not pleased at all. He was very angry indeed.

Yours sincerely,

John Hunt

Managing Director.

5. Boy to building company

Dear Standford Building Company,

I am very sorry that I took your bricks from a lorry. I needed the bricks very much but I know I should not have taken them without asking you first. I would like to pay for the bricks that I took. Would you please let me know how much I must send you?
Yours sincerely,
Tom Tom.

6. Monster to boy

Dear Tom Tom,

I am writing a letter to thank you for giving me lots of bricks. I have built a house with the bricks, and I would like to thank all the people who came with you to give me the bricks. I want you and Sam Bucket to come to my new house for tea.
Yours sincerely,
The monster.

The letters demonstrate the children's ability to write appropriately, bearing in mind audience and purpose. As might be expected from eight year olds, the role plays show more varied use of language in relation to the role of the speaker and the situation than do the letters.

What we learnt

We learnt that the children had a lot of implicit knowledge about language and that it was firmly based in their own experience. When we asked them about that experience, it proved to be quite diverse; for example, they had encountered a wide range of languages and accents, both in their everyday lives and through the media. Through the talk, they showed sensitivity towards the rights and feelings of others. If we hadn't created a context for their discussions, we would not have found this out.

The children enjoyed the story, and so did we. They were purposeful and involved in all aspects of the work and the level of collaboration was impressive. Their implicit knowledge was made explicit through this collaboration. Teacher intervention did move the children forward, but they did most of the learning themselves. Perhaps our most valuable contributions were giving them time to work and rework their ideas, setting up a model for groups and pairs to support each other, and explicitly informing the children that their thoughts and opinions were valuable.

Thanks to the children in the year 3 class at St Edmund's RC Primary School, London Borough of Enfield, and to their teacher, Jim Coffey.

This article shows children:

- discussing the range of purposes that spoken language serves (§9, Speaking & Listening);
- reflecting on and evaluating their uses of spoken language (§4, Speaking & Listening);
- exploring language variation in terms of such variables as occupation, age, gender (§14, Speaking & Listening);
- exploring the relationship between Standard English and the formality of situation and setting (§8, Speaking & Listening).

DRAMA AND KNOWLEDGE ABOUT LANGUAGE

CAROL BINGHAM

I teach a full timetable of drama in a secondary school. This entails a general drama course in lower school and a GCSE course in years 10 to 11. The teaching applies to drama in education rather than performing arts or theatre skills.

This article is an attempt to exemplify how drama offers situations and opportunities in which students can adopt appropriate language and register. I taped lessons and found numerous examples, such as:

Whatever you do, the choice is yours, but you must make your decision with care. There are many of you who have come forward, and I am grateful.

This was spoken by a student in role as the leader of 'Zardon', a city and civilisation that had been created in the course of the drama. The student had produced the formality of language and tone which the role required – much to my amazement, since the student in question was not a 'high achiever' academically, nor particularly articulate. It is perhaps excessive to say that he was inspired by the drama process, and yet the adoption of role, the perceptions of the required register for that role and the demands upon it within the drama medium – all of these can push students to use their knowledge to the fullest extent. There is a sense of urgency and a need to make meanings explicit.

Another example came from a year 10 student who was placed in the role of a headmistress:

I have invited you up to school to discuss Jane's behaviour. There was an unpleasant incident in the playground... I have no alternative but to place her on suspension.

Here, a more formal, social register was assumed by a far from articulate or intellectual student as a result of the demands of the drama.

However relevant, this only identifies one aspect of the relationship between language and drama. This relationship is not simply a one way process, with the drama situation enabling and facilitating language use and awareness. The link is reciprocal. Specific use of language has an impact upon the drama. Often it stimulates activity or creates mood; simply asking students individually to state what they see or hear establishes a clear, mutually understood context in which the drama can begin. Specific words and phrases can establish belief or bias. If the language is not compatible, the drama is impeded. Students perceive immediately when the language is appropriate: when it is inappropriate, it can interfere with their willingness to submerge themselves in the 'as if' reality of the drama medium. For example, a court-room improvisation or one set in the past cannot develop without appropriate language use, because the participants feel 'unreal' within the drama.

In this sort of situation, some dramatic strategies facilitate a sharing of language knowledge; when students are working with the dramatic convention of 'forum theatre' (in which certain students interact as a direct result of the wishes and decisions of the 'forum'), words and phrases are offered and adopted by the active role players. Alternatively, a group working together to create a ceremony will share their knowledge about language in order to find the appropriate tone. Students are very willing to share and experiment with language, because the dramatic context offers a 'safety net'; they won't be laughed at if they try out certain words and, equally, they can be taught words they did not know, without losing face in the peer group.

A group of GCSE students showed me how aware students at this level are of the use and power of language in creating and conveying meanings. One drama involved the creation of a character, Julie, who had suffered emotional deprivation as a child and was now an isolate. The drama required the students to establish what had happened when Julie was eight years old. It would have been theatrically artificial to adopt a childish voice or movement for the role, so the only appropriate and available strategy for presenting the child was her, and others', use of language. The mispronunciation of the word 'plague' and the abusive term 'smelly parts' were used effectively. In order to consolidate our awareness of the role, and the effect upon Julie of the emotional abuse, we used the following convention: students were given the opportunity to approach the central role in any of the roles that had figured in the drama; they were not allowed to specify who they were as this would have destroyed the tension and atmosphere. The convention thus forced them to 'fine tune' a range of lexical and grammatical choices in order to specify role:

You could have been an excellent student. We had great expectations of you.

She burnt the shed — she's naughty.

You've never given me anything but trouble. We should have gone to those CPS people in the first place.

You little slag! Keep your hands off my boyfriend.

I'm afraid you will have to accompany me down to the station.

A girl with such capabilities!

She hasn't half changed.

Another group experimented with using their knowledge of language to create specific effects. In a drama which incorporated an investigation into rape, the students worked on creating a surreal effect to present the dreams of the rapist. They managed to achieve this by building into it body language and spoken language which conflicted with each other: in the dream the victim spoke in terms of harsh accusations while at the same time using stroking and caressing body movements. Another piece of work produced a dream-like quality by contrasting the formality of the language of court with the informality of the rapist's language as he tried to justify himself within his mind. Specific emotive words were also combined with bodily movements to convey a state of guilt and turmoil. In their reflections on the work, students pointed to the reciprocal aspects of the link between the use of language and drama:

Student 1   It was like everything going round in his head – all the guilt.

Student 2   Like his head was spinning.

Student 3   It was like the circling of his conscience – no sooner had he pushed it away, it returned again like a revolving door.

If students are encouraged to consider the linguistic descriptions they have used in their reflection on the drama, they establish within their own minds the importance of language in encapsulating complex emotions. They are also perhaps more likely to be encouraged away from the staccato descriptions of emotion usually associated with adolescent pupils. Furthermore, one result of this emerging sensitivity towards language is that students start to use language as a device in the structuring of their drama work. For example, students combined body language and language with intent to make meanings explicit:

Mike *(rapist)*   I won't sack you. I'm reassuring you of that fact. It's just a mistake. You girls have trouble with hi tech stuff.

Nicky   I though you'd go spare. *(Use of colloquial register)*

Mike   Am I like that? Just because I'm usually seen as the hard-faced boss doesn't mean I'm not human.

Later, on the phone to his wife.

Mike   Look, I couldn't get home for six … It wasn't my fault that one of the discs got rubbed off, but then I'm the boss and I've got to take responsibility.

The morning after:

Mike   Sorry about last night. We both had a bit too much to drink — it was just one those things, wasn't it?

The students clearly identified the intimidation of the tag question 'wasn't it'. They also commented upon the way in which the silence and body language of Mike's victim encapsulated her anguish. This was echoed by her adoption of the language of the commonplace once her attacker had left the room. Her agony was apparent, but the language allowed a distancing protection for the girl who was in role as the victim.

The students' understanding of language and its complexities allowed them to express the violence of the rape. They used a multiple role strategy and placed all the emphasis upon the words leading up to the event. The atmosphere this created culminated in the words 'Don't ... please'. The language used to explore the thoughts of the victim after the rape entered an almost poetic mode:

I was so stupid
My fault for opening the door
Should I tell someone
I let him in
He seemed so nice
Who can I tell
What will my mother say
Where can I go
I feel so dirty
Filth, hate, sorrow, shame
Trust, bastard, anguish, pain
Anger, pain, hurt, confused
Agony, pain, unfair, unclean
Dirty, foul, unclean, forcing
Hurt, pain, rape!

Moments like these link knowledge about language and drama intrinsically. The teacher's role is to highlight and reflect upon the language used in order to encourage students to develop their awareness. The teacher can also challenge students' perceptions of appropriate register and accent and can use the dramatic strategy of Teacher in Role in order to offer alternatives and create meanings. For example, a more formal register does not necessarily call for a BBC accent. Students are actually helped in this context by the key words of the drama medium itself, which they adopt quite easily and which allow them to explore a register not often open to them:

Establish   Reflect   Can we assume?   We need to identify   Investigate   Can we focus on

Finally, I hope that working with the use of language so closely gives students a vocabulary with which to explore their own feelings with safety:

I felt threatened when ...
I felt moved when ...
I felt concerned that ...

not

I was frightened ...
I was upset ...
I could not cope ...

If pupils are able to verbalise their own emotive responses, they are perhaps able to deal more sensitively with themselves and others.

With thanks to pupils and staff at Norton School, Stockton-on-Tees, County Cleveland.

This article shows students:

- participating extensively in varied group work in a range of groupings (§18, Speaking & Listening);
- discussing the range of purposes that spoken language serves (§9, Speaking & Listening);
- reflecting on and evaluating their uses of spoken language (§4, Speaking & Listening);
- exploring language variation in terms of such variables as occupation, age, gender (§4, Speaking & Listening);
- exploring the relationship between Standard English and the formality of situation and setting (§18, Speaking & Listening);
- making explicit the ways in which language can act as a bond or a barrier and can be used to alienate, insult, wound, praise or flatter (§21, Speaking & Listening);
- using spoken language as a means of reviewing experience, and reflecting on ideas.

'WATCH WITH MOTHER' OR 'VIEW WITH MUM'? CHILDREN INVESTIGATING CHANGING STYLES OF TELEVISION PRESENTATION

FRANCES SMITH

Comparison is always a good way to focus on language features, so in our LINC in-service sessions we provided primary teachers with samples of children's television presenters from 1963 and 1990 as a means of looking at language change over time. These samples of language, while limited, worked well. Television allows us to examine not only the words, but also the paralinguistic features that contribute to spoken language: eye contact, gesture, facial expression, hesitations, intonation, pitch, volume and accent. All these were noted in comparisons and led to productive discussion on aspects of language and society – what kinds of language, voice and accent adults considered appropriate for presenting programmes to children at these dates.

Some teachers were keen to see what children could learn from a similar activity, so we used the videos with two junior classes in order to pinpoint aspects of language change.

What the children saw

Each extract lasted two and a half minutes. The first was taken from 'Picture Book', part of a *Watch with Mother* programme shown in 1963, which featured a woman presenter demonstrating how to make a paper lantern. The second was a clip from *Take Hart* in 1990. Here a woman presenter showed children how to use pastry scraps to make a brooch in the shape of a holly leaf.

The presenters contrasted sharply in appearance, style and language. The black and white transmission of the *Watch with Mother* programme probably contributed to the severity of some of the children's judgements. In it, the presenter was seated behind a table and, in the children's words 'sat up very straight', 'moved like a robot' and was 'very crouched up'. She spoke slowly and deliberately, in what we would recognise as a traditional BBC accent – Received Pronunciation or RP – which was described by the children as 'very posh', 'a proper English accent'. She fixed the viewer with eye contact at important moments (for instance, when conveying the life-threatening properties of a pair of scissors) and was seen to wear 'plain and boring clothes which were probably then the fashion'. She 'looked like an auntie'. Her opening words give the flavour of her language:

Hallo, children. Are you ready to look at the picture book? I wonder what we shall have today. Oh hallo, Sausage (*a string puppet dog*). What a splendid coat you've got on! Is it new? But why do you wear it indoors? And it does look very pretty, Sausage. Now you sit still and be good.

The *Take Hart* presenter was dressed casually, seemed younger and stood working at a table. The children saw her as 'a lot more relaxed', 'comfortable, able to move freely' and 'more friendly'. She spoke in a Northern Irish accent, which the children didn't identify ('a Scottish accent', 'speaking like Gazza') and spoke in a conversational way ('didn't sound as if she was speaking from a script'). Her opening words were (after she had hummed to herself for a few seconds):

Well, that's that. Biscuits are now in the oven, and this is what I'm left with, some old pastry sort of cut out things. I'm sure your mum's been making biscuits, and she's let you play with the pastry or whatever's left over. Well, I've got an idea, something I've just thought of, to do with old pastry, so don't throw it away.

What the children did

The teachers used the video in different ways. The first class, years 5 and 6 children from Bourn Parochial School, watched it and talked about it with their teacher. They then wrote individual accounts of similarities and differences between the two extracts, choosing their own format (lists, boxed columns, use of signalling devices like icons, straightforward exposition and so on). Two groups later talked to me about their responses.

The other class, year 6 children from Thorndown Junior School in the suburbs of a market town, were able to work with me and their class teacher over several sessions. Before we watched the video, we explained that we would be comparing two television programmes, one from last year and one from about thirty years ago. The class teacher organised the children in 'home' groups of five or six children to work on the assignment. We thought it would help the children in an unfamiliar activity if we gave them some headings on which to hang their comparisons. These also provided tasks suitable for the range of ability in each group. In their home groups, we asked the children to negotiate between themselves, so that there was one 'expert' in the group to concentrate on each of these headings:
- use of media technology (obviously black and white or colour, but also number of cameras available, close-ups and longshots, background setting, etc);
- presenter's body language (posture, gaze, movements);
- presenter's appearance (clothes, hair, make-up, etc);
- clarity of the instructions given;
- use of language;
- presenter's voice quality (accent, loudness, clarity, speed, warmth, etc).

We then viewed the video again, this time with all the experts for a particular heading sitting together, so that children focusing on the same aspect could exchange their ideas. We used the pause button fairly often to allow time for discussion and note-taking. The children then returned to their original home groups and compared notes, each expert reporting back to the others in his or her group.

Home groups discussed their conclusions over a few days, and spent some time over the next few weeks planning and working on ways to present them to a visitor (me). During this time they found they needed to watch the video again several times.

Some of the groups were ready with their conclusions when I returned. I was impressed by the children's hard work and the inventiveness with which they presented their findings. I was shown model televisions with writing pasted in, a model television with a concealed tape playing spoken comparisons, model clapperboards with unfolding written comparisons and even a giant dice containing the 'expert' analyses within it!

After enjoying these presentations, we discussed general features of the two styles of presenter. I suggested that the groups might like to role play the two presenters, perhaps making them explain something else. This was immediately taken up with enthusiasm and we all moved to the hall. Groups quickly organised themselves to produce two scenes and found props to simulate a TV studio. Plastic bottles and metre sticks acted as sound booms, while camera operators were wheeled in on a chair trolley. Groups chose to show their presenters giving various types of instructions: how to use an overhead projector, how to make a paper aeroplane, as well as reworking the actual instructions seen on the video. A very enjoyable way to finish!

Other activities went on alongside the main group work. At the end of the first day, a group of children talked to me and their teacher about some of the issues that arose as they watched the video. The talk focused on accent and dialect and their observations of attitudes to this in daily life. Children also did some individual work on comparisons between the two programmes.

What the children noticed

Implicit and explicit knowledge

One of our aims in helping children to learn more about language is to encourage them to make some of their implicit and half-formulated knowledge explicit and thus more open to reflection and analysis. The nature of this activity meant that children were led to reflect and comment explicitly on a whole range of language features, from slang and accent to body language and media uses. The children used both straightforward description and analogy: 'She explained too clearly. She could have cut down on some of the words', 'She spoke as if she didn't have a script'. Implicit knowledge of other language features was also evident, of course, for instance in children's sense of appropriate and conventional ways of organising their conclusions in the final report by means of headings, columns and paragraphs. Arriving at this end product also involved a process of negotiation, collaboration, practical work and open-ended discussion.

Main points

So, what did the children notice? The task we set them – to comment on the difference between two samples of children's television thirty years apart – was designed to encourage reflection on language change in its broadest sense. The children's comments in fact clustered round two main areas:

– change in the medium of television itself, including representation, technology, audience and the 'language' of the medium;
– differences in language, from gesture to vocabulary.

The discussion with small groups allowed further reflection on this last area. These were some of the points that they noted:

1. Difference in body language

Differences in gesture, eye contact, movement, etc. were noted as part of both media and language change. Children focused on the static nature of the 1963 presenter compared with the relaxed 'comfortable' movement of her 1990 counterpart. They noticed that the standing position of the latter allowed more freedom of movement. They also noticed that the appearance of the two women reflected the same contrast of rigidity and freedom: 'dull clothes', 'tight' and 'very brushed hair' as against 'jazzy clothes', 'dressed casually' and 'lots of jewellery'; some of these comments, such as 'prim and tidy' implied a knowledge of how we read appearance and body language as an indication of character.

2. Language of instructions

The children found plenty to say about the words and voices of the two women. Children thought that the way the first gave instructions was 'extremely precise' and that she organised her explanation 'step by step'. She 'explained very well' and was 'easy to follow' (in contrast to the second presenter). Some impatience with the first presenter was also expressed, however: she 'never missed anything out' and 'got boring'.

3. Changes in use of words

Children certainly saw the first programme as a historical artefact, far in the past: 'when the war was going on', '1963', 'before England won the World Cup'. They noted some uses of words thirty years ago that have changed today: the frequent use of 'pretty' and 'splendid', words which are not usual nowadays, and also the use of 'oblong' rather than the mathematical term 'rectangle' with which they were familiar.

4. Voice quality

Differences in emphasis, intonation and clarity were noted; the children generally judged the first speaker to speak more clearly.

5. Accent

The RP of the 1963 presenter was described, inevitably, as 'posh'. Some described it as 'like the Queen's English', 'formal' and 'clear'. The way she spoke was judged 'perfect English' (though it is unclear whether this referred to dialect or accent) and 'a proper English accent'. The *Take Hart* presenter, on the other hand, 'had an accent', 'mumbled' and 'had regional speech', though there was some difficulty in identifying this. There were some positive comments on her accent: 'relaxed', 'clear but soft', 'casual', but she was also described as having 'a funny accent' and criticised for 'speaking very common' and 'using words like 'ain't' (which she didn't!).

Issues arising from the discussions

I recorded discussions with two groups in one school and one in the other, which the class teacher joined. There was no agenda or list of topics, and in all cases the children moved beyond comparisons of the two programmes to relate some of the issues that had emerged which were pertinent to their own experience. Most interest centred on accent. They talked about attitudes to spoken language, the appropriateness of different accents to different situations and the relation of accent (and local dialect forms) to regions and social class. Levels of formality in both spoken and written language were also discussed, including the nature and use of slang and how this relates to local ways of speech.

Further outcomes of the activities

The activities, based on making comparisons between two language samples, proved to be productive and engaged the children's interest. The video, and a description of the group work, has now been included in a box of books, tapes and other resources, designed to promote reflection on varieties of language; this is now on loan to Cambridgeshire schools.

Knowledge about language

I was pleased by the children's willingness to engage in constructive discussion of complex areas of language, and impressed by what they seemed to know about many aspects of language, including the strength of social judgements of language and how language is implicated in one's sense of identity and in social class. They probably knew more about some aspects of language and media studies than their counterparts in 1963 would have done. They knew something of the composition of television programmes and how such texts construct the child viewer (in the case of the 1963 programme, one who is 'good' and an obedient listener), though it was not clear if they could extend this insight to present-day programmes. One or two children also showed an awareness of language and gender that would not have been likely thirty years ago. Their repertoire of regional and social varieties of language is certainly extended by their familiarity with the accents of television programmes, especially soap operas, though here again this may be at a fairly low level of conscious awareness – none of them recognised the regional accent of the second presenter.

Knowledge about language yet to be developed

There were also, of course, things the children didn't know. The taped discussions in particular showed that the children didn't have at their disposal much of the language (and some of the knowledge) they really needed to disentangle puzzling problems concerned with language and society.

They knew the words 'accent' and 'slang', and much of their meanings, but they had no word but 'posh' (together with 'slightly posh', 'very posh' and 'poshness') to describe RP, and no evident knowledge of the terms Standard English, dialect or non-Standard English. One or two of them realised this lack and made the comment that the very word 'posh' was itself a slang usage. This was clearly an example of a time when it would be productive to teach children certain linguistic terms – they were moving towards developing the concepts, and it would have helped to have had the language with which to discuss them.

The other area I might have pursued was Standard English. Activities based on the video would have been a way to fulfil some of the National Curriculum programmes of study; it would have been interesting to have gone on at a later date to help the children compare the rules shaping the non-Standard forms they describe as 'slang' with those of Standard English forms, and to spend a little time on the functions of the latter.

The Cox Report comments:

The simplest (justification for teaching explicitly about language) is that the world would be a better place if people were better able to talk coherently about the many language problems which arise in contemporary society.

Perhaps the discussion and reflection promoted by this kind of work is a step in that direction.

I wish to acknowledge the considerable help given to me by Chris Robinson, Bourn Parochial School, Cambridgeshire, and Julie Branch, Thorndown Junior School, St Ives, Cambridgeshire, in allowing me to work with them and their classes and in their perceptive comments on the work while it was in progress.

This article shows children:
- discussing regional and social variations in accents and dialects of the English language and attitudes to such variations (§9, Speaking & Listening);
- discussing the range of purposes which spoken language serves (§9, Speaking & Listening);
- discussing the forms and functions of spoken Standard English (§9, Speaking & Listening);
- discussing vocabulary that is specific to particular age groups (§14, Speaking & Listening);
- considering language appropriate to situation, topic and purpose (§18, Speaking & Listening);
- being introduced to media texts and considering their purpose, effect, and intended audience (§18, Reading);
- leaning about some of the ways in which English is constantly changing, and about people's attitudes to such change (§19, Reading).

Kinds of Writing

The case studies in this chapter reflect some of the many ways in which teachers are developing children's understanding of a range of text types or written genres. Common to most of these accounts are a number of features.

The teachers have introduced models of the genre for the children to engage with. With these models, teachers are able to tease out what the children already know about how writing is differentiated by audience and purpose, and how such dynamics influence the choices we make within the different 'levels' of the language system – layout, discourse structure, cohesion, grammar, vocabulary and so on. As far as the writing tasks themselves are concerned, these have been located firmly within the children's own orbit of interests and concerns – a well known fairy story, a favourite meal, an endangered environment, their own school. Where necessary, the teachers have supplemented the children's prior knowledge with opportunities for direct experience or research (cooking pizza, researching elephants, interviewing the intended audience) so that they come to the task of shaping their thoughts on the page as genuine experts. These teachers have built in opportunities for discussion, and for joint collaboration in the compositional process. Lastly, they have scaffolded the pupils' interaction with sensitive interventions, making the pupils' implicit language knowledge explicit at points where this will help learning move forward.

What is impressive here is not only the imaginative vitality of the starting points and contexts in which reflection on language takes place – enriching the learning experience rather than reducing it to arid formalism – but the quality of the teachers' own reflections. Having access to a shared framework for describing language learning enables these different contributors to identify specifically their children's understandings about language (see Liz Slater's precise notes on her learners' language achievements) and to plan further challenges to ensure progression (as in Jenny Monk's exploration of the language of argument).

This chapter begins with three pieces illustrating work from year 2 and 3 classrooms. Two short vignettes, Liz Slater's 'Writing newspaper stories' and Gill Clarkson and Hazel Stansfield's 'Writing recipes' are separated by a more extensive account of 'The language of argument in the writing of young children'. This case study draws directly from 'genre theory' in its analytical framework, and Jenny Monk establishes some useful hypotheses about early development in argumentative writing and ways of supporting youngsters in this genre. All of these pieces are worth reading by teachers of older pupils, since they challenge pre-conceived notions about the difficulty of non-chronological writing for young children.

The next two articles focus on writing story books for younger readers. In 'Writing stories for a younger audience', Julie Young's work with year 10 students provides a clear blueprint for anyone who has yet to use this activity as a way of focusing older students' reflection on the appropriateness of subject, form, and grammatical choices in relation to a specific purpose and audience. A closer look at the knowledge about language revealed when pupils are making such choices is provided by Holly Anderson's article, 'Dr Xargle's guide to Earthlet knowledge about language'. Her annotated transcript of year 5 children's collaborative talk during the process of composition reveals a remarkable range and depth of understanding.

The last two articles show the development of critical, reflective reading in classrooms where students are learning about different kinds of writing as authors in their own right. In 'The Newham Press', the experience of producing and editing newspaper stories takes Lynn Newton's year 6 class back to the newspapers they are reading with a new critical edge. In 'Karen's poems' Peter Nightingale shows the quality of reflection which is available to a year 9 writer when she is supported by opportunities to draft and refine her writing, sensitive comment from her peers, and the thinking space provided by keeping a journal.

WRITING NEWSPAPER STORIES

LIZ SLATER

The examples of writing used here are from three of the year 2 children who did this work in a vertically grouped infant class. The class topic was houses and homes – the school was new and surrounded by houses in various stages of building. The whole class – with the exception of the reception group – consisted of children who had already been to at least one other school; for most year 2 children it was their third school.

As a starting point, we looked at the story of The Three Little Pigs and the houses they had built. Children brought in their own copies of the story – mostly Ladybirds, but in two different versions. This gave rise to heated discussion (with a distinct lack of 'courteous disagreement!') about the 'truth' of each version. Eventually, one year 2 boy suggested it might have been a bit like the newspapers, with the stories being different in different papers. He had been involved in a local newspaper story himself. Someone else asked if they could make newspapers about the story.

Although it was year 2 children who eventually drafted and edited the newspaper articles, the whole class was involved in initital discussion, and reception and year 1 children wrote 'news stories' if they wished.

We looked at the front pages of many newspapers. Children noticed the varying sizes of print, the use of capitals by tabloids and the use of lower case by broadsheets for headlines. They talked about the headlines and the way some words are missed out, and what kind of words they were – although, of course, without using technical terms like indefinite and definite articles! They noticed the way the text was organised in headlines and columns. They noticed the way the front page stories weren't just narrative (although, again, they didn't use that term): some reporters quoted other people; sometimes comment, as well as news, was included.

The children worked on their newspaper articles individually and in pairs, trying out their news stories on each other. They wrote their final drafts in columns. (The class had no access to desk top publishing or even BBC Folio at this stage – nor would it have been appropriate, as our process of production was longer and enabled pupils to reflect together on aspects of newspaper layout as well as style.)

Pictures were drawn in black and white – with crayon and pencil – and some children added picture captions, as they had observed in the real newspapers.

It is obvious that many children took on the role of reporter with much understanding, and reflected a newspaper style and organisation of text. (We could have, but didn't, use role play and interviewing as a preliminary to this activity.)

For two children, the report was a chronological narrative, but most of the other children's writing was non-chronological and demonstrates characteristics of argument.

The children were very concerned to get their headlines looking right, and this caused some problems. At first, using two guidelines for the top and bottom of the letters seemed sensible, but some children found that difficult – I think because their capitals were also related to the white space outside the lines. When, instead, they were given strips of paper, and it was suggested that they simply filled the paper from the top to the bottom for each letter, the problem with spatial awareness – if that's what it was – disappeared.

The children enjoyed this work enormously. As an exercise in media awareness it was extremely valuable; it also gave children an opportunity to write in various forms within a general 'newspaper' style.

To summarise, the children had identified and talked about typical design content and language features of newspapers which they then went on to use in their own versions. Among the points they considered were:

- black and white pictures;
- picture captions;
- headlines;
- text organisation and print size;
- newspaper names;
- content and style of a story, and the way that sometimes advice was included;
- advertisements, indexes;
- 'more news tomorrow' – the idea that the story would continue.

Three examples of the children's work follow, with an accompanying commentary. The second example has been reset with the original spellings.

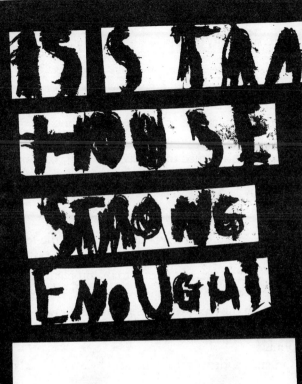

IS IS TRAW
HOUSE
STRONG
ENOUGH

You cant
use straw
for a
chimney
but you can
use brick
you cant use
straw. A
wolf
will blow

A straw.
chimney.
down
you cowid
put bricks
behind
the straw
maake it
stronger

reporter

William

Is Straw House strong enough (page 97)

William has chosen to discuss the suitability of straw as building material for a house. His writing shows the following:

- non-chronological organisation (comment and argument);
- newspaper style which is reflected by:
  — the omission of the definite (or indefinite article) in the headline;
  — William's identification of himself as a reporter;
- no statement to set the context (it is assumed the reader knows the context and that this is a continuation of a newspaper story).

The headline serves as introduction.

- Use of the present tense 'can't', 'can', 'can't' gives the statements the feeling of universally accepted truths.
- Use of the modal form 'could' in a suggested solution to the problem of having a straw chimney (not fire!) contrasts with the stronger 'can't' and 'can'.
- Strong coherence is achieved with the repeated use of the word 'straw' – as a subject in a noun phrase (twice), an adjective in a noun phrase, and as an indirect object in a prepositional phrase.
- Use of complete clauses, sometimes identified as sentences by capitals and full stops.
- 'But' is the only connective used. Other connectives he might have used later with more experience are 'however' and 'because' at appropriate places; without these, the writing is more like utterances in spoken language, but as a first venture into written argument, William has been successful in communicating.

Third Little Pig tells his story

I left my friend and I carried on I had just left the placs where the 1st pig and the 2td pig were building I come to a placs where a man was carrying some bricks and I asked the man if I could have some of the bricks to build a house of my own and he let me have some of the bricks to build a house of my own and I got a wheel barrow to put my bricks in and I wheeled barrow it to the place where I was going to build my house and I come to a place where there was a nice place where I was near the sea-side and I started to build a house there and I lived across the road where where the wolf and I didn't mind living near the wolf.

(Sharon)

Sharon's text is one of the only two pieces of narrative writing which any of the group produced. Briefly, particular features are:

- the writer has assumed the role of the third little pig and written in the first person singular narrative;

- the writing is organised chronologically as a recount with a comment at the end. There is one 'flashback' in 'I had just …';
- the text consists of a series of clauses joined by the connective 'and', mostly meaning 'and then', which, with further experience, would be more likely to be omitted;
- coherence is emphasised not so much by the connectives, which are largely superfluous, but by the repeated use of the pronoun 'I', the use of the past tense, the re-use of words like 'man' and 'he' in successive sentences, as well as 'bricks', and 'build' and 'house';
- the word 'come' is used instead of 'came' – this may be a near-correct spelling, or dialect or a result of early experimenting with the flashback strategy, attempting to write 'I had just left… (when) I came…';
- true to newspaper style, the headline has the definite article missing, and the text was originally written in columns.

Is Pig safe? (page 100)

James took great delight in organising his newspaper page. He has observed and used the following aspects of newspaper style:

- the headline has a missing definite article (and an unintentionally missed question mark);
- an advertisement;
- the index;
- black and white photo and police photofit;
- reporter's name;
- some text broken into separate sections.

James's writing is non-chronological with some aspects of recount, but comment and argument feature strongly. Without the chronological organisation, and no other linguistic device as an aid to coherence, his writing has a disjointed feel. He had problems concentrating, but the use of phrases like 'put himself at risk' and 'apparently' show the level of his language experience, so it is unclear how much of this lack of coherence is a result of short span concentration or an absorption of the feel and style of some tabloid reporting! There are some interesting points to mention:

- 'Apparently…' introduces a form of conjecture in argument; although the 'it' is not coherently linked with the previous sentence, the thought linking the two statements is very clear.
- 'He' at the top of the second column refers back to the wrong noun in the previous sentence. This is probably because James is experimenting with more complicated sentence structures and this has led to unclear pronominalisation.
- He has also ventured into the use of modals, 'would', where he has used a

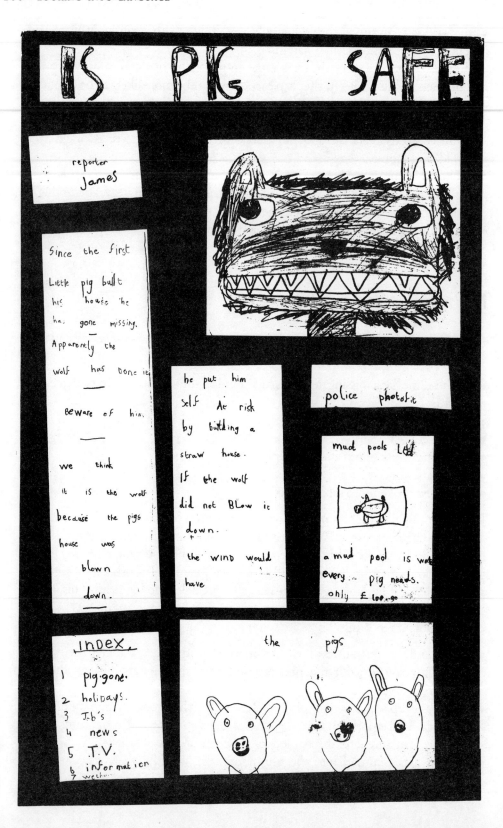

IS PIG SAFE

reporter
James

Since the first Little pig built his house he has gone missing. Apparently the wolf has Done it.

Beware of him.

we think it is the wolf because the pigs house was blown down.

he put him self At risk by building a straw house. If the wolf did not Blow it down. the WIND would have

police photofit

mud pools Ltd

a mud pool is wot every pig neads. only £ 100.00

INDEX
1 pig gone.
2 holiDays.
3 Job's
4 news
5 T.V.
6 information
7 weather

the pigs

conditional clause to support his proposition that the pig put himself at risk by building a straw house.

With thanks to the children of Chetwood County Primary School, Essex.

This article shows children:
- talking about stories they have read and comparing versions of the same story (§6, Reading);
- reading material related to the real world (§3, Reading);
- learning how to interpret and use organisational devices such as headings, print and type face (§13, Reading);
- differentiating their writing in relation to a specific purpose and audience (§2, Writing);
- writing non-chronologically (§9, Writing);
- discussing their writing (§12, Writing);
- drafting their work (§14, Writing);
- being made aware of grammatical differences between spoken and written (Standard) English (§20, Writing);
- being made aware of variations in vocabulary and grammar according to purpose, topic and audience.

THE LANGUAGE OF ARGUMENT IN THE WRITING OF YOUNG CHILDREN

JENNY MONK

Pupils should have opportunities to write for a range of communicative or informative purposes including: describing, explaining, giving instructions, reporting, expressing a point of view.

(*English 5–16*: para 17.48)

Background to classroom research study

The focus of my study was to find out more about the ability of children aged 5 – 7 to write in different genres for different purposes and audiences. I chose to examine one type of factual writing: the writing of argumentative text. There were two reasons for choosing to look at this kind of writing from young children. First, attitudes about what can be done in writing can be formed at a very early age. If continuity of experience is to be addressed in the writing curriculum, it seems to me that we should have some idea of what the starting points are for supposedly difficult forms of writing, which we nevertheless expect children to be competent in by the time they leave school. Secondly, I was attracted by the challenge implicit in the following observation made in the 1978 HMI report on primary schools:

It was rare to find children presented with a task which involved presenting coherent argument, exploring alternative possibilities or drawing conclusions and making judgements. While it is recognised that this is a difficult form of writing for young children, it could have been more regularly encouraged among the older and more able pupils .

(Primary Education in England: A Survey by HM Inspectors of Schools DES: 1978: 49)

In order to explore whether their analysis applied to the writing of young children, I collected evidence from two classes of 5 – 7 year olds involved in a topic on the environment. In their planning, the teachers decided that argument and debate were appropriate to the topic but rejected the idea that this kind of writing should be limited to key stages 2 and 3. They took the view that, given support and plenty of opportunities to explore, discuss, read and reflect, there was no reason to assume that argumentative writing should prove intrinsically more difficult than any other.

For their topic work, the children had been divided into two groups: one to research the argument against, and the other for, the killing of elephants. The teachers allocated children to each group so as to ensure that both sides were explored. Within the groups, the children brainstormed all their ideas as to who would be affected by their allocated policy. They then chose roles – craftsmen, lorry drivers, governments, elephants – and researched their arguments accordingly. Writing only occurred after the children had explored their chosen roles, discussed and exchanged their ideas, and questioned each other.

A framework for investigating language in classroom contexts

As a framework for my analysis of the texts written by the children, I chose to use the concept of 'genre' as it has been elaborated by educational linguists working in Australia (Martin, 1984; Martin and Rothery; 1989: Derewianka; 1990). In the work of Martin, Rothery and others, 'genre' is used to describe the patterned variation in language which writers exploit to make their communications purposeful. It is this patterning of linguistic choices that enables us to distinguish Descriptions from Explanations, Instructions from Reports or Expositions. Genre theory itself is situated in a broader framework of language description, taking account of the way language changes according to whether it is embedded in action or being used to reflect on more distant thoughts, events or feelings.

Moreover, this framework embodies a veiw of language as a cognitive not a mechanical process. Our choice of genre (something which we make quite unconsciously for most of the time when talking, but a matter of considerably more deliberation when writing) is broadly determined by three interactive variables: what we are communicating, who is involved in the communication, and the part played by language in shaping the text as speech or writing. More technically, these variables are referred to as Field (the subject matter of a text), Tenor (the interactive roles and relationships of speaker/listener, reader/writer), and Mode (the choice of channel of communication, dependent on how close or distant we are to the events in time).

With reference to the classroom in which I worked, the Tenor roles in the early part of this topic were casual and consultative, the Mode was spoken, exploratory and investigative while the Field was limited to the non-technical language of personal emotion and 'commonsense' descriptions of the subject matter. As the topic progressed, the language became more technical and subject specific, serving to redefine the Field ('poachers', 'ivory', 'man-made' were terms that entered the discussion). Children took on more authoritative roles prior to advancing more sustained representations of their points of view in writing. It was of course noticeable that in the more formal written mode, the technicality of the language varied with respect to the individual's level of understanding and command of the written form; the completed texts also varied in the extent to which pupils were able to structure their views into an argument.

Examples of children's work

As a whole, the outcomes suggested that the pupils would benefit from more explicit discussion of the genre they were aiming to write. In selecting examples of children's work for discussion, my aim is to highlight some of the linguistic features which give these texts the status of arguments. By looking closely at how children work on the construction of argumentative writing, we come closer to understanding their achievements so far and can start to plan what to do next to help them develop further.

Closeness to spoken language assertions and statements

In the work of the youngest children (aged 5–6), we typically find starting points which seem to arise directly out of the ongoing arguments of talk, taking issue with known points of view, or assuming at the very least shared familiarity with the controversy. Lacking the support of an interlocutor, the children produce statements which appear somewhat random out of conversation context.

The first three pieces of writing illustrate these points.

No, no, no, I want to save the elephants

I think that you should kill elephants so that the old people can buy food

If there's more elephants more trees will be knocked down

Beginning to negotiate a point of view

The next piece of writing (on page 106), by a slightly older child, shows evidence of more ability to sustain a definite point of view – that it is cruel to kill elephants – basing it on the following propositions:

1. elephants can't grow again, trees can;
2. elephants suffer;
3. elephants are helpless;
4. baby elephants need their mothers for five years;
5. elephants depend on each other.

Each proposition is exemplified and there is a final reiteration: 'I think it is cruel to kill elephants'. Counter arguments also appear and are disputed: 'Trees get knocked down, but they can grow again; They think ivory is attractive to women, but it is not', with an additional thread: 'It is not fair to kill any animal'.

At the level of specific linguistic choices, this young pupil has drawn on a range of features which are characteristic of argumentative writing at all levels. Thus we find reference to generic rather than individual participants – both human and non-human ('elephants', 'people'). The choice of conjunctions ('if', 'when', 'but') serves to forge logical rather than temporal connections, and the selection verbs ('make', 'knock', 'kill', 'grow'; 'are', 'have'; 'need', 'depends', 'love', 'think', 'matter', 'suffer') represents the complex processes of actions, relations and thoughts which constitute the case against killing elephants. By writing in the present tense, the pupil has emphasised that this state of affairs is an ongoing, urgent problem.

Importance of controlling 'themes' in writing

In the piece of writing we have just discussed there is little general development as the argument progresses, despite the promising material adduced. Simply by looking at the use of 'themes' – the material presented at the start of each sentence – we can see where part of the problem lies: if every sentence starts with a new thought, the effect of a coherent case is likely to be weakened. One way of supporting the writer might be to help the child to write a more inclusive introductory statement based on the text as it stands; another strategy, which might be developed from reading the text aloud to a group of peers, would be to insert more reminders to the reader that we were still pursuing the one main topic. As it stands, the text is closer to one person's part of a (spoken) dialogue than to an independent written text. Such revisions might be best developed through collaborative work, with the teacher acting as scribe.

The fifth piece of writing (page 107) shows a different strategy for presenting a case. There is one major argument: that we should not kill elephants because they will become extinct. The opening proposition is supported by a reason with exemplification: 'when new babies are born …they won't know what elephants are …' and

We do not think you should kill elephants. The trees they ~~knc~~ knock down can grow again but elephants cantgrow agin. It does not matter

if the trees get knocked down it does not matter beacause they can grow agin but it matters if elephant get killed —

they kill elephants for there ivory tusks They think the ~~tusk~~ tusks atract woamem but the do not. And theymake neklases and braclets and earings with it. They sufer from it. People some times kill elephants for fun.

In some countrys they use elephants for paradse and dress them up. They love there elephans like aphew of us. Elephants are a very speacle thing to us. When people come and shot us we can say please dont kill me and tell the police but elephants cant beacaus the cant taik. The are not lucky like we are. They have quit rought and thic skin. It is not fair to kill any any animal. There baby needs milk and its mother for five years. Other elephants depend on other elephants. They some times keep elephants in zoos I think it is cruel to kill elephants. elephants are nice.

∘The end

comparison: 'they would be like dinosaurs'. The choice of linguistic features is similar to those of the previous piece of writing with time referents: 'when', 'in…time', 'by then' and modalised expressions: 'should not', 'should make sure', 'would [have] forgotten', being used quite skilfully as the pupil draws contrasts between present and possible future scenarios. This child is using hypotheses to support his argument, and shows command of the language needed to engage the reader in speculation.

However, in this text too there are traces of spoken language interactions: having presented his main thesis, the writer goes on to suggest an alternative and potentially

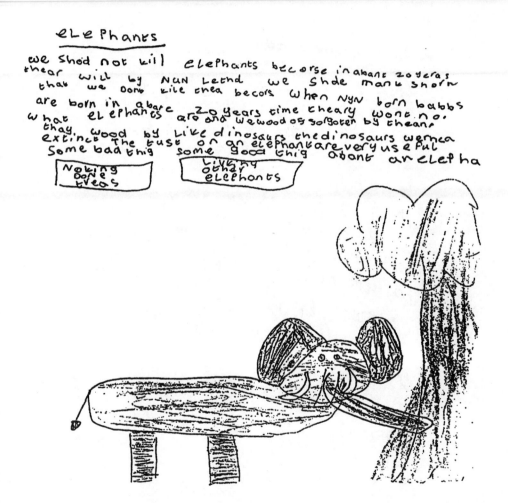

We should not kill elephants because in about 20 years there will be none left. We should make sure that we dont kill them because when new born babies are born in about 20 years time they wont know what elephants are and we would of forgotten by then. They would be like dinosaurs, the dinosaurs were extinct. The tusks on an elephant are very useful. Some bad things some good things about an elephant.

  Knocking down trees   *Liking other elephants*

distracting argument: 'the tusks on an elephant are very useful'. It seems fair to interpret this as an embryonic debate, in which another point of view is being entered but unfortunately not developed, as is the case with the boxed pro and contra points with which the text ends.

The difficulty of arguing for a contrary point of view

In discussion afterwards, all the children agreed that the hardest job was to argue a point of view which they did not necessarily hold. The next piece reflects the dilemma this causes.

The warden counts how many trees have been knocked over because he likes to keep the park nice and not horrible he likes to keep it nice all the time. You should kill some because it is cruel to kill them. They are very nice but we don't want them to keep knocking down trees. I like them, the park warden likes them too, the zoos like them too, they don't want them to be killed. They need to kill them to get their tusks, to make things. They sell the things they make to the shops, they need lots of things to have in the shops. I like the babies too and the big ones.

The argument develops as follows:

Elephants knock down trees, so you should kill some: but it is cruel.

We all like elephants but they are needed for their tusks to make things and to sell things.

but... 'I like the babies too and the big ones'.

There are of course many ways of presenting points of view with which one does not necessarily agree (one such way is shown by the pupil who used the rhetorical question: how would you like?). Another can be seen in the use of general propositions: 'some people ...'. Although pupils did find it hard to deal with conflicting points of view, there were signs that they were starting to develop the linguistic resources which would enable them to do so. On the evidence of their own work, they were ready for a more extended study of others' writing.

What constitutes 'personal experience'?

Dixon and Stratta (1986), who have written extensively on ways of helping older children write better arguments, contend that where an issue is complex and dependent on specialised knowledge, rather than on personal experience, then the students are doomed to failure. They give as an example the familiar type of examination question, 'Streaming in school is the best method for educating. Discuss'. It could be argued that, given these children's ages, the elephant debate was indeed specialised and complex. It was, however, an area of concern which generated sufficient debate for the teachers involved to consider it worth tackling and, in the way they organised their topic work, ensured that children were able to 'personalise' expert knowledge to a considerable degree.

Furthermore, the children were able to reflect on the significance of working on a controversial topic from the public domain. They explained to me that they argued at home with their parents about such things as choice of clothes and taking medicine. Each child could relate to the concept of domestic arguments, but when asked how this argument differed, they said, 'It is more important. It's a bigger argument'.

The significance of the elephant project

Given a meaningful learning context, young children can write using the language of discussion or exposition. Some of the features characteristic of mature forms of these genres were found in the children's writing: but more importantly, these language structures were generated by the nature of the task. In one sense these children were demonstrating a developing knowledge simply by using language and working with it. Beyond this their reflection upon that knowledge was as yet naive, but a more reflective frame of reference was shown by those who could quite clearly tell me that their previous work was not a debate but something more like an information-gathering exercise for the purpose of reporting to others. Informed and sensitive variation of social interactions such as these within the classroom help children develop expertise as language users.

Only by teachers creating meaningful experiences will this knowledge be made explicit to the children, and the necessary foundations for a wider repertoire of writing be laid.

Taking it further

In recent LINC INSET sessions, we have introduced this work to teachers, highlighting the fact that arguments and discussion are powerful means for decision making and conflict resolution in our society. As members of this society, children are exposed to current affairs programmes, news broadcasts, documentaries and health campaigns, to list just a few of the contexts in which children have a chance to observe and perhaps participate in controversial exchanges. Local and national issues provide children with a reason to express opinions; by voicing their concerns, children become aware that opinions may be judged according to the validity of the reasons which support them.

We have suggested to teachers working with very young children that it may be helpful to spend time developing this genre in the oral mode only. However, it is clear that a subsequent interim stage between a spoken argument and a free standing written one is the shared construction of a text with a teacher or another pupil acting as scribe. Working together can help to shape a text which approximates more closely to the structure of the genre than one written without benefit of support. For example, an introductory paragraph to the subject could be jointly written and then groups might add their differing points of veiw. Such a procedure allows teachers to demonstrate that argument is a dynamic process in which positions are successively explored and evaluated in the light of feedback and reflection. At the same time, the process of joint construction allows the teacher to highlight appropriate language features and also provides credible opportunities for drafting and editing. By showing children how to transform meanings expressed in spoken language into meanings expressed in written language, we are giving them access to a powerful written form, with long term ideals in view:

A democratic society needs people who have the linguistic abilities which will enable them to discuss, evaluate and make sense of what they are told, as well as to take effective action on the basis of their understanding. The working of a democracy depends on the discriminating use of language on the part of all its people. Otherwise there can be no genuine participation, but only the imposition of the ideas of those who are linguistically capable.

As individuals, as well as members of constitutencies, people need the resources of language to defend their rights as well as to fulfil their obligations.

(The Kingman Report, chapter 2, para 2)

With thanks to Sally Taylor and Rebecca Boyd and the children of Deddington Church of England Primary School, Deddington, Oxfordshire.

This article shows children:
- writing for a specific purpose and audience (§2, Writing);
- writing for a public purpose so that there are valid reasons for using Standard English (§20, Writing);
- writing non-chronologically and learning to order ideas to explain meaning clearly (§9, Writing);
- drafting and discussing their writing (§§12 and 14, Writing);
- becoming aware of the differences between spoken and written argument, e.g. use of tense, mood, logical connectives, generic nouns. (§§28 and 30, Writing);

WRITING RECIPES

GILL CLARKSON AND HAZEL STANSFIELD

Recipes, instructions and directions are a good place to start to be explicit about particular language use. The purpose and audience are clear – to explain a process to someone who wants to achieve a specific outcome.

Children can readily see the need to get the writing 'right':

- to explain clearly and unambiguously;
- to sequence the steps correctly;
- to include all relevant information;
- to meet the general expectations of the reader regarding the style and layout of their text.

On this occasion, year 3 children from Colebrook Junior School, all of whom had been used to cooking during their infant school years, were to make pizza as part of a project on Italy, and to write instructions for others to follow.

After looking at real models, and drawing on their own previous experience, the children drew up some criteria of how a good receipe should be written. One group noted:

a good Recipe must tell you

how Long to cook it

It should tell you what to get ready

It should tell you what numer you

should put it on. How much ofen

When to stir it

The pizza base would be standard, but, having decided that the pizza topping would consist of ham, cheese, tomato and tomato sauce, the pupils began to draft their own recipes individually. Group discussion of these drafts followed, then a report back to the class, when it was agreed that some indication of quantities needed to be given in the list of ingredients. Following that discussion, the following recipe was agreed upon and tested:

A Recipe for a Pizza topping

ingredients to make pizza topping

ham 2 slices

chease I lump

Tomato I

Tomato Sause 3 teaspoons

. . . .

What to do

1. cut the ham in stripes

2. and put it on the pizza

3. great the cheese

4. and put it on

5. pour the sause on the pizza

This 'trying out' revealed that the recipe instructions were flawed:

We should have said to put the oven on first. We had to wait for it to get hot.

We needed to say how long to cook it.

We should have said to put the tomato sauce on before the cheese, because it would look horrible.

Other changes were made too. After a discussion of the need for 'correct wording', 'What to do' was changed to 'Method', because this was the terminology the children had found while studying published recipes.

And the injunction to 'cut the ham in strips' was abandoned in favour of 'cut the ham and put it on', when it was found that 'the ham wouldn't cut in strips, it fell apart'.

Given the time and the opportunity to consider how they might use language more professionally, children show that they have high expectations and are prepared to work to 'get it right'. Not to give them these opportunities is to suggest that language use does not matter – and none of us would want to teach that lesson.

The recipe which was finally drafted (see page 114) included these amendments:

- the illustration was made more prominent to show the potential follower of the recipe the splendour of the finished poduct;
- the sequence was re-ordered to ensure that the cheese was added last;
- instructions for using the tomato and the cooking time were added;
- spelling was carefully checked.

Despite all this care, the children's final reflections showed that they recognised their omissions – most notably that they had forgotten to list the equipment which would be needed. This recognition of a small failure suggests, not how little, but how much they have learned. The opportunity for reflection, the 'I didn't do it but…' comment shows the teacher exactly how much explicit knowledge children have about this genre and shows children how and where they can achieve even more next time.

With grateful thanks to the children and staff of Colebrook Junior School, Swindon, Wiltshire.

This article shows children:
- reading and discussing good examples of instructions so that they can write their own (§18, Writing);
- writing for a specific purpose and audience (§2, Writing);
- writing for a public purpose so that there are valid reasons for using Standard English (§20, Writing);
- thinking about ways of making their meaning clear to their intended reader in redrafting their writing (§18, Writing);
- considering features of layout and variations in vocabulary and grammar, according to purpose, topic and audience (§18, Writing).

A Recipe for a Pizza topping

Ingredients

2 slices of ham

lump of cheese

1 tomato

2 teas tomato sauce

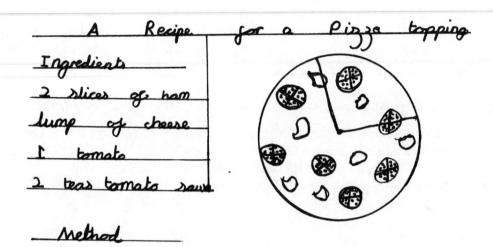

Method

1. Switch on the oven to 200 c
2. make the pizza base and roll it out
3. cut the ham and put it on
4. Pour on the sause on
5. Grate the cheese on the top
6. cut the tomato and put it on

Cook for 25 mins

WRITING STORIES FOR A YOUNGER AUDIENCE

GILL CLARKSON AND JULIE YOUNG

In setting up liaison initiatives such as the project described here, it seems important to ensure that intentions are clear both for the teachers concerned and their pupils. In this project, the year 10 pupils from George Ward School were not indulging in a bit of easy writing. The demands made on them were considerable and the results were to be an important part of their GCSE coursework assessment, written and oral. They were required to:

- review a range of children's books;
- prepare for and conduct interviews with the infants (Reception class – year 2) to discover the children's reading preferences;
- demonstrate what they had learned from both of the above, in drafting their own children's stories;
- prepare for the reading of their final stories to their very young 'readers';
- provide a full assessment of their own stories against the criteria which their general reviews had provided.

Throughout the process, the aim was to raise awareness of what 'matching style to audience and purpose' meant in practice.

The initial contact came from the infant class at Shaw Primary School. Individual children wrote to named individuals in the year 10 group, introducing themselves. The students then prepared to find out as much as they could about books for young children.

Reviewing children's books

Far from regarding this as a demeaning task, the year 10 pupils fell enthusiastically upon the books provided by the infant teacher from Shaw School and by the County Librarian. The problem was rather to tear them away. They were already learning a great deal because the reason for their reading was made clear: to learn something about the content, language and layout – knowledge which they were to employ later.

After reading and general discussion, pupils were to write a review of a particular book. Here is an extract from one of the reviews.

The book has a very attractive cover with the title clearly displayed, there are also many small illustrations of all the characters in the story. The story rhymes and repeats itself so that it is more fun for the children to read and there are not too many new words for them to learn in the one book.

On each page there is an illustration, a small picture above the writing and a large more intricate picture on the opposite page. In these pictures there is a lot going on and they are bright and colourful.

While such comments show implicitly what the writer understands as being 'appropriate' for the young reader, the teacher concerned wanted her pupils to make this knowledge about language explicit.

Pooling the experience gained from the general immersion in the genre and from articulating what they thought was valuable in particular books, the pupils were then able to move on to more objective criteria for what makes a 'good children's story'.

The extract which follows shows the fruits of this discussion:

Children's story criteria

In order to create a successful book it was important to consider more than just the story-line. We soon realized that a lot of planning and organization would be required to develop the book and this could be arranged according to a list of criteria.

Layout:- The layout of the book included whether the book was to open vertically or horizontally, where the illustrations would be positioned in relation to the text, whether the written content would be spaced around the pictures or together in large blocks. The use of a cover and title should also be considered, including the type of material to be used — paper or card and the use of illustrations on the front cover. The illustrations themselves could be colourful and simple or more detailed in order to retain the child's attention.

Length:- The length of the story is important as it has to be long enough to allow the story-line to develop, but yet not too long so that the text becomes monotonous and boring to the reader.

Language:- The language in the story is also of great significance as it is required to be both relatively basic so as the child can understand the plot and yet the interests of education and progessive learning have to be recognised and therefore new words might be included to extend the child's vocabulary. There are many methods of promoting learning such as continuously repeating words or by using subtitles to support the text which would enable the child to learn sentence structure.

The characters:- The choice of characters is a more individual decision directly related to the story/plot. One possibility is to create characters that the child can identify with and then use them to provoke feelings and a response to the story so as to involve the child in the story. Another idea is the concept of giving animals, plants or objects the same capabilities as humans so appealing to the reader's imagination.

Plot:- The plot itself presents a variety of possibilities. The theme of the story can be detailed or simple to accomadate the reader's intellect or realistic and fantastical to stetch the child's imagination.

Scene/setting:- The scene should provide the basis on which the plot can be developed. It is the scene which should create a successful atmosphere to encourage the validity of the storyline. Similarly to the plot, the setting presents a wide scope of possibilities such as adopting a familiar environment to the reader or alternatively an original scene, depending on the book's requirements.

Educational/moral:- The educational or moral value of the book should also be considered when contemplating the plot. The storyline might convey moral views without necessarily limiting the humour or fun of the story. The educational values of the book might be presented in the use of appropriate language and vocabulary or in generally good sentence structure.

Age suitability:- Although the author might have an age in mind during the compilation of a book there cannot be a stipulated level of intelligence for any age.

Before the year 10 pupils began drafting their books, they visited the infant class at Shaw School to meet the children who had written to them and for whom they would be writing a book.

To focus their attention, they had considered general areas of questioning, recognising, of course, that their infant interviewees would not be amenable to a formal question and answer session. The intention was to discover what sort of books the individual year 2 children enjoyed and whether they had any particular ideas about the sort of story they would like to have written for them.

At these interviews, the younger children shared their favourite books, explaining what they enjoyed about them. This gave the year 10 writers more information as to what made a successful children's book.

Producing the books

The writers were asked to produce their books during their summer holidays and to return with a completed text in 'publishable form'. That they all did so – and did so with such enormous care – is a testimony to their interest in, and enthusiasm for, the project.

To help the writers in this process they had:

* their own recent experience of reading many children's books;
* memories from their own childhood of favourite stories;
* the criteria which they had drawn up from reading and discussion;
* additional information from their recent interviews with their potential readers;
* 'real readers' of an appropriate age locally, on whom they could test their product.

Again, the teacher was not content to assume that the authors 'knew about' children's books because they had written them. She wanted them to be explicit about the extent of their understanding in relation to their own practice. She therefore asked pupils to evaluate their products, explaining and justifying devices they had employed.

The following are extracts from some of these evaluations which were to be part of the pupils' GCSE coursework.

The title on the cover is large and readable from a distance. It is also an alliteration, 'The Search for Sammy

Sharpener'. The alliterations like this will often attract children as they sound like fun. There is also a picture of Sammy on the front cover so as you know who the story is about.

The language content of the story was of more significance to me and my aim was to use generally basic language which would already be familiar to the reader. However in the interests of education and learning, which I recognised as being particularly important for a young child, I included a small number of more difficult words and frequently repeated them throughout the story to stimulate the child's mind. I hoped these would contribute to broadening the reader's knowledge. To assist the child with the text I included brief subtitles above each illustration supporting the storyline. I thought that the subtitles would remain in the child's memory more than the rest of the story and they could learn basic sentence structure using this method.

Story reading session

At last the books were to be delivered – an important opportunity, as one boy wrote, 'to test out our books on the real experts, the children'. The reading of the stories and the accompanying talk were also to constitute part of the GCSE oral assessment.

Time was given in class before the session to consider knowledge about language. What language issues should be borne in mind to make the session as successful as possible?

All the children had met before and had commuunciated by letter, but still the (now) year 11 pupils were concerned to use language – verbal and non-verbal – which would put the younger children at ease:

- It was suggested that all the pupils should sit on the floor so that height differences would be less obvious and so less daunting.
- It was felt that the younger children should also contribute to the session, and it was suggested that they should bring their own current reading books to talk about.
- Their talk would also help the older pupils gauge the sort of response they might expect to their own books.
- By now, the notion of 'matching style to audience and purpose' was so much a part of the pupils' thinking that they did not have to be reminded to make their vocabulary and syntax suitable for the occasion.

Finally, a written self-assessment of the session was required from the year 11 pupils to support the teacher's oral assessment.

Writing stories for a younger audience was, in this case, certainly not an easy option for older pupils – as it may sometimes be if insufficient time and planning is given to it. Here, every opportunity was taken to make the task of writing the book a peg for a thorough study of the genre and for meeting the central requirements of the attainment targets for writing, and speaking and listening.

With grateful thanks to students and staff at George Ward School, Melksham, Wiltshire.

This article shows students:

- working and discussing with other children and adults – involving listening to, and giving weight to, the opinions of others (§3, Speaking & Listening);
- reflecting on and evaluating their use of spoken language and planning activities collaboratively (§5, Speaking & Listening);
- reading aloud with fluency and awareness of audience (§6, Speaking & Listening; §20, Reading);
- talking about and analysing stories (§8, Reading);
- discussing the themes, settings and characters of texts (§20, Reading);
- discussing the effects in context of vocabulary, structural repetition, and grammar (§27, Reading);
- matching the form of their writing to subject matter and to readership ($22, Writing);
- reflecting on their writing (§22, Writing);
- creating, polishing and producing extended written texts (§18, Writing);
- handling key elements of story structure – opening, setting, characters, events and resolution (§25, Writing);
- employing a conscious control of grammatical structures and lexical choices (§31, Writing).

Dr Xargle's guide to earthlet knowledge about language

Holly Anderson

The context

This work took place with a small group within a class of 35 year 5 children. The class teacher, Lorraine Laudrum, encourages the children to be independent in their writing. They choose response partners when planning and reviewing their work, they publish their writing for themselves and other classes in the school and they are used to working collaboratively. It is unlikely that I would have been able to produce this work if the children had not had this rich background.

The activity

I read the latest book in the Dr Xargle series to the class, *Dr Xargle's Book of Earth Tiggers*. They had already seen the first two; *Dr Xargle's Book of Earthlets*, and *Dr Xargle's Book of EarthHounds*, and so were familiar with these amusing and perceptive books published by Andersen Press. The books are written from the viewpoint of an alien teaching his class about the antics of humans and their pets, and they are fortunately translated into Human by Jeanne Willis. The illuminating illustrations by Tony Ross play an integral part in the enjoyment and understanding of the texts.

I then asked a small group of children whether they would like to produce a book in the same genre, and they decided to write about their class hamster, the final title of the book being *Dr Anderson's Book of Earth Nibblers*.

The children worked for two days on the content. The first stage involved gathering information about hamsters by observation, discussion with classmates (response partners) and use of reference books. The second stage was to rewrite the facts they had decided upon in the style of the Dr Xargle books. This, not surprisingly, proved to be extremely challenging, and the children decided to work as a group to craft the language. Working collaboratively in this way involved the children in social, communicative and cognitive talk, which I taped for analysis.

The children's knowledge about language in action

The following annotated extracts highlight the wide-ranging understandings about the purposes, forms and varities of language which were elicited from young learners by the nature and challenge of this activity.

1   Extracts from the group's tape-recorded discussion

Extract 1. Discussing a subject
'In the Earth Tiggers they're all cats, like I mean...'
'Yes, they're all cats. They're the cat family.'

'...Could do Sharky fish. Except for whales.' → *knowledge of core words (generic, containing sub-categories)*
'Yes, that's a whale. A whale's a whale.'

Extract 2. Discussing hamsters → *poetic language — knowledge of book language*
'Rascals and adventurers.'
'Acrobatics.'
'Got a fur hat.' —— *use of reference books*
(Reading from reference book) 'It says babies don't open their eyes until they're at least 15 days old.'

TEACHER: 'Oh good, you've found out about that.'

'Live behind bars.'

(*Reading from reference book*) 'This long haired hamster has somewhere to burrow and somewhere to explore.'

Extract 3. Discussing appearance

'We've got lots of ideas and we're going to make it into a story.'

'Well, not a story, you can't...'

'Explaining about book.. Explaining about hamsters...'

knowledge of different genres — narrative being different in construction from information books

'Sort of explain about their colours.'

'I've put in they've got (*inaudible*) fur coats.'

'Yeah, and they come in all shapes and sizes.' (*laughs*)

'They do if they're babies...'

'...and they don't if they're adults.'

'Adults and babies.'

'Babies don't have fur coats do they?'

TEACHER 'How old are they when their fur grows?'

'About a month?'

'Two months?'

(*Sound of flicking pages*)

reference skills — scanning for information

'About 15 days?'

(*Reads*) 'Five days.'

(*Sound of flicking pages*)

'Ah.' (*Reads*) 'The longest fur is found in the male, but it doesn't reach its maximum length until at least six months old.'

Extract 4. Discussing sections

knowledge of how information can be categorised

TEACHER: 'What other sections could there be?'

'Habits.'

'Babies.'

'Er...the food.'

'How they could be cared for as well.'

TEACHER: 'Right, that's important, isn't it?'

'Caring.'

'Would the appearance be about how the babies were?'

'Just put babies.'

'You could have appearance when older and appearance when younger.'

sub-dividing information into appropriate sections

'Where they live.'

'Prison.' (*laughs*)

'Cages.'

'No, prison.'

observation of original language in texts — inventing ways to rewrite own language to fit in appropriately

Extract 5. Crafting the appearance section

(*Reads work*) 'When grown up they have open eyes and whiskers.'

→ *using simple present tense (common in information books to give sense of permanence/ universal truth)*

'Yeah, well, we're going to do the language after...'

'You could say open buttons.'

'Yeah, OK.'

'I think you could start off with the young, and then gradually get older, then it's in order then.' →

(*Continues reading*) 'When babies they are pink and blob. When they are five days old, they grow fur coats.' (*Stops reading*) 'What I think you could do is, umm, when they are, umm, how can you put Earth Nibblers into babies?'

→ *ordering information logically*

TEACHER: 'What about, Earthlings were the grown-ups, what did they call the babies?'

'Earthlets.'

'Nibblets!'

'Nibblets and Nibblers.' ——→ *knowledge of morphemes*

Extract 6. Deciding on order

'With this, you know like we started...' (*Reads*) 'Good morning class, today we are going to learn about Earth Nibblers...'

'So can we start with that?'

TEACHER: 'If you want to.'

'Are we going to put appearance first, like they usually do?' → *close observation of original book structure*

'Yeah, cause they usually do...'

Extracts 6, 7, 8, 9, 10. Finding the right expression
Extract 6

close observation of original text

(*Reads from work*) 'She got in the wool, she slept there, and she'd wee over it.'

'Hold on a minute, it says in here something for, another word for "wool".'

TEACHER: 'Yes, it does.'

(*Looking through book and reading*) 'Very old Earthlings, or Grannys, unravel the sheep.'

→ *scanning for relevant information*

'Sheep?'

'Hairdo of... Hairdo it says here. Hairdo of the sheep.' ——→ *finding precise vocabulary*

Extract 7

'Put it on the spade.'

'What would it seem like to the hamster? It's all right saying that it's a spade, but...' (*tape runs out*)

→ *ability to take on another's viewpoint*

Extract 8

'What could you say instead of water?'

'Liquid.'

'They suck the liquid from the...' —→ *use of present tense, timeless, giving a permanent status*

'It doesn't have to be from the, it could be out of the...'

'...Clear plastic thing.'

'Clear worm...'

'No, cause the end bit they suck is metal.'
'Silver worm?'
'Silver bowl?'

collaborative, cognitive talk – each child building on from others' contribution, and reasoning out own ideas

TEACHER: 'I think that's a very hard bit, that bottle. I can't think of anything much for bottle.'
'Why don't they just...'
'Bowl...'
'Oh what...it doesn't have to be bottle, Tipsy has a bowl.'
'Yeah, but then it would have to be drink the water, cause you can't suck it out of a bowl.'
'They lick the water.'
'They slurp the water.'
'Yeah – slurp!'

realisation of need for specific language

Extract 9

crafting idea, choosing words for special effect – onomatopoeic

'Now we're on caring.'
'Oh no! I've done the first bit.'
TEACHER: 'OK. Tell me what the first bit is.'
(*Reads from work*) 'Earth scholars usually clean out the Earth Nibblers' prisons every week.'
TEACHER: 'Why do they have to clean out their prisons?'
'Otherwise they'll pong.'
TEACHER: 'Yes, to stop the pong!'
'To stop the pong from...'
'To stop...'
'To stop the pong for staying long!' (*laughs*) → *playing with words – rhythm and rhyme*
'Yes – that is good!'
(*Repeats*) 'Stop the pong for staying long.'

Extract 10

(*Reads from work*) 'They live in cages.'
'He's put "prisons".'
TEACHER: 'So, we've already chosen a word to represent cage, haven't we?'
'We could have "live", sort of... "they live in"...'
'No, I don't think we... I don't think we'd better change too many... words that, umm ... like if we go around changing words like "live"...'   → *specific vocabulary / terminology*
'They won't know what it means.'
'They won't be able to understand it because... we can't show "lives" in the pictures.'
TEACHER: 'Right. Do you want to use "they", though? Do you want to use the pronoun "they"?'
'Umm. Why don't you just put the Nibblers?'
'No, "they".'
'I've got four "theys".'
'Yeah. Nibblers, that's what I'd use, I'd say.'

deciding how to link sentences for cohesion

2 The final draft of their written text

Cover:
Dr Anderson's Book of Earth Nibblers and Nibblets

knowledge of signatures, use of full stops to denote abbreviations

Published by
J.A. Gibling, N.J. Woor, H.E. Curtis, E.P. Hilditch, J McNN and Philip Stylar.

Illustrated by Y5 ⟶ *knowledge of abbreviation*

Page 1.   Good morning class, today we are going to learn about earth nibblers and nibblets.

Page 2.   The nibblets have an automatic fur coat. When five days old they press a button and it gardually (sic) starts to grow. Instead of shoes, nibblets wear sponges on their feet. When 15 days old, Mummy nibbler opens the blinds so they can see the prison bars.

Page 3.   When grown up they have open blinds and long pieces of thread attached to their sniffers. They have different coloured coats and a stump wag at the back.

lexical cohesion (linked vocabulary)

Page 4.   Nibblers (eat) earth scholars' morning grub.

Page 5.   They (eat) greens from the growing patch.

simple sentence structure - syntactical cohesion, with each sentence following same grammatical structure - initial use of a subsequently pronouns

Page 6.   They (eat) the grey tunnels which are placed in the prison.

Page 7.   They (slurp) the liquid with their pink flannel.

phonological cohesion - similar sounds, both onomatopoeic

Page 8.   Nibblers explore the water pipes where the (gurgling) goes down.

Page 9.   The earth scholars stroke the (nibblers) with their (wrigglers).
            Don't hold tight with your wrigglers or else you will splatter your nibbler.

phonological cohesion

Page 10.   They like to sleep in (sheeps' hairdo).

knowledge of original text

Page 11.   They run in their spinning wheel but their fur coat does not turn into gold.

knowledge of books/fairy stories (Rumplestiltskin)

Page 12.   The nibblers live in (prison) with (lofts) on top. Their (prison) is metal with woody bits in it.

lexical cohesion

Page 13.   Earth scholars bring them out in their (castles)

Page 14.   Nibblers trian (sic) to join the circus by climbing on top of the (prison) bars.

lexical cohesion contrast 'castle' with 'prison'

Page 15.   They jog to the (loft gym) every Saturday morning.

playing with words – rhythm and rhyme

Page 16. Earth scholars clean out the earth nibblers' prisons every week to stop the pong from staying long.

playing with rhythm and rhyme - patterned and systematic lexis cohesion through (oops, whoops, poops, etc), syntax (repeated sentence structure), morphemes (nibbler, nibbo) and phonemes (oops, whoops, poops)

Page 17. Repeat after me:

'OOPS I have splattered my nibblers!' 'OOPS I have splashed my nibbol!' 'WHOOPS I have nibbled my squasher!' 'POOPS I have whooped on my squasho!' 'WHOOPS I have squashed my nibbler!' 'WHOOPS I have wriggled my splutter!' 'OOPS I have squared my squasho!'

Page 18. Oh, class, is that the time? Get your disguises on and we'll zap to planet earth.

lexically linked from science fiction genre

Page 19. Be careful not to nibble your squashers!

playing with parts of speech to create humorous ending (nibbler - noun; to nibble - verb) – observation of original texts which end with puns and jokes

Postscript

After completing *Dr Xargle's Book of Earthnibblers and Niblets*, the earthlet authors asked me if they could send a copy to Jeanne Willis. Their first effort at a letter to accompany the book was rather turgid in its intense sincerity, and they were far from satisfied with it. At my suggestion, in their redraft of the content they pretended that it was a letter from Dr Xargle him/herself.

Their eager anticipation was more than rewarded by Jeanne Willis's gracious and inventive reply: both letters follow, on pages 127 and 128.

Summary

The purpose and value of this activity transcended 'knowledge about language'. In selecting the five children for me to work with, the class teacher had in fact been more interested in how the individuals would interact in a collaborative context. These were usually the 'leaders' in other groups, and the exercise illuminated how they got on in the challenging company of other extroverts. My own chief interest had been to explore an activity which involved children in speaking, listening, reading and writing effectively for a range of 'real' purposes. In these terms I was most pleased by the way in which the children's discussions and their use and knowledge of books helped to structure and extend their writing, producing an outcome which was 'vigorous, commited, honest, and interesting' (English 5–16, 17.31).

However, a significant by-product of the task is the evidence it provides both of the children's implicit knowledge about language (revealed through the choices they make as speakers and writers of texts), and their explicit understanding of the purposes and patterning of varieties of English (revealed through their dialogue and decision making).

A brief summary of some of this knowledge concludes the analysis:

Awareness of genres and text types, e.g.
- how reference books work and how to access them: 'What other sections could there be?' 'Habits…Babies … Er …the food';
- non-chronological principles for organising text: 'well not a story you can't';
- intertextual jokes relating to other genres: but their fur does not turn to gold'.

Awareness of principles of cohesion, e.g.
- lexical cohesion to guide reader through the text: 'prison, lofts, castles';
- use of pronouns: 'I've got four theys';
- phonological cohesion giving text a 'fun' aesthetic: 'oops, whoops, poops'.

Awareness of syntax, e.g.
- use of simple and more complex sentence structures, as appropriate;
- use of simple present tense in information genre: They have different coloured coats'.

Awareness of vocabulary, e.g.
- sustaining metaphorical mode for key words: 'sponges, sniffers, prison,' etc;
- morphological awareness: 'nibblers, nibblets'.

Awareness of phonology/graphology, e.g.
- use of rhyme: 'to stop the pong from staying long';
- page layout: 'use of abbreviations in authors list'.

With thanks to the children and teachers at Elsenham County Primary School, Essex.

This article shows children:
- presenting their ideas, experiences and understanding with an increasing awareness of audience and purpose (§6, Speaking & Listening);
- discussing texts which make imaginative use of English, in order to bring out the ways in which the choice of words affects the impression given by the text and considering the way word meanings can be played with (§13, Reading);
- discussing their writing frequently, talking about the varied types and purposes of writing (§12, Writing);
- thinking about ways of making their meaning clear to their intended reader in redrafting their writing (§18, Writing).

Elsenham C of E Primary School
Elsenham
Bishop's Stortford
HERTS. CM22 6DD

21st May 1991

Dear Jeanne Willis

Yesterday I saw 6 earth scholars named Phillip, Hannah, Elliot, Jenny, James and Nicola discussing your books. I overheard them saying how brilliant they were and I think they are brilliant too. The earth scholars said that they liked the pictures and the way the story was written and thought it was amusing. They liked all your books but especially the one of earthlets. They decided to make their own book. I heard them saying they would write a book about earth nibblers and niblets (hamsters and baby hamsters) because they have a nibbler in their scholar's castle (classroom) and they know all about them.

First they thought about the nibbler's habits, caring for niblblers, appearance, diet, exercises and environment. The earth scholars went off and worked on a subject each. They wrote about their subject and then translated it into my language (alien talk) which I thought was very nice. The earth scholars had help from an earthling called Mrs Anderson. The earth scholars said that the book would be nothing if the earthling hadn't help them. Some of the other scholars in the castle did the drawings.

The earth scholars told me to enclose a copy of the book for you to read. Please let them know if you enjoyed the story.

Yours alienly

Dr Xargle

Dr Xargles
Planet Zubb
Outer Space

Lunar Month 6

Dear phillip, Hannah, elliot, Jenny, James and Nicola!
greetings Earthlets. I have recieved your amusing story about the Earthnibblers and niblets. Jeanne Willis sent it to me when that British spacebeing went up in an Earthrocket. It was such a very small vehicle at first I mistook it for one of your sherbet fountain sweets and almost swallowed it.

On Planet Zubb we have something like your Earthniblets. only larger. And greener. And scalier. And with many more feet. Matron is not very fond of them.

On my last visit to your tiny planet we landed in the playground of Elsenham C of E primary School but nobody was there. Mind you, it was very dark. I dropped some secret papers. If you find them please send them to the above address or bring them personally. We are only two thousand light years away. Do excuse my writing only the spaceship has hit a bit of turbulence as we are going through a black hole

THE NEWHAM PRESS

LYNN NEWTON

'You can certainly tell this newspaper doesn't like Prince Charles', pronounced Nickie adamantly as he finished reading the front page of the The Daily Mirror. 'Yes, they've called him a 4-star Charlie – are they allowed to do that?' queried Kerry. 'But they're right', chipped in Linzey. "He told US not to use our cars and now he's using more petrol than anyone.'

This interest in the mass media all began when my year 6 class was given the opportunity to produce a newspaper as part of the North-East News Day. The children had no experience of writing for a newspaper with all the awareness of style, writing to tight deadlines, drafting on a word processor, sub-editing, selection and presentation that it entails, but they were eager to have a go. And I was eager that the paper would be all theirs.

In the week that followed we lived and breathed newspapers. Using the three criteria we refer to whenever we are writing (Function: What is its purpose? Audience: Who will read it? Form: What type of writing will it be?) we brainstormed ideas. Small groups of children read and analysed a range of printed material from newspapers and comics to special interest magazines. This proved to be an excellent way of looking at styles of writing for different purposes and audiences. Each group reported back with their findings and as the list evolved, so did the gradual realisation that each paper's content fell broadly into the same categories: writing to inform, to entertain and amuse, to give you 'instructions' (TV programmes, competitions), writing to persuade you (adverts, opinions), and the cartoons which give you a 'good laugh'. In arriving at this list, the class had been involved in analysing, discussing, questioning, sharing and justifying opinions and finally preparing a consensus view to present to the other groups. What gave it all such dynamism was that the work was inspired by a genuine need to find out.

The final contents list included 'hot news' for the front page – 'We'll have to get fast writers to do that bit' – feature articles – 'we'll need people who write long stories' – sport, a review page, local news snippets, competitions, word searches and puzzles. Groups offering to try out America for us or to test-run trial bikes were good naturedly rebuffed, and action started. Category headings were put on the wall and the class signed up according to the kind of contribution they wished to make. Again, there was a lot of informal discussion on the pros and cons of each writing style and on what would be demanded of the writer before final commitments were made.

Individual preferences for writing styles were already quite pronounced. 'I don't like writing short things like instructions cos you can't write what YOU want to say,' mused Caroline, while Graham only wanted to write short sports articles 'because that's all sports readers would read'.

Page editors were chosen, together with a rotating group of sub-editors who would check copy to ensure it made sense, was spelled correctly and had its full quota of punctuation marks in place.

The features team got started straight away. They decided to take as their main theme the learning of foreign languages (we have recently started a French club in which many of the children are involved). A survey of everybody in school was carried out. Children were asked if they wanted to learn a foreign language and, if so, which one. Entering wholeheartedly into the spirit of the occasion, half a dozen bemused reception children obligingly signed up for Japanese. As one group collated and wrote up this wealth of information, another prepared a questionnaire for parents and other adults around the school, carefully trying it out on each other first to check that 'the questions work'. Several amendments were made before a final version was painstakingly keyed into the computer ready for sending out to parents.

A further group investigated the possibility of interviewing well known people. Owing to shortage of time it was decided the Queen might not be a good idea, but we settled for Paul Daniels (the magician), the Mayor, our local MP, and British Steel and ICI – the two industries where many of the children's fathers worked.

Again, a questionnaire was formulated and test-run and we were just about ready to make initial phone calls when a worried group of interviewers arrived to see me at lunchtime to confess that they were 'scared – what do we say on the phone?'. We raided the younger classes for 'real' telephones (why don't older classes have these?), and started a series of role plays. It was Matthew who pointed out that all of us, including me, spoke in a 'posh voice' when we used the phone. This, of course, provided a brilliant opportunity to explore the need for Standard English. As Kelly pointed out, 'when you're speaking to people you don't know, you've got to speak clearly because they might not understand the common talk you use with your friends.'

The celebrity interview times were well known and, as each pair of interviewers returned, they were greeted like heroes having survived a dreadful ordeal. The debriefing by the rest of the class was thorough. For a class who had previously rarely asked questions, they were unstoppable. And the reporting back had all the flow, the drama, the facts and impressions of a BBC news team reporting from the front line.

News day arrived and we set off, armed with wallets of notes, photographs, graphs, part-written reviews, articles, dictionaries, a thesaurus and a never ending supply of Polos.

For six hours, broken only by a short, snatched lunch, the children avidly absorbed news bulletins, wrote, redrafted, corrected, punctuated, cut, stuck and pasted. Page editors read everything submitted and made judgements: 'This can go at the bottom of the page. We'll have this as our main story because it's the most important.' Pictures were selected for clarity and interest, and were carefully cut to size.

And finally, by 3.15 each child had a copy of the seven-page *Newham Press,* hot from the presses, and like all real journalists, they scoured the paper for their own work, re-reading it with enthusiasm.

The return coach home was full of cries of, 'I've read yours, it's wicked', and 'Oh no, I've left in a spelling mistake'.

And that brings us back to today and Nickie and *The Daily Mirror*.

So many important language issues had arisen from our media experience that it warranted further exploration. Which is why, one Tuesday morning the class had been invited to bring in a copy of Monday's paper. Fearing an overload of tabloids, I had invested in some of the 'heavies' for comparison.

Working again in small groups with two contrasting styles of newspaper, the children were reading and comparing styles and content. What was the main front page story, how many words did the article have, what size print, what did the headline say? How did they differ?

Using our own format, I asked them to look at the purpose of the article and the type of writing used. Some children read and accepted at face value: 'It's telling everybody about Prince Charles' car going away.' Others were looking further. Consider this analysis:

In The Daily Mirror they don't write as much as they do in other newspapers. They have more pictures than writing and they use more common words and they try to write it so it sounds sarcastic. We don't think the Mirror likes Prince Charles – you can tell from their writing.

Others reading tabloids agreed and I asked how they knew this. 'It's the words'. Which words in particular? Lists were compiled, citing 'gas guzzling', 'thirsty vehicles', 'cars as monsters', 'cars gulping petrol', and Andrew was quick to point out that calling the Prince 'green' was being sarcastic and not talking about his colour. How about this for highlighting inference and deduction, and appreciation of meanings beyond the literal, not to mention discriminating between fact and opinion?

As we head off into the sunset of another school year, considering as we go how the pen could be mightier than the sword, I catch Anthony saying, 'they only want you to take their side, it's just like the adverts on the tele'. Our next direction, perhaps?

With thanks to pupils and staff at Newham Bridge Primary School, County Cleveland.

This article shows children
- being shown how to distinguish between fact and opinion (§13, Reading);
- considering purpose, effect and intended audience in relation to media texts (§18, Reading);
- using contextual cues to deduce authorial points of view (§24, Reading);
- identifying persuasive and rhetorical techniques (§26, Reading);
- working and discussing with other children and adults – involving listening to, and giving weight to, the opinions of others (§3, Speaking & Listening);

- learning that Standard English is generally required in formal settings (§18, Speaking & Listening);
- reflecting on and evaluating their use of spoken language (§4, Speaking & Listening);
- matching the form of their writing to subject matter and to readership (§22, Writing);
- reflecting on their writing (§22, Writing);
- drafting, polishing and producing extended written texts (§18, Writing);
- exercising conscious control over lexical and grammatical choices (§31, Writing);
- correcting spelling and punctuation (§22, Writing).

KAREN'S POEMS
COLLABORATION IN THE WRITING PROCESS

PETER NIGHTINGALE

Learning about the construction of effective text is much better done... through writing than through literary analysis. It has the further advantage that writing is a skill whose usefulness pupils can appreciate, whereas literary criticism is not.

(Marsh, 1988, quoted in *English 5-16*, 7.9)

Several writers have shown that the purpose of much writing in school, especially at key stages 3 and 4, is more for testing than for learning.

In many settings [writing] was not being seen as part of the learning process, but as something that happened after learning was supposed to have taken place.

(David Crystal, *The Cambridge Encyclopedia of Language*)

Karen's teacher and the rest of the Carleton High School English department wanted to establish instead the notion in their students that writing is in itself a rewarding and worthwhile activity. To this end, establishing a sense of audience outside the classroom was important. This audience, it was believed, should not just exist as the recipient of the product of writing, but also, where appropriate, be involved in the process of writing. This case study describes one strategy by which this was achieved. The principle 'speaker' is Karen Snowden, a year 9 student.

Karen was being encouraged by her teacher to draft her work in her journal, and also to keep some record of her intentions and decisions each time she altered a draft.

War poem (draft)

Boys, men, women too
Fight the wars for me and you
Can't put if off cos of weather conditions
They fight away with their ammunition.

In the air in their planes
Soon someone will blow out their brains.
Are the government totally docile
When they they shout 'fire a missile'

In the land war in the tanks
Split up into army ranks
Who starts the wars? Well someone does.
Who fights the wars? In the future – us?

I wrote this poem because the Gulf War was on at the time. I hate war. I think it is totally unnecessary.
They tell kids not to fight and to talk of their problems, but they [adults] can't even go by their own guidelines.
I made it rhyme so it sounded obvious.

It seems that the usefulness Karen has perceived for her writing is real enough. She is aware of an hypocrisy and can use writing to give vent to that awareness. Furthermore, she is explicit about using a conventional literary device to give form and force to her thoughts. Her choice of a conversational tone, use of contracted phrases and the dialectal 'docile' to help achieve it, her decisions about punctuation – as yet incomplete – and her decisions about where to begin a new stanza, imply further use of her knowledge about the language and structures of verse.

When Karen felt reasonably happy with a draft, she then shared it with other pupils in a drafting conference . The teaching intention here was to encourage students to discipline and shape their writing through shared and collaborative criticism with a real audience. In the case of the following poem, Karen's teacher put the draft into the cloze procedure program, 'Developing Tray', on a BBC microcomputer. Year 8 students worked on the poem during independent reading time, and their notes (on the program's 'scratchpads') were passed back to Karen for her consideration.

Their final scratchpad read:

LIKE A RAP.
WHEN THEY SAY LINE IS TOO SHORT.
WE LIKE THE ENDING.
DOES/US IS A GOOD RHYME.
IT'S NOT JUST ONE SIDE THAT'S DOCILE.

These comments seem to pick up the strength of the rhythmic shape of the poem, also the point at which that fails. There is an assumption that the final part rhyme is deliberate and a judgement that it is an effective device. Also, there is disapproval of the implied blame of one side in line 7. The brief comments cover a lot of ground and provided Karen with a sincere and helpful reaction to her poem. The year 8 students had got to know the poem by working on it 'from the inside' as a cloze procedure. They were writing about the poem's effectiveness, not offering judgements about its literary merit.

Karen's final draft shows the impact of these comments and her reaction to them as a writer.

War Poem

Boys, men, women too
Fight the wars for me and you,
Can't put it off cos of weather conditions,
They blast away with their ammunition,
In the land war in their tanks
Split up into army ranks.
Are these governments totally docile
Telling the armies, 'Fire your missiles!'?

In the air in their fighter planes,
Soon someone will blow out their brains.
Who starts the wars? Well, someone does!
Who fights the wars? In the future —
Us.

There are some very obvious manipulations of the text. The changes in line groupings seem to offer a more coherent order of the points being made, and the reorganisation of the stanzas presents them differently, perhaps more forcefully. Karen is again implicitly demonstrating her knowledge about the organisation of language to make meanings.

She has responded to the comments of her readers in two clear ways. Accepting the criticism of loss of rhythm, she has lengthened line 8 so that it now more successfully fits the rap style of the whole. Also, she has acceded to the criticism of content by generalising line 7 from 'the government' to 'these governments', incidentally avoiding the problem of whether to treat the collective noun as singular or plural.

More subtle and perhaps more profound is her alteration of the line break and punctuation at the end of the poem. The addition of the exclamation mark to the penultimate line strengthens the statement. The removal of the final question mark and the placement of 'Us' on its own line, combined with the incompleteness of the part rhyme, adds a definiteness absent from the previous draft and certainly increases the final sense of pessimism.

It is clear that these decisions are being made for a real purpose – to refine the communication of feelings and attitudes which it is important for the writer to express. They are also being made in a real context – the submission of her writing to a real audience. Judgements about the effectiveness of the text are to some extent subjective, but it is evident that learning has taken place and that Karen is using her knowledge about language to facilitate her writing.

What seems to me to be important here is the establishment of a dialogue between Karen, other students, her teacher, other teachers, parents, etc. Karen clearly perceives herself as a writer: yet her performance in English was described as well below average at transfer to high school (key stage 2). Now, two years later, there is evidence of considerable progress, a high level of motivation, and a realisation of the importance of writing in the monitoring and exploration of her own attitudes.

Incidentally, Karen kept a writing journal which contains a series of written dialogues between herself and her teacher. These constitute exactly the kind of 'evidence' for 'assessment and record keeping' required by the National Curriculum, thus obviating the need for the arid grid-based (sometimes computer-driven) recording sheets which have been independently and wastefully piloted and abandoned in English departments throughout the nation. More importantly, this process has established a sound basis for Karen's work in writing at key stage 4. Rather than writing for the mysterious and sinister 'examiner', Karen can just add another person and another layer to her already established expectation of audience.

With thanks to students and staff at Carleton High School, Pontefract, West Yorkshire.

Karen is:
- writing poetry and experimenting with different layouts, rhymes, rhythms and verse structures (§18, Writing);
- thinking about ways of making her meaning clear to an intended reader in redrafting (§18, Writing);
- consciously controlling the structure and organisation of her writing (§22, Writing);
- reflecting on her writing (§22, Reading).

Her classmates are responding to literary language, patterning, and figures of speech §24, Reading).

Spoken and Written Language

Nobody speaks — or writes — in the same way on all occasions. We alter our language according to who we are talking to or what we are writing about, whether it is for social, transactional or literary purposes, and so on. The most obvious variations are the contrasts between speech and writing and between formal and informal registers in both modes. An understanding of such variations should help pupils to select the appropriate vocabulary and grammar for a given purpose and to recognise why communication sometimes breaks down when inappropriate choices are made.

(The Cox Report, 6.19)

Investigating the characteristics of spoken and written language and the differences between these two language modes represents a rich new area of curriculum content for many schools. The three critically reflective case studies in this chapter demonstrate that there are many interesting, exploratory ways of working with pupils on these issues. In doing so, they confront a range of challenging pedagogical issues:

- planning and providing contexts for pupils to analyse and reflect on differences between speech and writing;
- generating resources and data for pupils' investigations of language variation;
- distinguishing between pupils' implicit and explicit knowledge;
- exploring the complex relationship between pupils' knowing about how spoken and written language work and being able to use each mode more effectively;
- considering whether pupils need a metalanguage if they are to describe language, and how and when to provide this terminology;
- building in differentiation in the knowledge about language curriculum;
- embedding language study in the study of a literary text;
- devising discrete units of language study.

Although these case studies describe 11–14 year olds at work, they are worth reading by teachers of both older and younger pupils. Infants will have already started to learn about differences between spoken and written language; we go on learning about these differences into our sixth form years and beyond. As pupils become more experienced language users, their progression is characterised by the way in which their descriptions and analyses of spoken and written language become more systematic and sustained, in their written and spoken reflections. Whereas younger pupils will be able to describe relevant but isolated examples of differences between spoken and written language, older pupils will progress to discussing the principles underlying examples.

In the first case study, 'Written and spoken versions of the same situation', Elaine Hines describes how over five 70 minute periods, her mixed ability year 7 pupils produce improvised speech and compare it with written versions of the same dramatic situation. Her pupils' analysis of differences between spoken and written language is embedded in their shared reading of a literary text, *The Iron Man*. Their spoken and written reflections of the differences which they notice, and their teacher's evaluation of these reflections, make interesting reading. This case study provides a clear example of the difference between teacher's and pupil's knowledge: drawing on her knowledge, the teacher is able to highlight and develop her pupils' knowledge. She shares with us her insights about some of the difficulties which she observes her pupils experience, as they move from the spoken to the written mode, and outlines strategies which she will adopt to support them.

Kim Wilkinson's case study, 'Getting the message across', outlines a five week unit of work (two 50 minute periods per week) with her year 9 pupils. As with the previous case study, regular opportunities are provided for pupils to reflect upon and to make explicit the nature of their language choices.

In the final case study in this chapter, 'Differentiation in the knowledge about language curriculum', Nigel Kent raises questions about:

- how an explicit knowledge about language focus can be embedded in units of work;
- how to construct a knowledge about language curriculum which provides differentiation, while allowing for pupils to revisit areas of language study.

Nigel's account is based on two units of work on differences between speech and writing, the first offered to a mixed ability year 7 class and the second to a less able year 10 GCSE group. Nigel, like the two other writers in this section, is interested to see if pupils' explicit study of the differences between spoken and written language will help them to produce more effective written texts – will their knowledge *about* improve their competence *with* written language?

Written and Spoken Versions of the Same Situation

ELAINE HINES

Lesson 1

We had read *The Iron Man* up to the end of Chapter Two. I told the class the next part of the story: the Iron Man has been buried under a hill for a year; one day a family goes on a picnic; they are enjoying themselves when the ground shakes, and a crack appears growing wider and wider; an iron hand rises through the ground!

I asked small groups to dramatise this scene and, if they wished, to show the rest of the class their version. They were only given 15 minutes to do this – it wasn't refined or rehearsed much. I taped their versions without telling them in advance that I would do so. The groups enjoyed this activity!

At the end of this lesson, I asked the pupils to talk in groups about the ways in which *telling* a story this way was different from *writing* a story. They wrote down the main points of their discussions:

In some ways it's better to read a story in a book, because you can read it again and again.

It was different because writing a story takes much longer.

Acting it out you just say things, practise and make it better and you can do that easily, but you can't always think of better words when you write to make the story interesting.

When you act it out you can show your personality.

Their comments seem to show that they were aware of many of the differences between speaking and writing: the more ephemeral nature of speech; the immediacy of feedback; the more reflective nature of writing; the contribution made to speech by facial expression and body language. I was becoming more aware of some of the difficulties they find when writing: the isolation of the writer, the lack of immediate feedback, the difficulty posed by the need for greater explicitness in writing.

Lesson 2   Analysis of contrasting versions

In the next lesson I played back the tape of the class's improvisations and gave them a transcript of the key moment in the scene when the iron hand appeared. The main reaction was laughter! I asked them, in groups, to read the next chapter of the book together and then to discuss the differences between the written version of the scene and their improvised version. Their comments were:

There were more details in the (*written*) story.

The words were different.

You didn't know why people were screaming (*on the transcript*).

Ted Hughes' story was more dramatic.

When we were acting our expressions told you that we were scared but you can't do that when you are writing.

You have to write the details down because in a play you can see the things but in a written story you have to describe them.

Lesson 3

In the next lesson I asked the class to write a script of the same scene for a radio play which we would tape. They did this in their original groups and then recorded the plays. Once I had played back their tapes, I asked the pupils, on their own, to think about the differences between telling the story, writing the radio script, and improvising it. The comments below are taken from their subsequent evaluations and reflect the full ability range:

They put more detail in the radio script.

In the play we knew who the baby or mum was because the baby was crawling, but in the radio play the baby had to speak like a baby.

(*In the radio script*) You need to describe who you are and what you are doing, but when you are performing they can see who you are and see what you are doing.

(*In the script*) When you are scared of something, you have to say what you are scared of.

We had to describe everything more in the script.

I think acting is much better because you can see expressions and immediate reactions.

In the written version you can read through and change the bits you don't like.

In the written version you have to describe things more carefully.

If you are writing the play you can change it but if you are saying it out loud in front of the class you just have to say what comes into your head.

(*In the play*) People made it up as they went, in the radio script it was much better because it was planned out.

In the play you could say 'look at this' without saying what it is. But in the radio play you had to say what it is e.g. 'look at that hill'. And if you were in the countryside you would have to describe the countryside.'

When acting out you can tell by the audience's faces if they are enjoying it or not. When you are acting out a radio play you cannot see the audience's faces so you cannot tell if they enjoyed it or not. You don't hear the audience's comments.

By comparing the different uses of language in these three contexts, pupils had the opportunity to reflect on how language changes according to the needs of each situation. The pupils' final comments and the comments they made during the work showed that they had a considerable amount of knowledge about the differences between speech and writing. I am not sure whether the work enabled them to learn anything new (although there seems to be development when their first comments are compared to their final comments), but the work did enable them to reflect more consciously and to articulate their thoughts. Their knowledge seems to have become more explicit. Their final comments show, I think, their awareness of the following:
– the need for greater explicitness in writing;
– the more solitary nature of writing;
– the way the writer lacks the stimulus of interaction which is available to the speaker;
– the way the writer has to work harder to convey emotions;
– the more spontaneous nature of speech;
– the contribution made by non-verbal gesture and expression;
– the interaction between the speaker and audience.
I felt I had learnt a lot! I was more aware of these differences and more aware of the difficulties facing these young writers. They need audience feedback, it seems, and the stimulus of interaction and response. Writing is more solitary than talking, but it seems more important than I had realised to ensure that the writer does not work in complete isolation. Our responses, as pupils write, are important. These pupils enjoy reading their own work to others as they write; it seems that this needs encouragement.

With thanks to pupils and staff at Lyng Hall School, Coventry.

GETTING THE MESSAGE ACROSS

KIM WILKINSON

The aim of this series of lessons was for 9AL to gain an appreciation and a more advanced awareness of the different registers of language required to communicate effectively and appropriately in both written and spoken English.

Unit of work (Lesson 1)

The class was introduced to the unit, and on the blackboard we looked at examples of written and spoken language performing the same function. One example used was a guarantee:

Bring it back if anything goes wrong. (Spoken)

Should this product or any part of it become defective under normal use within 12 months of the date of purchase, the defect will be rectified, and defective components repaired or replaced. (Written)

Written and spoken directions (Lessons 2 and 3)

The object of these lessons was to focus closely on the differences between the language of written and spoken directions.

- Directing a stranger. The pupils were asked to work with a partner and to take it in turns to tell each other how to get from their house to three of the following places. They were to choose at least one which was near (and therefore easy to describe) and at least one which was much further away. They were also asked to tape their efforts:
  - the doctor's surgery
  - the church
  - the park
  - their school
  - the dentist
  - a place of their choice.
- The class was then asked to produce written directions for the same journeys.
- The class listened to a sample of the tapes and the written instructions being read out loud. They were encouraged to add to a table summary of the most obvious differences they could note between written and spoken directions.
- The class studied the transcripts produced more closely later on.

Written and spoken instructions (Lessons 4 and 5)

The object of these two lessons was to focus closely on the difference between written and spoken instructions.

The class was requested to bring in a variety of games e.g. Scrabble, Draughts, Trivial Pursuit, etc. The class was then arranged into groups of four or five according to the games they were not familiar with. One member from each group – an expert – was to teach the game. The brief they were given was: to instruct their partners as clearly as possible in the rules and objects of their game, while the rest of the group was encouraged to ask questions to help their understanding.

Three or four volunteers put their instructions onto tape. There was no time for rehearsal.

The second part of the task required the groups to produce written instructions for the board game they had participated in. Illustrations were allowed, but the class was discouraged from referring to any manual or instruction leaflet which accompanied their game.

Finally, the two pieces of writing which follow (a transcript of a spoken explanation of the game Scoop, and a written explanation) were made available to the groups to compare and discuss the differences between the two examples chosen. They were asked to jot down further observations in their books.

Teaching a group how to play Scoop – a board game: excerpt from pupils' transcript

This is how to play Scoop. Right – um – everybody gets a board with a newspaper, of a newspaper. You get 500 each, you have a pile of cards, another pile with exclusive scoops, etc ... You get, er, there's a telephone in the middle. Every time you get three of a, three of the same type, like, for example three crosswords, you'd phone up and, if you got three stars, it would mean your story's given three stars status, and in other words you could keep the story, get a card of a crossword. On the back it would say how much you get, and you put it in the space on your card – um, you'd carry on the game. If you got, if you got um, it you've got an exclusive scoop, you go that go and, and you bank it, right, and you can bank your cards to say you've got three, three cards and you want to bank one, you pay a 00 to the bank, you put it there so everyone can see it and you pick up another card, and that will be the end of your go and every time you pick up a card, you can put another one down besides the pile – right – um anyway, em. Does everyone understand how to play it?

What happens if you don't want to pick up a card?

You can pick up an exclusive scoop – read it. If, like this one says keep this card, it may be used to complete any articles, then say if you had two, two artists, you could use this to make, you'd put the other two, you'd scrap the other two, you'd keep the other one, you'd keep this and you'd er – phone up. Good. Right, that, er ...

But what do you do with the board?

Your board. Oh, every time you go, every time you get a scoop, you put your crossword on there. When you've completed it, the game ends and you can, er, you – you collect your money, you count up all the money on the back of your thingy ...

Carmel Davitt   <u>Rules on how</u> to play the board game Scoop.

This board game is for two to four players aged seven to adult.
The equipment for 'Scoop' is you should have = 4 newspaper boards

1 telephone (play)

4 telephone instruction cards

2 packs of scoop cards.

Paper money

The object of the game is to have 8 various newspaper articles placed on
the newspaper board which include ones like crime, sport and scandal.
Also the person who does this is the winner yet they have to not have
there story scrapped as all articles are taken from the board.

How to play:

First every person gets a board headed with the name of a newspaper
It will be either 'The Sun,' 'The Times,' 'The Today' or 'The News of the
World.'
Then £500 is given to every player, now the game starts a dealer gives out
three cards to each person on those will be various job like for instance :
a photographer, an artist or a crime reporter.
The rest of these cards are placed face upwards in the middle of the table,
also you are given a telephone instruction card which I'll say about more
later. Yet also in the middle of the table are some chance cards now when
it is your go you can either pick up the card that is on top of the job
cards and put down one of your cards you don't need, because say you
wanted a scandal story and you have got say the 'Telephone' and 'photographer' cards
and the scandal report is the one on top of pile you can pick that one up.
So now you have a story, you shout out 'scoop' so play immediately stops
and you go on the play telephone. For this you dial a number then pick
up the telephone receiver which will have written something like 'Yes' you
look down your instructions and find yes and see what it reads. Now yes
actually says your

Making a complaint (Lessons 6, 7 and 8)

The focus of these lessons was the language we use to make a complaint. A scenario was given, and three tasks followed. In Numbers 1 and 2, the class was asked to think very carefully about the sort of spoken English required by each situation; Number 3 was a formal written exercise following on from this.

Instructions to Pupils

Scenario
A   Householder
B   Plumber

Duane Pipe Plumbing Co have recently called at your home to replace a piece of piping in the bathroom/ kitchen. The job does not meet with your satisfaction, and you are very angry. The piping runs alongside the top of the cupboard instead of behind it, therefore damaging the cabinet. The plumber has also left a very bad mess.

How do you express your displeasure most appropriately in the following situation?

1. Act out the scene where, having left the plumber to do the job, the householder returns. Think of the various ways you (as the householder) can display your annoyance: i.e. language, voice, bodily gestures, pointing. The scene should end with the plumber giving you the phone number of the firm so you can make a telephone complaint.

2. **The Phone Call**
   A   Householder
   B   Secretary

   You ring Duane Pipe Plumbing Co to make a complaint about the piping job. What sort of spoken English is required in this situation? What sort of things will you have to bear in mind about the speaker on the other end of the phone? What is the purpose of the call? The scene should end with the secretary advising you politely to write a letter making a formal complaint to the company.

3. Letter of complaint Write a formal letter of complaint to Duane Pipe Plumbing Co. How are the aim and function of the language used in this task different from that in 1 and 2? What sort of language is required here (dates/facts/work undertaken/workman involved)? Be clear, informative and courteous.

   Do you think there is any place for sarcasm or anger in your letter? How does the task become more difficult if you are feeling depressed, angry or annoyed about something?

4. After you have completed your work, write about the differences in each situation in terms of the language, tone and attitude. What are the advantages of being able to give:

— a spoken account?
— a written account?
Are there any advantages?
In your own words explain the aims and functions of the language used in each activity.

(An alternative to the plumbing scenario could be a complaint about a recently purchased pair of shoes where the sole has come loose.)

Evaluation

After the pupils had completed the three different assignments, I wanted them to consolidate what they had learnt. To help them to structure their evaluations, I provided them with the following questions:

Written and Spoken English: 9AL – Evaluation

Using the table 'Differences Between Written and Spoken Language' that you have built up in your exercise books to help you, answer the following questions:

1. What are the advantages of being able to give spoken directions to a place?

2. What are the main things required to give successful written directions?

3. What were the main difficulties in listening to and trying to understand the spoken instructions given on how to play the game Scoop? Give at least three reasons and try to explain the difficulties.

4. When devising written instructions on how to play a game what do you think are the five most important things that the writer should do?

5. a) Can you suggest reasons why we repeat ourselves and use expressions like 'you know', 'er', 'um', 'thingy', 'like' in spoken English?

   b) Why do these expressions not crop up in written work?

6. Look back at your work on Making a Complaint. What were the differences a) in the language used and b) in the tone of the language in each of the situations you were given?

7. In a paragraph or two say what you have learnt about written and spoken English from your involvement with this project.

One pupil's responses to these questions follows as an indication of what had been learned about differences between written and spoken language.

Written and spoken English.

1. The advantages of being able to give spoken directions to a place are that you can use your hands to point directions, because you can see, you also can use phrases like "round the corner" and "on your left" or "on your right" and "next to the traffic lights" and "over the road". There is also an advantage in that you don't have to give as much detailed directions, as when you are writing directions on paper.
It is also alot easier for the person who is wanting to know the directions to a place, because they can ask questions if they are not sure.

2. The main things required to give successful written directions are that you require clear precise road names, and specific language like "then you turn right round the Island" must be used to ensure readers understanding.
A little simple diagram could be used

So the readers can check if they are in the right place, in the diagram you could have detailed descriptions of landmarks, like tower clocks or statues.
Written instructions are easier to describe because the writer has time to consider how to phrase instructions clearly, therefore making it easier for the reader.

3. The main difficulties in listening to and trying to understand the spoken instructions of how to play the game 'scoop' are that the describer kept repeating the same instructions over and over again she kept pausing in between each sentence which made it hard to keep track on what had been said. The describer also didn't use precise language instead said "if you've got it, if you're got um" and "you go, that go ands" also "you get 500 each."
500 what? clear precise language must be used.
Another difficultie in understanding spoken instructions are that the speaker used words

like er, um, youd, thingy, right er anyway, these words can cause confusion for the readers. The spoken piece isn't very clear, the instructions leap from one part of the game to another without explaining the stages properlly.

4. The five most important instructions the writer should do when devising written instructions on how to play a game are what equipment is needed, how to win the game and the object of the game, what equipment is given out and the start of the game i.e money and at what times in the game do you pick up cards etc

5a. We repeat ourselves and use expressions like "you know" "um" "er" "like" and "thingy" because this shows that we are thinking about what we are going to say next, we also sometimes repeat ourselves because we have run out of things to say.
When we use words like "thingy" it is caused maybe because we are quite nervous or it is a common use of language.

b. These expressions aren't used in written work because the writer has time to use precise

Speech, therefore making it clearer to understand.

6a. In "Making a complaint" the language used to the plumber was more direct, and the householder used alot more slang words, than on the telephone where he used proper and precise words. The householder and the plumber both were very sarcastic to one another.

b. The tone of language used in each situation were very different, in the complaint with the plumber, the householder went suddenly from a very loud voice, to a very quiet voice to display his anger but on the telephone he was quite civilized but still got his point across.

7. In this project I have learnt that there are many differences between written and spoken English, in written English we use precise vocabulary, but in spoken English we use slang words and often pause for thought on what we're going to say next.

With grateful thanks to the pupils and staff of Cardinal Newman School, Coventry.

DIFFERENTIATION IN THE KNOWLEDGE ABOUT LANGUAGE CURRICULUM

NIGEL KENT

Like all other English departments in the secondary sector we are currently engaged in constructing an English curriculum that fulfils the statutory requirements of the National Curriculum and takes account of the fact that language development is non-linear and recursive. No easy task! We have tried to achieve this by requiring our pupils to revisit language experiences explored in the previous year in a fresh and more demanding way in each of the secondary years. At the same time we have been striving to place knowledge about language at the centre of our curriculum, embedding within the majority of our units of work opportunities for explicit language study, in the belief that this should support pupils' development as language users. There was considerable agreement within the department on how the curriculum in each year should differ: for example, there was no real argument when we were deciding how narrative work done in year 9 should differ from that done in year 8. However, the department felt less secure when attempting to differentiate the strand concerning knowledge about language. We may have wished to return to the issue of the difference between speech and writing on several occasions during the secondary stage, but we had little experience of doing this in a way that was fresh, more demanding and yet supportive of our pupils' language development. This study was an attempt to provide some answers to that question.

The study is based on two units of work: one for a mixed ability year 7 group and one for a less able year 10 GCSE group. In both cases, pupils were required to reflect upon the differences between speech and writing.

The year 7 unit

The focus of this unit was instructional language. It was felt that the main area of difficulty with pupils' instructional writing was their inability to identify and anticipate audience need and the inappropriateness of the language used. Too often their written instructions read more like spoken instructions with their lack of precision and reliance on deictic expressions. Could explicit study of the difference between spoken and written instructions remedy these deficiencies?

In the first lesson, pupils were asked to make a simple paper model, in pairs, using some poor written instructions. As problems began to manifest themselves, and before the frustration level rose too high, each pair was asked to note down the problems it was experiencing and the reasons for those problems. These were then shared during a plenary session. At the end of the lesson I explained that we would be looking in closer detail at why these instructions did not work.

For the next session, each member of the class was asked to prepare a spoken demonstration of some fairly complex task – for example, how to perform a card trick. These demonstrations were taped, and at the end of the session the pupils were asked to describe the features that made a good spoken demonstration.

One of these tapes was then used as the basis for the next lesson. A transcript of one of the most successful demonstrations was made. It was reproduced on a sheet of A3, and in pairs pupils were invited to underline anything which told them it was spoken rather than written language that they were reading. They were then invited to try to describe each of the features they had spotted.

One fortunate bonus was that the boy who had given the demonstration showed me the book on which he had based it. I reproduced a page from this book for the next lesson and asked the class to spot the differences between the spoken and written versions. This enabled them to consolidate and summarise what they had learnt from the previous lesson and to make explicit the differences. At the end of the session pupils shared what they had learned and produced the following summative description:

WRITTEN	SPOKEN
no pauses	pauses for thought
more specific and descriptive	less precise, uses phrases like 'you know what I mean', 'like that', 'you do this'
no slang	uses slang
no mistakes	keeps hesitating, pausing for thought and going back and correcting himself
diagrams in stages	one continuing diagram, added to as he speaks
explanations split into small parts/paragraphs	one bit of explanation goes on into the next
a bigger range of words used	keeps repeating himself
sound like 'a robot'	definitely Simon speaking
not many personal pronouns	lots of personal pronouns included things which had nothing to do with the subject

When asked to explain the reasons for these differences, various pupils offered the following explanations:

When you're writing you've got time to go back and correct it so your mistakes don't show.

When you're speaking you know whether they understand it or not, so you can say it again if you have to using different words.

In written instructions if you don't understand it, that's it, like when we were making the angel — we couldn't do it — when you're speaking, if you don't understand you can ask. You've got to get it right when you're writing.

I (*Simon, the demonstrator*) said some things, which didn't have much to do with the drawing because I felt nervous and I wanted to ... like break the ice.

To focus on the importance of structure in instructions, pupils were then given a sequencing exercise based on effective instructions for the same paper model they had been asked to make in the first session. In pairs, they sought to find the best sequence for the instructions and test it out by attempting to make the model.

The programme finished with pupils being invited to produce an entry for a class anthology entitled 'Things to do on the rainy days in the holidays'. The book was to be published and marketed to the pupils within the class.

Evaluation

During the programme, pupils manifested a considerable implicit knowledge about the differences between spoken and written language. Even with their limited metalanguage they were able to make this implicit knowledge explicit and in doing so articulated and made accessible a clear set of guidelines for their own writing. Furthermore, the collaborative redrafting undertaken during the manufacture of the anthology was effective because these guidelines produced a shared set of criteria by which they could assess each other's work. They were able to look for and comment on specific aspects of their partner's work in an efficient, well-informed and supportive manner.

The year 10 unit

Within a module looking at the nature of autobiography and diary, pupils had been asked to read Valerie Avery's *London Morning*. The aims of the part of the module described below, in which the class spent a two week period looking at the use of dialogue in the text, were: to develop the pupils' response to character; to help them understand the nature of autobiography and the craft of the writer; and to provide a supportive context for their own writing.

In the first of these lessons, three pupils, each taking the part of a different principal character, were hot-seated about their response to the events in Chapter 8. This helps to establish and focus discussion on the nature of the characterisation in the text. This was followed by a plenary session which gave the class as a whole the chance to challenge or support the interpretations they had observed by specific reference to the text.

In the second lesson the class was reminded that an autobiography purports to deal with real people and real events. They were then invited to consider the relationship of the text to reality through an exploration of the dialogue. To facilitate this exploration, the class was given a worksheet containing an example of an authentic transcribed anecdote and an anecdote related by one of the characters in the text. The class was split into groups of three and asked: to identify the authentic speech; to highlight and describe the features of the language used that enabled them to recognise it as such; and, finally, by comparing the authentic speech to the dialogue drawn from the novel, to suggest changes a writer might have to make to authentic speech if he or she wishes to use it as part of a novel.

The summary on the page opposite was produced in the plenary session that followed.

Having established that even writers of autobiographies are in the business of editing, shaping and making sense of the experience, in the next lesson the class was asked to examine how Avery does this, with particular reference to the way she creates a distinctive voice for each of the principal characters they had explored in the first session. A second worksheet was produced which consisted of seven speeches spoken by four of the main characters: three of the characters were represented by two speeches and the fourth by only one. The groups were asked to identify the pairs of speeches and the odd one out, justifying their decision by highlighting and describing the common, distinctive language features of each speaker.

This unit was concluded by a writing exercise in which the pupils were asked to take these four main characters and put them in a new situation, and relate that situation in script form, replicating the distinctive voice that each has. On concluding the piece, they were asked to analyse and evaluate what they had intended and achieved in their scripts.

Evaluation

The general quality of the scripts was exceptional for this less able group. Many of them revealed characters with the distinctive voices of the original. That evaluation of their scripts suggested that this may have been a product of the high degree of consciousness with which they approached the writing process and of the heightened sensitivity they had acquired during this unit to the nature of authentic and crafted speech. For example, in his evaluation one pupil writes:

I have captured the different personalities by using slang and different accents. E.g. The Grandad is always moaning, so I used things like stage directions saying 'he moaned', 'he shouted' or 'he yelled'. For grandad I have also used a cockney accent which misses out some sounds ... Val's personality has been captured by sentences running into one another and the speech going on and on. Yet the

Features of real speech	The writer's changes
we need to be there to understand it	have to include descriptions of actions that accompany the speech to make the meaning clear
unplanned: quick subject changes	might have to make cuts to make it relevant to what the writer's trying to say at the time
attempt to find a more exact word/phrase	use exact words first time
pauses and hesitations	reorganise to make better sense: put background information first?
longer, takes more words to say same thing	make it shorter to hold the reader's attention (cut repetitions, pauses, etc)
thinking words ('well', 'anyway')	pauses, hesitations etc might be included if they have something to say about the character/situation
signalling words (I'm about to start talking — e.g. 'Well')	make up for intonation with punctuation/phrases of saying/descriptions of actions etc.
tendency to exaggerate: choose words to make immediate impact	
sentences run into one another	

grandad speaks in short, sharp sentences ... I've used hesitations and pauses because of the situation some of the characters get themselves into. E.g. when Val goes back to the jeweller's and gives back the brooch she comes home and she says, 'Y...y...yes I've taken the brooch back'. She speak like this because she is in two minds of what to say.

Their scripts produced at the end of this unit revealed a genuine command of dialogue and an ability to shape language to create a strong sense of the original characterisation and situation.

Conclusions

What then can be learnt about knowledge about language and differentiation? While it must be acknowledged that in both cases the focus on the differences between spoken and written English was new for the students, it would appear that there is sufficient evidence here to suggest that the knowledge about language elements in the English curriculum can be covered in exactly the same way as we would wish to cover other elements such as poetry or narrative. It would be possible to construct a knowledge about language element in an English curriculum with, for example, historical knowledge in the lower years working towards sociolinguistic knowledge in the later years; but such an approach would limit the potential for language study to support pupils' own language development. This study suggests that pupils have a wealth of implicit linguistic knowledge which we can exploit in the interests of their development as language users continuously throughout their school career. It is possible and, indeed desirable, to return to aspects of this knowledge which we have raised earlier, from new perspectives and for different purposes, consolidating and extending that knowledge on each occasion and using it to support the skills of reading, writing, speaking and listening. In the year 7 unit we saw how a comparison of the differences between spoken and written language con provide elementary insights into the nature of language, which can be used to support pupils' writing. In the year 10 unit it was possible to build on such insights to prompt quite sophisticated observations on the style and meaning of text and to stimulate appreciation of the creative process which in turn had a tangible impact upon the pupils' own writing. Obviously this study represents one small step towards the evolution of an English curriculum based on this principle. It is now our task as a department to determine which aspects of language we return to, when we do so and how – a not inconsiderable task!

With thanks to pupils and staff at Bournside Comprehensive, Cheltenham, Gloucestershire.

These articles show children:
- reflecting on their own effectiveness in the use of the spoken word (§6, Speaking and Listening);
- focusing on the range of purposes which spoken language serves (§6, Speaking & Listening);
- considering language appropriate to situation, topic and purpose (§18, Speaking & Listening);
- recognising that speech ranges from casual spontaneous conversation to more formal forms (§20, Speaking & Listening);
- discussing contrasts in how vocabulary is used in speech and writing (§21, Writing);
- understanding that, as speech typically takes place in a situation where both

speaker and listener are present, it can be accompanied by gestures and words like 'this', 'that', 'here', 'now', 'you', etc., whereas writing generally requires greater verbal explicitness (§28, Writing);

- understanding that, at its most characteristic, speech is interactive, spontaneous and informal which means that topics of conversation emerge in an unplanned and unstructured way; in contrast, writing needs a more tightly planned structure (§30, Writing).

Language Diversity

For many years we have underestimated and undervalued the rich variety of languages and dialects in our society. The status of English as a major international language and the status of Standard English as its written form have led to the sidelining of other languages and other dialects of English. Teachers now recognise that accepting and valuing the experience of children in other languages and other dialects is one of the most potent means of developing their abilities within English and within Standard English.

Language is a crucial feature of personal identity – an understanding of language is an understanding of oneself. The case studies in this chapter are all concerned with encouraging children to reflect on the part that language plays in the formation of their own identity. Children are able to relate complex and abstract issues such as language and power to their own experiences, and they are able to discuss language in the safe knowledge that they are the experts.

The work featured in these case studies makes children aware of influences – regional, educational, and cultural – on their own language, and it encourages them to reflect on and to value those influences. It leads them towards an awareness of both the commonality and diversity of language experiences: they see that both adults and children use language for broadly similar purposes in a wide range of different contexts, and they see the richness and variety of language skills and language experiences among their peers and in their community. The work takes them from an awareness of self to an awareness of others – as, for example, in the year 2 class which goes on to question parents and grandparents about their language profiles.

The teachers involved emphasise the importance of teacher modelling, with teachers producing their own language profiles to set alongside the children's. They show the value of using children as researchers as well as the need to provide both external comparisons and clear frameworks to help children analyse and reflect on their data.

In 'Children describe their own experience as language users', Carolyn Boyd describes work with three different classes in years 2, 3 and 4. The teachers involved begin by exploring their own language profiles, and use these as models for the children to explore and present theirs. The year 2 children go on to interview their parents and grandparents and to present their language profiles.

In 'Home and away', Gaik See Chew explores the potential of building on the rich knowledge and experience of bilingual pupils in years 5 and 6. She shows the importance of acknowledging the children's first languages and talking to them about their languages in relation to their home lives.

In 'The two worlds of language', Shabanah Waheed argues that exploring language diversity is not enough; we need also to look at the power relationships that are embedded in language. She describes how a year 9 class used poetry as a starting point for looking at language variety in a social context, and for reflecting on the status of different languages and how this affected their own lives.

In 'Many voices', Angela Jensen explores ways of reflecting on accent and dialect with year 3 children. The pupils begin by considering dialects other than their own, and this 'distance' enables them to identify and reflect on their features.

In 'Researching accent and dialect', Kate Parkes demonstrates the resourcefulness and independence of year 8 pupils researching into accent and dialect. Using the resources of teachers and other pupils, groups research:
– attitudes to Received Pronunciation;
– the attitudes of speakers to their own accents;
– the effect on people's accents of moving to another part of the country;
– the specific differences between regional accents;
– the dialects of the old and young.

In 'The language of *Miguel Street*', Linda Croft introduces the GCSE coursework of a year 10 pupil who studied the dialect speech used by characters in V S Naipaul's *Miguel Street*. This case study demonstrates very effectively the value of studying a regional dialect in terms of developing an understanding of Standard English.

CHILDREN DESCRIBE THEIR OWN EXPERIENCE AS LANGUAGE USERS

CAROLYN BOYD

Children use language and see language being used in many different situations in their daily lives, in and out of school. Many of their experiences will be shared by the wider community, and some will be personal to them as language users. How can we encourage children to reflect on and value this wealth of experience?

Language histories

The year 2 class at Hounslow Heath Infant School had watched *Geordie Racer*, the BBC Schools television series, and discussed the accents in the film. An actress from Newcastle visited the class and talked about Newcastle and her dialect and accent with them. The class also discussed accents when an American student worked with them.

Sheila Novak, the class teacher, Sofia Mughal, from Hounslow's primary language service, my colleague Kulvinder Lidder and I shared our language histories and experiences with the class, in which numerous languages are spoken. This led to interesting conversations and observations by the children on their language use:

Akif	You have to say 'thank you' to big people.
Aftab	I say 'arp' (*polite form of 'you' in Urdu*) at the temple.
Teacher	Would you say 'arp' to your friend?
Aftab	No. 'Toom'.
Sandeep	I say 'satsriacal' (*greetings*) to the old people. My papaji lives at my sister's house and I always say 'satsriacal' to him.

The following day the children decided to see how their relatives use language in different situations for different audiences. As a class they compiled a list of questions they would like to ask their parents and, if possible, their grandparents. Sheila quickly scribed their questions onto large strips of card. Questions regarding the different languages spoken were quickly formulated. Questions which related to tone of voice and accent called for more teacher direction. The children then spread the cards out on the carpet and sorted them into a logical order. There were comments such as, 'No, you can't put that with that', 'Well, that goes with that'. They placed the cards in a long line on the carpet and spent ten minutes reading and checking the order. Then they numbered them. Sheila wrote them out on a banda sheet. Each child took three copies of the questionnaire home. Here it is:

Dear Parents,
Class 9 are finding about how we speak. Please could you help us by answering our questions?

1. Were you born in another country or were you born in England?

2. What language did you speak a long time ago when you were little?

3. Was your school in India or Pakistan or Africa or England?

4. Did you use a different language when you went to school?

5. What language did you speak to your teacher? Did you speak to her in a different way?

6. How did you feel when you started to read and write in your language?

7. Do you speak a different language to your Mum and Dad? Do you speak to them in a different way?

8. How do you speak to your grandparents?

9. Do you speak to babies in a sweet voice and say different words?

10. Do you speak differently when guests are here or at your house?

11. What language do you speak at your friend's house?

12. Do you always speak differently to your friends? Do you change your accent? Do you use different languages?

13. What language do you speak when you go to the temple? Do you speak in a different way?

14. What language do you speak when you go to the shops?

15. Do you speak in a different language at work, or with a different accent, or in a different voice?

16. Can you write us a story that you were told when you were little?

As they brought the completed questionnaire back to school, the children excitedly shared them with the class. They then began to collate this information in poster form. The work evolved until all 30 children were working at various stages of their language profiles. Some children rewrote the answers in sentence form onto their posters; some formulated parts of the sentence and added it to the parent's answers in a cut-and-paste fashion, so that both the children's and the parents' writing appeared on the posters; some cut and pasted both the questions and answers completed by their parents onto the poster. Because the nature of the activity allowed children to work at their own pace and level, and the children were so engrossed and busy helping each other, Sheila was able to observe and collect samples of the children trying out different forms of language and reflecting on their knowledge of language.

Bindi commented when writing 'alive' that it could be pronounced in two different ways, but was spelt the same, as 'I live in England' and 'I am alive'.

Rakki decided to combine the answers to the two questions, 'Do you speak a different language to your mum and dad?' and 'Do you speak to them in a different way?' She wrote, 'My mum speaks to her mum politely in Gujerati'.

Reeena was copying down a question. The following conversation occurred:

Ashmi	That's not proper writing…write…sentence…answer…That's copying the question.
Reena	Oh…(*Reads hers, reads Ashmi's*) Can you help me? 'What language do you speak when you go to the shops?'
Ashmi	Does your mum say English in the shops?
Reena	Ye…es.
Ashmi	'My mum speaks English at the shops.' Write that.

Reena wrote, 'When my mum is going to the shops she speaks English'.

The teacher was available to support children's explorations:

Gurpreet	Is this a sentence? 'My mums speaks to babies polite and simple.' No—oo, it's wrong.
Teacher	You could use 'politely and simply' or 'in polite and simple language'.

| Gurpreet | 'Polite and simple language' – no – 'polite' – 'in politely simply language' – no – 'in politely simple language' – no – ' 'in polite and simple language' – that's best. |

Children's conversations ranged across the curriculum:

Ashmi	My mum comes from Madagascar and my dad from Tanzania.
Krandeep	Where's that?
Ashmi	It's a little bit near India and a little bit near Africa.
Teacher	Shall we get the globe from Class 11?
	(Ashmi returns with globe and the group spend some time locating Madagascar.)
Ashmi	Look! It's near Tanzania. My dad went to Madagascar and he married my mum.

The children explored their concepts of time – and of reality:

Anupam	It's not long ago, we're new.
Teacher	It's longer ago for me, and for your mums and dads. Is that long ago?
Anupam	Not as long ago as the dinosaurs.
Teacher	No. I'm not extinct.
	(All laugh.)
Mandeep	That's long long ago, once upon a time.
Anupam	No that's stories – once upon a time – like Littlefoot – but he might be real. Is he real?
Teacher	Well, it was part of a film. What do you think?

The children proudly showed their language expertise. Monolingual English-speaking children were interested in and respectful of the wealth of languages in the class:

Lee	This is Chinese. I can write it.
Vijay	I can write my name in Gujerati.
Leroy	I can't. That's good.

Samantha remarked, 'I know a lot of French and I know a bit of Urdu'.

The teacher discovered a wide range of language expertise. For example, Farid knew three languages (Gujerati, English and Punjabi); Anupam's father speaks six languages (Urdu, Hindi, Punjabi, Swahili, Gujerati and English).

Compiling the language histories was a fruitful way of exploring children's knowledge about language. It was beneficial at the broad level of showing that languages are systems that do roughly the same job of communicating broadly the same concepts and understandings; and it allowed the children to reflect on the surface features and structures of the languages they use, and how the languages are written. They began to make explicit their understandings of the languages they use, and how they change their language or tone of voice according to the context of the language being used:

My grandma speaks Punjabi when she goes to the temple.

My mum speaks in a different way on official phone calls.

My dad speaks differently when he plays with Linus and me. He speaks in a funny voice.

The children continued to discuss how they heard language being used around them. As they read each other's profiles, they were sometimes prompted to add another observation to their posters. The work gave support and prestige to the children's multilingualism. The languages and experiences they brought to the classroom were genuinely valued and celebrated. The teacher often came into the room to find parents sitting down reading the work that had been done.

Telling stories

The last question on the children's questionnaire was 'Can you write us a story that you were told when you were little?' Parents responded by writing real events they remembered or stories they were told. The stories were typed up and translated into a number of languages. Some parents visited the class and told stories. One of the children commented after being told a story in Portuguese, 'I didn't know of that language before. That was good.' All the children's understandings of and respect for languages were increased in a way that closely linked home and school.

Traditional stories also proved to be a stimulating link between home and school for year 2 children at Heston Infant School, with Gaby Brent. The children compared different versions of Little Red Riding Hood and decided to write their own versions. They compared the adventures of Raj Rasalu with St George and the Dragon. Parents were then invited to write or tell their children stories they remembered from their childhood. Some parents also responded by writing stories at home with their children. These stories were printed on the computer, translated and published. Comments about the authors and illustrators accompanied their photographs. The parents and children made bilingual tapes. All the children became interested in story telling, drawing in grandparents, aunties and older sisters. The children recounted traditional stories told in assembly, which were then published. They were able to see that more than one language can do approximately the same job of describing the same events, and that books are made by authors.

In all these examples, understandings were generated as part of the act of producing language. In a subtle but powerful way, the understandings that are developed when children can both show their competence and reflect on that competence will inform their future language use.

Thanks to all the teachers, children and parents involved in this work at Heston and Hounslow Heath Infant Schools.

This article shows children:

- reflecting on and evaluating their use of spoken language (§4, Speaking & Listening);
- focusing on regional and social variations in accents and dialects of the English language and attitudes to such variations (§9, Speaking & Listening);
- focusing on the range of purposes which spoken language serves (§9, Speaking & Listening);
- being encouraged to respect their own language(s) or dialect(s) and those of others (§11, Speaking & Listening);
- considering language appropriate to situation, topic and purpose (§18, Speaking & Listening);
- talking about ways in which language is written down (§6, Reading);
- observing writing in their own first langauge (§4, Writing);
- considering some ways in which writing contributes to the organisation of society, the transmission of knowledge, the sharing of experiences, and the capturing of imagination (§20, Writing).

HOME AND AWAY: RAISING AWARENESS OF MOTHER TONGUE IN THE CLASSROOM

GAIK SEE CHEW

This language project was conducted throughout a whole term with year 5 and 6 children. There were twenty-two children altogether with a spread of nine languages among them. The class was a very lively one. There were only two children in the first stages of learning English as a second langauge. Both, however, were literate in their first language. Languages spoken in the class were Bengali, Farsi, French, Creole, Arabic, Serbo-Croat, Yoruba, Spanish and Portuguese.

The idea was to bring together through the language project all the cultural and linguistic richness that these children possessed and to make them aware that these are positive assets. I also wanted to introduce new experiences for the children so that each week there would be a new activity which would always have a language focus. To summarise, I had four aims with the project:

1. Acknowledging the children's first language and using their mother tongue as a positive support to all-round intellectual development and to the development of the children's second language.

2. Developing confidence and self-esteem through their first language and background by talk about language(s) and home life as part of everyday life. Giving recognition and status to mother tongue that is central to the children's life.

3. Introducing and encouraging language awareness, gaining new insights into

language for bilingual and monolingual children towards a more positive view of languages.

4. Through these aims, increasing knowledge about language, and about English as a mother tongue. Knowledge about other languages and knowledge about English will give us valuable insight into language as a whole. It will give children the opportunity to work collaboratively in order to share experiences and learn from one another.

'It's so Chinese!'

We started with a language questionnaire, the first part of which plunged the children straight into an encounter with other languages. They had to listen to the story of *The Very Hungry Caterpillar* in five different languages (Spanish, Chinese, Cantonese, Arabic and Farsi) and to guess which language it was in. As I played each tape, they became very excited – another kind of language was being communicated in the class. Nods, winks, nudges and gesticulations were directed at children who were bilingual. Amazingly, although there were no Chinese speakers among the class, everyone recognised the Chinese version of *The Very Hungry Caterpillar*.

'Why was that?' I asked the class. Answers came flying back at me:
'Because it goes up and down, that's why!'
'It's so Chinese!'
'It just sounds like Chinese'
'But how do you know it's Chinese?' I asked.
'It's Chinese because it's sing-song.'

This led to more questions and a lively discussion about what makes one language distinct from another; to the identity that each language brings to each person and to the fact that language is central to life and communication.

The children then completed the second part of their questionnaire (see below). Once they had done that, they looked at the English text of *The Very Hungry Caterpillar* and tried to retell it in their mother tongue. Tapes were made by the children in Serbo-croat, French and Arabic. I also brought in written translations of this story in as many languages as I could find, so that the children could examine different scripts as well as different texts of the story of *The Very Hungry Caterpillar*.

Language questionnaire (Part II)

1. Do you speak a language other than English? What is the language?

2. In what part of the world is your language spoken?
   If it is English that you speak, have a guess where English might be the national language.

3. How well do you speak this language?
   (a bit, quite well, very well)

4. Who do you speak this language to?

5. Can you read and write this language?

6. If you had the chance, which other language would you like to learn to speak?

7. Can you think of five words or expressions in your language and translate these into English?

Home and away

The second session of the project was aimed at the children's experiences at home and away from home. I read to them from Trish Cooke's book '*Mammy, sugar falling down*', a poignant passage where a child relates her experience of leaving her home country and travelling to England where she is to make her new home. I told the class that, in their piece of writing, they could write about what they wanted: about home experiences, travel, distant places, what there is outside their front door, members of family they miss.

Here are a few examples of what they wrote about:
  – Wayne wrote of his grandfather and of the differences between Dominica and England.
  – Rade compared Yugoslavia to England and talked of his family in Yugoslavia.
  – Paulo's piece was written in Portuguese. (He is one of the pupils in the first stages of learning English. The piece was accompanied by a translation in English done by Paolo and myself.)
  – Maria's piece was about her father in Spain.
  – Ferdousi described her family from different parts of the world.
  – Clare's writing was about her father in Yorkshire.

Names and places

This was the third session of the project. It was clear that the countries of origin of the children and their families became more personal to them from writing about these places and their home experiences. It was time to look at maps and atlases. A display was put up using the map of the world, and ribbons linked names of class members to places of origin. Each child also had a blank map of the world on A4 sheets and they filled in their respective places of origin. They worked in pairs and 'visited' other pairs to find out which countries other children were from, until the whole class had all their places marked in. The class is made up of children from Yugoslavia, Grenada, Dominica, Jamaica, Nigeria, Kenya, Portugal, Ireland, England, France, Spain, Iraq, Iran and America.

This activity led us on to our next three sessions of the project: stories from different countries. I wanted these sessions to involve children in talk and to gain confidence in telling and retelling stories. I also wanted them to know that every culture has a rich store of stories and that they also had stories to tell.

I started with a story from East Africa called *The Wishing Tree*. An earlier LINC course on storytelling had taught me a good form of group work with storytelling, which involved collaborative work between the children. The story was told to the whole class, and then the class was divided into two groups; the children had to retell the story in a circle but were restricted to two sentences each. Both groups had then to come back and retell their story. The children became familiar with this format of storytelling, and this activity was extended to working in pairs with more stories.

On another occasion, we had eight shorter stories from different parts of the world. These stories were given to small groups of two or three children. Each group was given fifteen minutes to read and 'fix' each story in their heads and then each group had to tell their story to the whole class. Stories that were used were:

The Bamboo Princess (from Malaysia)
The Good Sister and the Mango Tree (from India)
The Tree in the Moon (from Tahiti)
Trees of Fire (from North America)
The Woman and the Rice Thief (from India)
The Magic Kettle (from Japan)
The Dragons of Peking (from China)
King Jahangir and the Baby (from India)

From this session, children began to see similarities and differences between stories and could appreciate how different stories from different countries could carry a similar moral. Children were also encouraged to bring stories from home or to retell their own stories, something they had made up themselves.

At this point, I also wanted something visual and tangible for them to handle. I am fortunate to own a small puppet collection from the Far East in the form of Indonesian rod puppets and shadow puppets, and Chinese hand puppets. When showing the children the shadow puppets, I told them of the great oral tradition from Indonesia and of the Dalang master storyteller who could tell the epics of the Mahabaratha and the Ramayana and manipulate puppets at the same time from behind a lighted screen. I also showed them a video of the story of Prince Rama: some children with whom I had worked before had made this with their own shadow puppets, similar to the original shadow puppets that I owned. We also looked at Brian Thompson's colourful book *The Story of Prince Rama* which has some beautiful prints of Mughal miniatures from the Victoria and Albert Museum.

Language awareness session

No language project is complete without a language awareness session. David had earlier asked the question, 'Are you going to teach us Chinese?', and this had been nagging at me. It was time to teach him some Chinese. I told the story of The Three Little Pigs in Chinese (Hokkien, which is my dialect), without telling them what the story was in English, but my huffing and puffing gave away some clues. Then I retold the story using picture cut-outs and visuals, and all was soon made clear to them. The children began to see how difficult it was for the two children in the class who were just beginning to learn English.

We also looked at borrowed words in the English language. We played the Word House Game (from *World Studies 8–13,* Oliver and Boyd) and then had a quiz from the section 'All languages are thieves' from *The Languages Book* (ILEA English and Media Centre) so that the children began to realise that language does not remain static, but borrows from other languages in its development, and changes all the time.

Our project culminated with a visit to Leighton House museum in Holland Park Road, where the children observed Arabic writing on ancient tiles from the Middle East brought back by Lord Leighton. Standing under the moorish arches of Lord Leighton's Arab Hall, with the fountain quietly gushing in the background, Salima said to me, 'My grandfather would love to see this. I shall bring him to see this wonderful place'.

With thanks to the pupils and staff at Avonmore Primary School, Hammersmith and Fulham, London.

This article shows children:

- reflecting on their own effectiveness in the use of the spoken word (§6, Speaking & Listening);
- focusing on the range of purposes which spoken language serves (§9, Speaking & Listening)
- being encouraged to respect their own languages and those of others (§11, Speaking & Listening);
- making their own translations from original sources (§9, Reading);
- helped to increase their control of story form (§18, Writing).

THE TWO WORLDS OF LANGUAGE

SHABANAH WAHEED

I have discovered new words and different ways of communicating with others around this environment. I have learned...new words which I didn't know...ever existed and ways of co-operating with each other in different languages.

From the beginning, I saw in 9SN the possibility of creating a learning environment in which social awareness of language could be fostered, and in which multilingualism could grow and flourish.

Ours is a single-sex girls' school in Bradford; the majority of the pupils are Asian in origin. The class in question is a mixed ability class of 20 pupils, aged 13 and 14. This particular class is composed entirely of Asian girls who possess a rich linguistic background; for most, English is their first language, and other languages spoken include Punjabi and Urdu. As well as these, the girls are exposed to other Asian languages, for example Hindi (which is learned from films), Arabic (of which they have a reading from the Koran) and, finally, European languages learned in school. I wanted to explore the rich linguistic resources of the class and to build on their intuitive receptiveness to language issues. I wanted also to make my own contribution to the study of language in the English classroom: unlike many white monolingual teachers, I share languages (English, Punjabi and Urdu), religious upbringing (Muslim) and cultural background (British Punjabi) with my pupils. I am also trained to teach French as well as English and throughout my academic life have been a bit of a polyglot, with an intense interest in language issues and a desire to communicate my enthusiasm for language in the classroom. Finally, I had always wanted to explore the potential of the computer in the classroom. An opportunity to do this arose during my second term with the class, when I was able to draw on the expertise of an advisory teacher who would be working with the class to develop both their IT competence and mine. I wanted to integrate the computer into normal activities, as a secondary, 'invisible' element, to be used, for example, in the drafting process. Wherever possible, it would also be used to underscore language issues, such as the relationship of handwritten to typewritten texts and their comparative status.

The foundations of the 'project' were laid in the first term when I endeavoured to encourage multilingualism by speaking Punjabi myself to create a relaxed, non-threatening environment. Pupils on the whole responded enthusiastically to this:

When she first started to speak in Punjabi I felt really happy towards her. Even though Ms Waheed does not speak proper Punjabi I still understand what she is saying.   (Tahira)

Inevitably, there was resistance – even outright hostility – towards the use of Asian languages in the class, but it was confined to one girl, whose responses will be discussed later. However, the rest of the class were already feeling positive and looking forward to the second term.

The language work embarked on during the spring term focused on the main aims of the project: to study language and varieties of English in their social context, to encourage pupils to reflect on language and status, and to develop their multilingualism and their competence in more varieties of English. I wanted pupils to arrive at an explicit knowledge of language and of its operation in society, and to start from the base-line of their vast intuitive experience of language – surely the best way of ensuring a contextualised study of language. Because the pupils themselves were the context, I felt the work could best evolve its own shape if it were freed from the usual demands of the class reader, for one term at least. However, the role of literature was not neglected, and the work moved along through a variety of mini-contexts – both literary and non-literary – each closely related to the theme of linguistic diversity and status.

The changing focus of the term's work can be expressed as follows:

Spoken language	→	Written language
Multilingualism	→	Varieties of English
Personal experience	→	A social/political context
Intuitive awareness	→	Explicit knowledge of language

Naturally, in practice, issues recurred and the focuses often overlapped; in retrospect there seems to have been a spiralling awareness of language, as I shall demonstrate.

Edwin Morgan's poem, 'The First Men on Mercury', provided an engaging first task: that of preparing a reading/interpretation in pairs. In the readings themselves, pupils explored the role of gestures, body language, intonation in language and speculated on the switch in power relations that occurs halfway through the poem. Significantly, some pupils made an instinctive link between 'Mercurian' and their 'home' languages as a result of picking up on the 'colonial' aspects of language (English) in the poem: 'I really enjoyed "The First Men on Mercury",' reflected Jabeena. 'It's like when I go home. I have to change the way I speak to my mum.'

The themes of power/alienation/communication in the poem were fertile ground for anecdotal reflection on similar language situations in the pupils' personal experience. In group and class discussions, various observations were made: one girl noted that in public places like shops, 'talking Asian' does not command respect, but 'talking posh' (English) gets quicker results. The anecdotes were then drafted on the computer, and many pupils related with relish how they frequently used their multilingualism to shut out monolingual speakers – either white people or Asians – and thereby empowered themselves. One anecdote entitled 'An Embarrassing Day' ran thus:

Once I was in a bus with my friends, and this English lady came and sat in front of me. She was smoking. I just couldn't stand that cigarette smell, so I said to my friend, 'Look at that old witch – she's got a cigarette on' in Punjabi. The lady looked back at me and then turned the cigarette off. I was quite embarrassed, thinking to myself, 'How on earth did she understand me?' Maybe she understood the word 'cigarette' even though I said it in a Punjabi accent. Maybe there should have been a word for 'cigarette' in Punjabi, so she wouldn't have understood me.

After Sakina had drafted most of this, I was able to direct her attention to revealing details, such as her unconsciously literal translation of Punjabi idioms: 'she's got a cigarette on' and 'turned the cigarette off'. The last two observations she makes reveal a sophisticated intuitive knowledge of language: accent can disguise or obscure meaning and, for cultural reasons, all languages have areas of lexical deficiency. Most importantly, she had translated the issues raised by the poem to her own experience: language can protect and empower, but its subtleties can occasionally defeat you.

The focus then shifted to issues of language and power within English itself. I felt it would be appropriate to explore pupils' feelings about the relative status of varieties of English by contrasting Yorkshire dialect with Standard dialect in the context of *Kes*. We read the section of the book in which Billy describes his kestrel at length to an enraptured class and teacher. The pupils were very perceptive about the shift of power from the teacher to Billy as he began to talk with confidence, employing specialist terms like 'jesses'. Intuitively they began to realise that Billy was like them in some respects: he brought with him from home an expertise in language that had previously been devalued because the dominant dialect in the classroom was Standard, which even the teacher – who had a Yorkshire accent – spoke. The connection was neatly articulated by Waheeda: 'Miss, because of our language, we all live in two worlds – one at home and one at school….' Such unprompted conscious reflections on language were deeply satisfying.

The passage afforded valuable opportunities to develop pupils' competence in Standard English, while at the same time encouraging them to value other dialects. This was the aim of the computer task which followed. Pupils were asked to 'standardise' a paragraph from the extract which they had already read, enjoyed and understood in context. This proved difficult at first, and, as pupils began to change almost every word in sight, I became worried that they would see the task as the 'translation' of a foreign, unintelligible language into a more socially acceptable and prestigious one. One of the reasons for this could be the pupils' perception of Billy's Yorkshire dialect ('missen'; 'thee' etc.) as being far removed from their own. In fact, some even failed to recognise that they do use Yorkshire dialect and that it forms a part of their linguistic repertoire. As this work progressed, I prompted them with questions like: 'How would you say to a friend, "I haven't got any?"' The reply, 'I ain't got nowt', helped them to recognise the variety of English they spoke. However, I felt the issue needed further exploration, especially as I did not feel I had fully achieved the aims of this task: I have increasingly had misgivings about the task itself.

I felt one of the best ways of encouraging pupils to acknowledge the varieties of English and of language which they were regularly using with great facility in their everyday lives was through a series of code-switching role plays. Entitled 'A Day in the Life of 9SN', the role plays explored many different permutations of language and context; they were also characterised by the uninhibited use of so-called home languages by virtually all pupils. Here is a breakfast scene from one of the role plays:

Safina	What time is it?
Jabeena	Half-past eight.
Safina	Oh no!
(Waheeda) Dad	Mehn tumeh kitni bar kaha keh raat mehn video na dekho? (*How many times have I told you not to stay up so late watching videos?*)
Jabeena and Safina	Oh shut up!
Dad	Bak bak kehtiahn! Mehn engine chalata hoon — aap khana kha kah jaldi aoh. (*Stop jabbering away! I'll start the car up – you come as soon as you've finished eating.*)

The transcript reveals the girls' unconscious understanding of the way multilingualism works in their daily lives, particularly the father's order to 'stop jabbering away!' The girls both understand their parents' language (Urdu) and can speak it, but choose not to for complex reasons to do with developing their own cultural identity, precisely because it irritates their parents and undermines their cultural values.

Waheeda's contribution was particularly interesting. Early on in the project, when she had displayed a great deal of resistance to languages other than English being used in the classroom, she commented in a written reflection:

We do get told off in school by some teachers not to speak our language. It's rude to speak Urdu when it's an English school. At home my mother does tell us off not to talk English all the time but we can't help it, so that's why I don't like to say "gee".

Most pupils liked it when I took the register in Punjabi, and answered 'gee' for 'yes'. It seems that pressures from home and school combined to make Waheeda resistant to speaking Urdu/Punjabi in any context. In addition, she probably saw me, an Asian teacher, as an agent of parental control in school. However, as it became apparent that *all* languages were being encouraged, and as she saw the obvious pleasure being derived from the work by other pupils, she softened. Eventually, in the secure context of a role play, playing her own father, she enjoyed airing a louder, brasher alter ego in Urdu. In a much later reflection which followed group discussion, she revealed:

I feel very strongly that our language is not just "dirty curry" or "Paki" language. When we speak English at home we get told off, but English is like a drug — you get addicted to it.

Most of the credit for this attitude change goes, I believe, to the power of peer pressure and the opportunities for oral group tasks that were central to the project.

The code-switching role plays were enjoyed by nearly all pupils, who took great delight in gently sending up the linguistic mannerisms of parents, friends, and white teachers in particular:

Teacher (Aquila) I	Come in!
Azra	Sorry, miss.
Teacher	Is that a way of entering?
Sakina and Abda	Kaminee — kitni kaminee heh! (*Mean old thing!*)
Teacher	What gibberish is this? I demand to know what you are saying right now!
Sakina and Abda	We were saying you're so nice and so kind!
Teacher	Huh! (*pointing to board*) Right — you have to write about [Queen] Elizabeth...
Sakina and Abda	Kitna boring! Kitna boring!
Teacher	I am talking here — what are you doing?
Sakina	Miss, I was just explaining to Abda...
Azra	Miss, she didn't understand — she's shy.
Teacher	Well why didn't she ask me?
Sakina	I know! (*Aside*) Pagal — shakal nehn — kakh nehn! (*The idiot — she's not even much to look at!*)
Teacher	Right — here's your books.
Sakina, Azra and Abda	Gisit, gisit here!
Teacher	Use proper English!
Sakina, Azra and Abda	This is English.
Teacher	This is a History lesson.
Sakina:	I can see that. (*As teacher walks away*) Ehnvehn basharam! (*Ought to be ashamed of herself.*)

The above transcript shows pupils displaying an impressive range of multilingual skills, an awareness of the lower status of Asian languages compared to English, and an ability to use Standard and non-Standard forms for the appropriate speaker.

Again, in an interesting parallel to the status of English within the pupils' homes, the pupils here demonstrate how they use language to subvert power relations in school. They employ either clear terms of abuse ('kaminee') or hybrid constructions ('kitna boring'), deliberately designed to undermine the teacher. Many white mono-lingual teachers are understandably worried by the 'abuse' of 'home' languages by pupils, and rightly wish to encourage them to use these as part of their normal transactions and learning strategies in the classroom. However, I believe too much emphasis has been placed on the pupil side of the equation. After all, it is teacher attitudes that often provoke such reactions by pupils in the first place. For example, the teacher's question in this role play ('What gibberish is this?') provides a revealing insight into the pupils' experience of language in the social context of the school. Very early on in the project, the same girl that plays the teacher here used the word 'gibberish' to describe the non-English lines in 'The First Men on Mercury'. Then, a few weeks after the role play, the word 'gibberish' cropped up again in another pupil's news report; it was used to refer to languages with low status. When casually questioned, a number of girls revealed they had all been to the same middle school as Aquila. One particular teacher there was in the habit of using the word 'as a joke, Miss' to proscribe the use of Asian languages by the girls. Interestingly then, it seems that Aquila had, through her role play, been exploring her experience of language and had begun to reflect on the comparative status of languages in school. For the girls, the teacher's description of Punjabi as 'gibberish' is also the mirror image of their parents' command to stop 'jabbering' in English. Underlying their role plays is the basic principle that the language of those in power over them is to be rejected, but the language of the powerless embraced.

Central to the theme of language and power relations in society was the work undertaken in the second half term, work which is still in progress and which has grown organically from a single seed: the science fiction story of *Krall City* (from *The Languages Book*, the ILEA English and Media Centre). The rulers of Krall oppress their workers (who speak many different languages) by imposing language rules which establish the supremacy of the Krall language. The story provides infinite possibilities for exploring language as a social phenomenon in an imaginative, dramatic context. The initial oral activity (a role play in which workers break the language rules) could furnish all the raw material for various types of writing, audience and bias: a worker's diary using slang and other types of informal language; a tabloid newspaper account giving the Krall rulers' point of view on the 'crime'; and a continuation of the original, unfinished Krall story, in which pupils present their own conclusions about language.

The beauty of this term's work has been its adaptability to any age and ability level. Work centred around the Krall scenario would provide a particularly unified GCSE unit incorporating a 'literary' stimulus, oral group work, and informal and formal writing in varieties of English for different audiences – diary, newspaper, narrative. Most importantly, there would be scope for an examination of the nature of the bias, the way the media manipulates language, and its role in society.

I personally felt that I was reasonably well equipped throughout with a working knowledge of language and a clear understanding of basic linguistic terminology. It soon emerged, however, that, despite being able to distinguish intellectually between accent and dialect and between Standard dialect and other dialects, in practice this was more difficult. For example, I felt the simplest way of defining 'dialect' was as a regional variety of language, with 'Standard' as a national variety. The task which required pupils to 'standardise' a passage from *Kes* unfortunately implicitly contrasted Standard and dialect, whereas, of course, the message I had tried to convey was that Standard English was simply one particular dialect – one that was more appropriate in some contexts.

It would be easy to be disheartened by the confusion that arose. However, I think it simply underlines the futility of pumping knowledge about language (for example, vocabulary from different regional dialects) into pupils without an examination of how language operates in society – that is, by looking at issues concerning bias and status. Secondly, it demonstrates that the study of language has to be a cumulative process. Pupils in 9SN seem to have found the work stimulating and enjoyable, so language issues will underpin all future work and will be reiterated regularly. The pupils are learning to respect linguistic diversity: Tahira commented, 'We have learned that you should not make fun of someone else's language.' Some pupils' self-esteem and oral skills blossomed through multilingual work: Aquila, for example, particularly enjoyed the 'A Day in the Life of 9SN' play, saying: 'When I watched the video, I realised how much confidence I had gained.' Unfortunately, given the particular make-up of the class, the problem of transfer remains: two pupils, Naiyar and Shazia, wrote, 'If there was an English student in my class I would not speak Urdu or Punjabi...because they might make fun of our language.'

Although the pupils greately enjoyed and appreciated their work with me, they were well aware that we were operating in a vacuum. However much they may feel oppressed by parental injunctions against the speaking of English, they know from experience that, in society as a whole, the power balance is tilted heavily in favour of English, and of particular varieties of it.

For this reason, it is vital that more language work of this kind is undertaken in racially and socially mixed classrooms (especially by white, monolingual teachers), and that multilingualism is actively promoted. To repeat the point made earlier in the dicussion on *Kes* and knowledge about language, encouraging diversity on its own – the 'How many languages can we speak?' approach – is not enough. Issues of power and status need to be simultaneously addressed. The best context for this is the genuinely diverse classroom, since it will be a microcosm of society, a real context in which pupils can observe and attempt to redress power imbalances in language.

Ultimately, it will be the pupils' future behvaiour in socially and racially mixed contexts – in school or outside it – which will show how effective this project with 9SN has been. For the time being, I think the last word should go to Jabeena, who saw the value of multilingualism in the English classroom.She decided the code-switching plays 'were really good, because it is the way we really are in our daily lives'.

With thanks to the pupils and staff at Belle Vue Girls Upper School, Bradford, Yorkshire.

This article shows pupils:
- reflecting on their own effectiveness in the use of the spoken word (§6, Speaking & Listening);
- using and understanding the use of role play (§6, Speaking & Listening);
- focusing on regional and social variations in accents and dialects of the English language and attitudes to such variations (§9, Speaking & Listening);
- focusing on the range of purposes which spoken language serves (§9, Speaking & Listening);
- focusing on the forms and functions of spoken Standard English (§9, Speaking & Listening);
- being encouraged to respect their own languages and those of others (§11, Speaking & Listening);
- considering people's sensitivity to features of pronunciation (§17, Speaking & Listening);

- considering language appropriate to situation, topic and purpose (§18, Speaking & Listening);
- learning about the situations and purposes for which people might use non-Standard varieties rather than Standard English (§18, Speaking & Listening).

MANY VOICES

ANGELA JENSEN

The study of language itself is an integral part of a pupil's knowledge about language. I was particularly interested in investigating the areas of variety in and between languages, and of language and power in society. I wanted to see how much implicit knowledge younger pupils had of these areas and how much of this knowledge could usefully be made explicit. I decided to use stories and poems written for children as my starting point.

I approached the headteacher of Coppermill Primary School in Waltham Forest and, after staff discussion, the year 3 teacher, Lesley Mogadhassi, invited me to work with a group of children in her class. The school topic for the term was 'Communication', and Lesley thought that some focus on speech and its variations would add valuably to the class's work. The children were watching *Look and Read* during the term, which included a dramatisation set in Newcastle upon Tyne about a carrier pigeon. The story was called 'Geordie Racer' and some of the children had commented on the different ways in which some of the actors spoke in the story.

The class teacher chose six children whom she felt would contribute in a positive way to the investigation, and I spent five morning sessions with them. One child was white, one was Afro-Caribbean, one was Maltese. The remaining three had backgrounds in the Asian sub-continent; English was their second language.

Session I

The class watched the *Look and Read* programme which contained the next episode of 'Geordie Racer'. The presenter highlighted some words spoken in Geordie dialect including 'mam', 'canna', 'gan' and 'mebbes'. At the end of the programme, Lesley asked the children to distinguish between accent and dialect, and with her help they came up with the following definitions:

accent – the way people speak
dialect – the use of different words and phrases.

After morning break the six children and I listened to a recording of Roald Dahl's

Revolting Rhymes. His version of The Three Little Pigs was of particular interest. The children all expressed enjoyment of the poem; then our discussion turned to the voices we had heard. The discussion went as follows:

Teacher	What about the voices? What did they sound like?
Michael	The man who told the story had a low voice.
Teacher	You mean the narrator?
Michael	Yes.
Vicky	She speaks royal, you know posh, like she rules the world.
Teacher	Do you mean Red Riding Hood?
Vicky	Yes. She speaks clearly, slowly like this.. 'How...do...you...do?' She sounds flash.
Darren	The wolf sounded American like, 'Hey man'.
Teacher	Why might he sound American?
Michael	Because they sound more fierce, or to make him sound like a cowboy.
Teacher	That's an interesting idea. What about the pigs?
Darren	They sounded squeaky. (*Kabir demonstrates a squeaky voice*)

It is interesting to note that Vicky is making a connection between a 'posh voice' and power over others. Towards the end of the session, we listened to a tape of the first three chapters of Dahl's *George's Marvellous Medicine*, and in this recording the characters have Dorset accents. The children were excited by the beginning of this story, which they did not know, and were keen to speculate on what would happen to grandma. Vicky mentioned that George said 'O'il' instead of 'I'll' but offered no explanation for this. I decided to begin to explore accent in my next session with the children.

Session 2

The whole class watched *Look and Read* including a further instalment of 'Geordie Racer'; when I got my group together, they commented that the people in the story spoke differently to 'us' because they came from somewhere else. I picked up on this point later in the session.

The group and I read the first few chapters of *George's Marvellous Medicine*; they read the character parts while I read the narrative. Afterwards we discussed the voices they had used while reading and whether they were similar to those on the taped version. Darren suggested that those on the tape sounded more 'countryish' and that we sounded more like people from London. This was interesting, as only one of the children, Michael, and myself could have been said to have originated from the London area. Vicky also noticed that the speech in the book was written in 'ordinary' English and that the spelling did not reflect the different accents used by the characters.

We listened to the next two chapters of the book, and I replayed a couple of the phrases where the accent was pronounced: 'I'm not forgetting you, Grandma, I'm thinking of you all the time'. The children all noticed that George said 'Oim' instead of 'I'm' and 'toime' for 'time'. Vicky suggested that we all spoke differently because 'that's how God made the world'. We brainstormed all the different accents we could think of, and I noted them down. They included: Australian, country and western from America, country type (like George), Lincolnshire (like their teacher), Newcastle (as in 'Geordie Racer'), 'posh', London and Jamaican.

We then briefly played a game which I had prepared. On cards were written the names of people, or television characters: Scott in *Neighbours*, the Queen, Bugs Bunny. The children took it in turns to choose a card and attempted to sound like that person and very often they attempted a phrase which they thought was typical of the character: for example, 'G'day' for Scott. The children were enthusiastic about the activity and requested to play it again later. We then had a discussion, prompted by me, on accent. Part of it is transcribed here:

Techer	What sort of accents do we know about?
Vicky	Countryish...Dorset...like George in the book. He says 'Oil' instead of 'I'll'.
Sahar	You can get an Australian accent like Henry in Neigbhours. He says 'G'day, Clacky' instead of 'Good day, Clarky' when he talks to Des.
Teacher	Anyone else?
Michael	Country and western in America. 'Howdee, partner'.
Darren	Our teacher. She says 'stond oop' instead of 'stand up'. She comes from...er...Lincolnshire, I think.
Teacher	That's right.
Sahar	Spuggy (in 'Geordie Racer') speaks different. His dad says 'daft man' (soft 'a').
Vicky	And posh people speak like royal.
Darren	You can get a Jamaican accent like me.
Teacher	(To the whole group) What sort of accent do we think we've got?
Shaukat	Ordinary.
Michael	But we live in London, so perhaps we sound like that.
Teacher	So what accents have we got?
Darren	English.
Teacher	What about Spuggy or your teacher? They come from England, but they've got different accents to us.
Sahar	We've got London accents then.

Following this session I reflected on what had happened and I found that the children were exhibiting not only a knowledge of different accents and who might use them, but also an understanding that accent may reflect social class.

Session 3

Michael and Shaukat were absent for this session, but the remaining children and I turned our attention to dialect. I asked them to define dialect and they offered: 'a different word for something, depending on where people come from'. We began to compile a chart of the dialect words the children knew and their equivalents in 'ordinary' English as follows:

Newcastle: (from 'Geordie Racer')

mam = mum

mebbes = maybe

gan = gone

canna = cannot

Jamaican: (from Darren)

me no know = I don't know

Liverpool:

pumps = plimsoles

We then listened to a piece of prose recorded in Scottish dialect by a colleague. The text was taken from *Language Live* by John Seely (Heinemann). Afer discussion we added these to our charts:

Scottish:

bairns = children

oot = out

wi = with

stanes = stones

wee = little

beasties = insects

bide = live (the children thought this might also mean 'hide', as it sounded closer)

I then read a number of poems by John Agard and we added to our chart as follows:

Caribbean:

mek = make, let

yah, yuh = yes

bout = about

homewuk = homework

I din do nuttin = I didn't do nothing

wink up = blink, squint

me = my

fowl = chicken

dih = the

At the end of the session this chart was put on the classroom wall for the children to add to during the week. The remainder of the session was spent listening to some more of *George's Marvellous Medicine* and then discussing a play which the group wanted to put on for the rest of the class about the work that they had been doing. In the play the children would use some of the accents and dialects we had discussed. The bilingual children were keen to use their mother tongues, which I encouraged. This led to a discussion about where and when the children used dialect, or other languages.

Darren said that he used Jamaican when he spoke by telephone to his grandfather, who lived in Jamaica. On the other hand he used 'ordinary' English with his mum and his friends. Kabir said he used Urdu mostly at home, but English at school so that everyone could understand him. Vicky suggested that their play could be set in a school like theirs, because then it would be natural to use a variety of languages, accents and dialects. I felt that this was a compliment to the school and to the value the teachers placed on children's language and languages.

Session 4

At the beginning of this session Darren showed the group a page from his copy of the book, *Ging gang goolie, it's an alien* by Bob Wilson (see below), which he said showed aliens speaking a dialect of English. We read the page aloud and discussed how the author had used misspellings to make the aliens' English sound and look different, yet remain understandable to the reader.

We reviewed the dialect chart from the previous week, and I asked the children whether people could change their accent and/or dialect and, if so, why they would. Vicky remarked that Spuggy in 'Geordie Racer' would change his accent if he lived in London, but that he would be able to understand 'ordinary' English, as he would hear it on the television. The children, on further questioning, thought they spoke 'ordinary' English as used by television presenters and that they had no accent or dialect. Michael suggested that we might change our accent to speak to the Queen or Prince Charles, so that we would sound posh. Darren felt that the Queen wouldn't understand his Jamaican, so he would need to use 'ordinary' English. Sahar thought that we might change our accents or dialects if acting in a play. The remainder of the session was spent in practising our play. At their suggestion I played a posh teacher welcoming her new class to a school, and the group played new pupils coming from various parts of Britain and the world: Darren from Jamaica; Michael from USA; Kabir from Pakistan; Sahar from Lincolnshire; Vicky from Scotland; Shaukat from Dorset. The play was shown to the rest of the class on my fifth and final visit to the school.

On reflection, I think the texts and tapes we shared were a useful introduction to our discussion of accent and dialect, although in future I would use video clips as an extra resource. An investigation of accent and dialect with children could valuably come from stories and poems read by the teacher and the children, as well as those heard in the listening area. It is vital that any work on language variety serves to build the children's respect for their own language(s) and dialect(s) and those of others. This respect needs also to be apparent, as at Coppermill, in the language resources and displays in the school and in everyday interactions – between teachers and children and among children themselves – which reveal the range of language competence present in the school.

Thanks to the children who worked with me at Coppermill Primary School, Waltham Forest and to their teacher, Lesley Mogadhassi.

This article shows children:
- focusing on regional and social variations in accents and dialects of the English language and attitudes to such variations (§9, Speaking & Listening);
- being encouraged to respect their own languages and those of others (§11, Speaking & Listening);
- considering people's sensitivity to features of pronunciation (§17, Speaking & Listening).

RESEARCHING ACCENT AND DIALECT

KATE PARKES

This project began with the viewing of two programmes from the *Language File* series which focused on accent, dialect and Standard English. During each programme, the pupils were encouraged to note down any ideas, comments or points which interested them. This led to a pupil-centred discussion following each programme, which explored each interesting feature and developed comment and opinion. Following each discussion, the pupils carried out two pieces of research homework. In the first week, they had to record all the regional accents and accents of people who spoke English as a second language that they came across in one week; in the second week, they had to record sources of Received Pronunciation and Standard English. These two simple activities raised the pupils' awareness and motivated them to begin their own research projects, as they discovered the very active mix of regional accent around them and the possible influences it could have upon them.

The next stage in the project was the group projects.

Group projects

From the outset, the pupils were encouraged to identify any areas of the topic which they would like to pursue. After the introductory discussions and research, pupils offered such ideas for consideration, and groups formed to investigate them. The areas of research chosen by the pupils were as follows:

- to record examples of Received Pronunciation and investigate the reaction of a cross-section of other pupils to such examples;
- to record examples of regional accents and investigate their particular characteristics;
- to compare the variation between an 'old' and 'young' local accent;
- to compare the changes in accent experienced by sisters in one family as a result of moving to a different region.

The groups planned their research with the help of record sheets and, growing more confident, broadened the scope of their investigation to involve a number of members of staff, both teaching and non-teaching. I had told the pupils that I would act as a support only, to give them access to equipment, such as the photocopier, and that the progress and problems they experienced were for their evaluation, not my solution.

Findings of group projects

Group 1

The area of research chosen by the pupils in this group was Received Pronunciation. Their aim was to investigate the reactions of a cross-section of other pupils in the school to an RP accent, and the reasons which lay behind these reactions.

The group began with a tape-recording of two volunteer members of staff whom the group, having watched the *Language File* video, felt to possess the clearest examples of RP. Having successfully recorded the teachers reading a set passage, the group then designed a short questionnaire to be distributed to a sample group of pupils. After much deliberation and calculation, they decided upon a $2^{1}/_{2}\%$ sample of each year group in the lower school. The required number of questionnaires was produced. Each sample group was then asked to listen to the recordings and to present their reactions in the form of answers to the questions put foward.

The group felt that the results were fascinating because they were wholly negative. They had expected some responses to be open-minded, particularly from the year 7 pupils, whom they had thought would not have such a 'fixed' idea or prejudice. However, none of the pupils in the sample felt that the accent was attractive or that they would like to adopt such an accent. Comments included:

It's not right for round here.
It's clear, but it sounds artificial.
I think it's all right for acting, but it doesn't sound like real talk.

The group drew the obvious conclusion from their findings that the pupils at the school felt that the RP accent was an alien 'language' and that they therefore did not respond to it favourably. The group added the thought that these responses were probably based upon the narrow range of accents experienced by the pupils and the presentation of the stereotype of RP on television. They also considered the possibly limiting effect of a script which may have exaggerated the 'acting' effect, and expressed an interest in developing their project in the future through further recording and sampling of reaction.

Group 2

The aim of this group was to gather a sample of the accents of people in the school in order to try and identify their different qualities.

They began by identifying from a list of their own teachers those whom they felt spoke with a strong regional accent. They chose from this list a Northern Irish accent, a second language English accent, a Black Country accent and a Liverpudlian accent. In order to carry out their comparison, the group decided first to collect samples of the accents and then set about asking the teachers involved for their consent. When that was given, the group made recordings of their subjects. They decided not to present a script but to ask a series of set questions to try and discover the pattern of sounds in each accent.

After recording their subjects, the group found the analysis of the recordings difficult and needed quite a lot of guidance to identify areas for comment. However, when they had begun to break open an accent they worked enthusiastically. Their findings were along the lines that they had witnessed in the *Language File* introductory programme, but it was clear when observing the group at this difficult stage that they enjoyed discovering the subtle sound differences for themselves.

They found the Northern Irish and the second language English accents to be the most interesting. The clipped vowel sounds in the former were a significant discovery, and they also enjoyed the 'song' of the accent. They could not identify the reason for this specifically, but the word they use to describe it ('song') is, I feel, an attractive and accurate one. In the second, and most revealing, recording they identified straight away the habits of acquired language (for example, the unusual and unnecessary use of 'Isn't it?') and they heard positive traces of a Black Country accent influencing the speaker in phrases such as 'my dad was a doctor, but I couldn't make it'.

The group eventually felt pleased with what they had achieved but decided that they would have liked more time to spend on analysis. A fair point; so would I.

Group 3

This group had outlined their aim as a comparison of 'old' and 'young' Black Country accents, following a discussion of this issue in the LINC material, which they had responded to with interest.

They had no shortage of volunteers for the 'young' accent! Eventually, after careful thought, they decided upon the most relaxed example, thereby trying to overcome any tendencies of the volunteers to exaggerate. This example was then recorded, and the group set about identifying an equivalent 'old' sample. They intended, having gathered their samples, to spend time comparing the qualities of the two recordings. There were problems, however, in arranging a recording time with their older speaker, the school caretaker. His duties took him all over the site and therefore made him difficult to trace…! They resorted eventually to notes on conversations with him, seizing any opportunity that presented itself, as they could not persuade him to wait while they collected a tape-recorder.

The group first analysed the two 'samples' of the chosen accent to identify its particular qualities. This was a time-consuming and challenging task, but they worked hard. Their findings were, as with the second group, in line with the investigations of *Language File*, but they, too, enjoyed the process of discovery. They felt that the most significant feature was the flat, lengthened vowel sounds, more obvious in the 'old' example, and they described this quite interestingly as a 'chewed sound'. They also found, after discussion, that the 'old' example was heavier and faster but, in their view and despite their peer knowledge, more authentic. They wondered if this was because the younger speaker could still be influenced by outside elements – quite a perceptive point. They were disappointed that they would not record both examples for posterity, but my observations of their work supported the feeling that they had chosen an interesting and challenging area for research which had carried out thoughtfully, given the constraints they encountered.

Group 4

The pupils working together in this group were cousins and both second language English speakers. Their thoughts and preparatory discussions had led them to wonder if their elder sisters had experienced any change in accent and, through this, change in 'identity' as they had moved away from the area. They had responded with interest to the discussion in the *Language File* programme on the subject of language and a sense of self. This is a subtle and quite complex area to research, and it was fascinating to watch the methodical approach which the pair took.

Having contacted their two sisters, who had moved to South Birmingham and Scotland respectively, and persuaded them to take part, they then decided to design a questionnaire to investigate the finer details of their subjects' feelings and experiences. The questionnaire began by establishing whether the subject felt that she had had a local accent before she had moved away. It then moved on to gather reaction to encountering new accents in the new home towns. Questions were asked about pressure to conform, difficulty in understanding and their sense of personal identity. The interviews were carried out personally by the pupils, although a visit to Scotland had to be cancelled, and this intereview was carried out by telephone.

Their efforts were rewarded by the interesting responses given by the two subjects. The sister who had moved to South Birmingham felt that there was an interesting difference in accent, although she was reasonably close to home, and this introduced the pupils to the idea of community rather than regional accent. She also commented on different dialect words that she had encountered and acquired, again only a short distance away from her home town. Although she acknowledged such changes in her own vocabulary, she was adamant that her accent had not changed. This was an opinion which the pupils questioned, as they felt that some changes were already occurring that she was perhaps not willing to admit.

The sister who had moved to Scotland responded most positively to the idea of the accent/identity link. Clearly, she had had more difficulties in communicating than the other sister and she had felt the pressure to modify her accent to Standard English. The point which interested the pupils most, however, was her effort to sustain her regional accent, in the face of these pressures, by modifying it only for specific purposes – an interesting way of introducing the idea of a sense of audience.

The pupils felt that their project had been interesting and rewarding. They had both thought more about the idea of identity and the factors which influence it, which was a significant achievement for pupils of their age.

Group 5

Working as a breakaway group from another larger one, the pupils here also wanted to examine the diversity of accents in the school, but preferred to focus on the attitude of the speaker to their accent. The group wished to explore the experience of accent diversity among members of staff, to gather their reactions to pupils' accents and to compare teacher's feelings towards their own accent and dialect.

The group began their investigation by gathering data on the diversity of accents in the school, based on the teachers with whom their year group had contact. Having collected this information, they then discussed which of the staff would be the most interesting subjects. They chose three members of staff who exemplified an RP accent, a Southern Irish accent and an accent from the North-East of England. Having received a favourable reaction from these members of staff, the group worked eagerly to design a questionnaire and arrange interviews. The focus of their questions was intended to gather background information upon accent experience and to investigate the ways in which the members of staff had preserved or deliberately changed their accent.

The interviews were carried out carefully, developing the courage and the organisational skills of the pupils involved. The group recorded their interviews and then patiently set about the task of listening and noting down points of interest for their reports. This process was delayed a little when one of the members of staff involved asked if she could re-record her interview. The pupils' questions had prompted her to think for several days after the original interview, and she had more comments to make!

The group resumed their discussion after the re-recording and began to identify some specific and very interesting points. All the subjects were contented with their accent and stated that they would not deliberately foster another, although they had all experienced pressure to do so. In the first case, the subject had spent some time teaching abroad and had experienced the need to modify his accent to Standard English in order to teach effectively. He had also made the observation about his father's accent that it varied according to his companions, and could be separated into a 'village' and a 'professional' accent. The pupils felt that the same thing may have happened to him: although they had chosen him to exemplify an RP accent, he felt that he had a Lancashire accent. This may be attributed in part to the pupils' inexperience in such research, but I feel, having observed their work, that they were making a valid point.

The second subject spoke with a soft Southern Irish accent about which she, too, felt very positive. This interview provided interesting details about the idea of acquiring a mixture of accent and dialect through working in very different regions. The subject also acknowledged the pressure she had felt to 'reform' her accent at times, and also the difficulties she had encountered with new dialects. However, she, too, was making a concerted effort to preserve the special qualities of her accent which she felt was very much part of her self.

The final subject had been re-recorded and introduced several valuable ideas which the group discussed at length. The interview developed the pupils' understanding of community accents when the subject very carefully defined her accent as from Sunderland, not from Newcastle, as many had assumed. Moving to work in the West Midlands, she had also encountered dialect differences and the need to 'translate' particular words, such as 'clarty', which she used automatically for 'dirty'. Other examples greatly interested the pupils, and this interest was also stimulated by the subject's affirmation that she had not deliberately adopted a Standard accent. In fact, she said that, whenever she felt herself to be losing her accent, she made a concerted effort to rekindle it, as it was part of her identity.

The group had therefore received several positive ideas. They felt that they had established a good understanding of their subjects' feelings towards their accent and the need to make a determined effort to preserve it.

Conclusion

What has the project achieved? How can it be developed in the future? Reviewing the project highlighted a number of key areas for further action. The resources, taken chiefly from *Language File*, were very valuable. They were accessible and interesting to the pupils, even though the majority of the students filmed were older than the group. The videos stimulated interest and identified specific areas which the pupils could very quickly key into for their own projects. The time allowed for the project gave the pupils an opportunity to discuss, negotiate, research and, very importantly, stretch their understanding. Their confidence visibly increased, and they learned some very subtle concepts through this active approach, which I am convinced would not have been as successfully conveyed through more formal 'lessons'. Ultimately, I was the designer of their research module, but they guided their own learning and provided a valuable basis for extending investigations into knowledge about language in year 8.

With thanks to the pupils and staff at Willenhall Comprehensive School, Walsall, West Midlands.

This article shows pupils:
- focusing on regional and social variations in accents and dialects of the English language and on attitudes to such variations (§9, Speaking & Listening);
- focusing on the range of purposes which spoken language serves (§9, Speaking & Listening);
- focusing on the forms and functions of spoken Standard English (§9, Speaking & Listening);
- being encouraged to respect their own languages and those of others (§11, Speaking & Listening);

- considering people's sensitivity to features of pronunciation (§17, Speaking & Listening);
- considering language appropriate to situation, topic and purpose (§18, Speaking & Listening);
- learning about the situations and purposes for which people might use non-Standard varieties rather than Standard English (§18, Speaking & Listening).

THE LANGUAGE OF *MIGUEL STREET*

LINDA CROFT AND AMY WOOLFORD

I studied *Miguel Street* by V S Naipaul with a class of mixed ability year 10 GCSE pupils in the Easter term. The class seemed to find the book humorous and refreshing, and certain characters, particularly Man-Man and Laura, captured their imagination.

Once the majority of stories had been read in class, a list of ten ideas for work was given to the pupils for their consideration. These ideas ranged from newspaper reports and diaries to a study of the lives of women in the street, and even a separate study of Caribbean poetry.

The tenth idea was the one I was particularly interested in developing for the LINC project:

Study the language used by the characters of Miguel Street. Try to identify any patterns or grammatical rules which seem to emerge, and examine how they differ from Standard English. Also, try to find any inconsistencies in V S Naipaul's creation of their language.

Finally, once your findings have been presented clearly, create a piece of writing in which you examine a particular character's viewpoint on an event or situation. Your character should 'speak' in the language you have identified.

I expected a small group to be interested in this idea, but only three took it up, and only one of these (Amy) reached the stage of finishing it. I was able only to spend up to ten minutes a lesson with them. They were given three reference books: *The Usborne Book of Grammar*, Dennis Freeborn's *A Course Book in English Grammar* and his *Varieties in English*.

Amy directed her study by extracting as much of the dialogue as possible from the book. She colour-coded those aspects she thought would be of relevance, and, once she had identified something in her own words, I would (perhaps) give her the grammatical term for it, which she would then look up and learn about in more detail. For example, once she had identified that the verb 'to have' was used irregularly, I told her about auxiliary verbs. Once she had looked up auxiliary verbs in her reference books, she was able to look for more examples and to understand their irregular use more accurately. I found it appropriate to supply the term once the rule had obviously been grasped. No other advice was given (otherwise Amy could not have used this part of the work as her *own* for GCSE purposes).

Amy wrote up her findings during the Easter holidays. In her creative piece of writing, written through the eyes of Laura (from 'The Maternal Instinct') it seems as if Amy has understood perfectly the language that V S Naipaul created for his characters. Specifically, Amy recreated Laura extremely effectively; I found it easy to believe Laura was speaking and, I was very moved by the end.

Although Amy was more than capable of tackling this task alone, I can now see that it would be an exercise valid as a whole class assignment in years 7–9. We have other class readers, such as '*Isaac Campion*' or '*Nature of the Beast*' by Janni Howker, which provide enough dialect speaking for groups to examine, create the whole picture and reproduce writing in the dialect they have studied.

Study of Language used in 'Miguel Street' by Amy Woolford, year 10

The following account shows our findings when studying the spoken language of the occupants of 'Miguel Street', Trinidad, as recalled by V S Naipaul when writing about his childhood.

The aim was to see if any patterns could be established and if the way the language differed from Standard English followed any rules. The end product was to be a written piece in 'Miguel Street' language.

Findings

A compilation of patterns (or rules) for 'Miguel Street' language follows, with the most common patterns first.

1 **Auxiliary verbs** are either missed out, or the plural is singular, or the singular plural. In 'to have', the verb takes the wrong form according to the tense, or the person. 'To have' and other auxiliary verbs are particularly dropped in questions:
'I tired.'
'How the cows, Hat?'
'He have a soul just like we.'

2 **Negatives** – 'can't', mustn't' and 'wouldn't' – are usually used correctly, but 'to be' in the negative is usually expressed with 'aint' for the first person singular and first person plural. 'Aint' is always substituted, where 'do not' or 'did not' should be, except with the first person singular and the first person plural:
'He quiet just because he aint have anything to say.'
'Father, forgive them they aint know what they doing.'

3 Often the **person** and the **tense** do not agree:
'Is he who vote for Man-man?'
'He didn't married.'

4 **Suffixes** to indicate the **past tense** are dropped:
'What happen?'
'He fix any new cars lately?'

5 **Suffixes like '-ly'** are dropped, and 'a' forms a suffix at the end of a word instead of 'have':
'Go brave.'
'you find that you don't care for the things you woulda like if you coulda afford them.'

6 **Personal pronouns** are always used in their subject form:
'He give she a baby.'
'Let we wait and see.'

7 The **'-s' suffix** to indicate possessive or the second person is dropped:
'It is all God work.'
'God make them that way.'

8 **Double adjectives** are used to express level of description (instead of 'very', etc.):
'I know him good, good.'
'I hear your husband talking in his sleep last night, loud loud.'

9 **'A'** is used rather than **'an'** with words beginning with vowels:
'My son Elias forgive me and he is a educated boy.'
'A old man like me aint have much to live for.'

10 With **questions** the word order is very often wrong with 'you' and 'don't':
'Why you don't let the man talk?'
'Why you don't like Bigfoot?'

11 To express the **future tense** 'go' is often used:
'If you don't leave me right now I go go call Seargeant Charles for you.'
'But you go mind your children?'

Those are the rules that we have found. There were some exceptions. V S Naipaul was writing from memory so there was bound to be. However, considering this, there were very few.

There do seem to be an awful lot of differences between English and Miguel Street language, until you appreciate that you might find some Miguel Street type language spoken here. For example, we might say something like: 'You going shopping?' or 'You know what I mean?' On the other hand, policemen and high class people in Miguel Street speak as we do, as do the papers. And to impress people, or in a large crowd, or when speaking to important people, the Miguel Street people speak almost 'proper' English!

What were the hardest and easiest parts of the task?

The first stage — taking down speech and colour-coding it — though long-winded, was comparatively easy.

Explaining the rules and finding them all was quite a bit more difficult! This took perhaps the longest but with all the textbook references, etc., one could be almost sure we were correct.

Writing up our findings was not really what I'd call easy either, but most of the hard stuff had been done in the work above.

Writing something in the new language was hard, because you had to remember all the rules and quirks which, however, wasn't as difficult as I'd expected once I got going. The really difficult part was getting to the depths of Laura and trying to write as her!

What have I learned?

Probably, the main thing I learned were some words that enable me to talk properly about language and its patterns, etc.

I must've learned a little more about our language sentence structure and the way it works in order to talk about other languages or forms of our own.

I discovered how much difference one wrong (or, should I say, different) word can make. Even if you know the context sometimes you can't tell exactly what they mean — you would have to know the language. That's why I say different rather than wrong: in Miguel Street, their different way of speaking is not wrong. Perhaps that's another thing I learned or at least came to consider.

Something else I had cause to think about is how one form of language can vary from country to country or even town to town. I also came to appreciate a little more why English might be such a hard langauge to learn!

Writing in 'Miguel Street' language:

LAURA

The baby come in the morning. What sort of luck you think I have? It looks like I really blight. Is another girl, another girl! Life hard like hell for girls — I should know. Boys they get life easy easy. They think they can do whatever they pleased.

Nathaniel think he own me just because he give me one baby. That baby only come by accident! He think he is a man but I know he just playing man. I say I go call Sergeant Charles if he aint leave me right then.

'But who go mind your children?' he say.

'That is my worry,' I say.

I didn't want he, he just one more mouth to feed. He go. But what he do before he leave? He give me baby! Two by he! I have six babies by six man before he.

When my eight baby drop, Lorna (oldest is she) work as servant in house in St Clair and take typing lesson from man in Sackville Street. That my last baby.

Lorna come home one night late late.

'Ma, I going to make a baby,' she say.

I shriek when she tell me and I cry all night. She say to me when the morning come:

'But, Ma, you does do the same thing lots lots.'

She aint see the problem. She think is cruel like anything. I can't explain to she. I try.

'When I is a girl,' I say, 'it have no school for me. I don't learn a brass peanut. I stupid stupid. I ain't able to do work and then I is poor poor. I can't live with parents forever and they go need support. I need money to live! I sad til I find money. I does please men and them.'

Now I has children, money, house and I can support my parents. I say:

'You is happy, you is happy, you got what you want!'

I can tell myself I happy, I can think I happy — I can make think I is. But I know inside me I aint happy. Is helluva life pleasing men and them. If only I could be a educated woman I woulda got job in a office, but I aint so I must make best I can. I love my children though people tell me different. 'Laura,' they say, 'why you does call Lorna black bow-leg bitch, you love her?'

But they know I only trying to make them good good so they have better life than me.

'What! Is someone knock on door?'

'What you want?'

'Laura,' Sergeant Charles say, 'It have bad news, I fraid.'

'What?'

'Lorna...she dead. Drowned at Carenage.'

I think of my little girl. She not want to be like me. It have nothing like education in the world. I don't want my children to grow like me. She have no life if she turn out like me. I sure sure she be better now. She save.

'It good, it good. It better that way,' I say.

With thanks to students and staff at Beaminster School, Beaminster, Dorset.

(This article first appeared in *Strong Language: the Journal of the South West Language Project*, Autumn 1991.)

This article shows Amy:
- focusing on regional and social variations in accents and dialects of the English language and attitudes to such variations (§9, Speaking & Listening);
- focusing on the forms and functions of spoken Standard English (§9, Speaking & Listening);
- being encouraged to respect their own languages and those of others (§11, Speaking & Listening);
- considering people's sensitivity to features of pronunciation (§17, Speaking & Listening);
- considering grammatical differences between a regional dialect and spoken Standard English (§17, Speaking & Listening);
- considering language appropriate to situation, topic and purpose (§18, Speaking & Listening);
- learning about the situations and purposes for which people might use non-Standard varieties rather than Standard English (§18, Speaking & Listening);
- learning how to recognise and describe some of the lexical, grammatical and organisational features of a text (§35, Writing).

Making Changes

Our recommendations on the teaching of knowledge about language had to be accompanied by an insistence that our policies did not necessitate any change in good teaching practice.

(Cox on Cox)

At the heart of the educational process lies the child. No advances in policy...have their desired effect unless they are in harmony with the nature of the child.

(The Plowden Report)

'Who's in charge of the language?'

(William, aged 8)

The aim of this chapter is to support language coordinators, headteachers and heads of departments, as they work with colleagues in their systematic planning to meet the knowledge about language strands in the English National Curriculum.

The National Curriculum requires more teaching about language than has been customary in many classrooms over the last few decades. Language study does not appear in the statements of attainment until level 5, a level within the reach of some primary children and beyond the reach of others. However, pupils do not start to know about language only at a certain age or stage. Primary aged pupils are interested in and capable of reflecting on linguistic issues, as the case studies in previous sections demonstrate.

Primary school staffrooms are rich with anecdotes about what children show that they know or suspect about language. For example, in one Cirencester staffroom, a teacher described how, in the context of reading and writing labels for tins in the class shop, five year old James thought to ask, 'Is the writing on a can in a shop still called writing if there is no one there to read it?'

As pupils become more experienced language users, so their reflections on language will be incrementally more analytic and systematic, written as well as spoken. Regular opportunities for pupils to reflect on language in use have to be built into a school's or a department's language curriculum.

No single 'model' for planning for knowledge about language has particular merit since, like other examples of language in action, models tend to be written for specific purposes and specific audiences. When undertaking a curriculum audit, schools have found it a useful starting point to map their current curriculum against one of the following models. This activity has proved to reassure them that much is already being offered. Any gaps in current provision can quickly be identified. Each of the following models provides a perfectly valid way of representing knowledge about language. Each is consistent with the requirements of the National Curriculum.

MODEL 1 – THE PROGRAMMES OF STUDY SIMPLIFIED

This model is derived from the programmes of study, which include knowledge about language elements as 'strands' within Speaking and Listening, Reading and Writing. It is possible to simplify the task of making sense of knowledge about language by grouping the strands together under major themes. Working from within the programmes of study, such a list might look like this:

Accent, Dialect and Standard English
- Vocabulary differences between local dialects and Standard English
- Grammatical differences between local dialects and Standard English
- Situations and purposes for which people might use Standard and non-Standard English
- Attitudes to Standard English, non-Standard dialects, and different accents; the need to respect one's own language and that of others

Purpose of speech
- Vocabulary used in different contexts
- Appropriateness to situation, topic, purpose
- Range of formality
- Language and identity; language as bond, barrier, weapon, salve

Literary language
- Sound patterning; figures of speech; word-play
- Rhetoric effects in context of different types of vocabulary, grammatical features such as structural repetition, ambiguity, grammatical deviance for effect

Language change
- How and why vocabulary changes; where new words come from
- Changes in grammar
- Attitudes to the fact that language continues to change

Purposes of writing
- The history of writing and the way writing contributes to society
- The range of functions of writing
- Features of different types of text
- Appropriateness to function and audience
- Functions and features of impersonal writing
- Patterns of organisation of formal expository writing
- Criteria for evaluating different types of writing

Differences between speech and writing
- Differences in vocabulary
- Differences in organisation
- Greater verbal explicitness of writing
- How writing achieves effects of intonation
- Differences in relationship with audience

MODEL 2 – WHERE THE GRAMMAR FITS IN

The National Curriculum acknowledges that the key to language competence lies in increasing the range and variety of the user's language repertoire. This requires the ability (often exercised at a subconscious level) to match choices of intonation, vocabulary, and grammar to the requirements of wide-ranging speech or writing situations in which we are involved. In reflecting upon language in use, pupils will be identifying and investigating the kinds of patterning which typify these rich varieties of language. This is in every sense 'grammar teaching', but it links structure and pattern firmly to their uses and functions within 'real' language settings. Some teachers have found it helpful in this respect to distinguish between 'Big KAL' (Big Knowledge About Language)

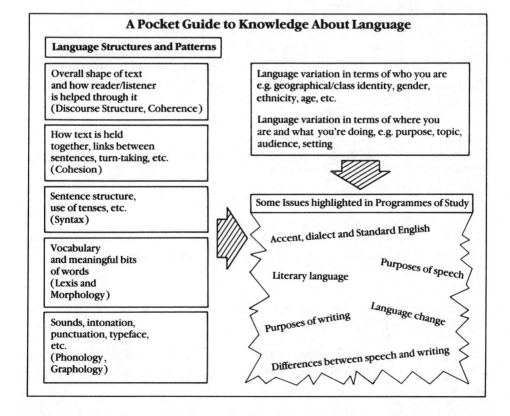

A Pocket Guide to Knowledge About Language

Language Structures and Patterns

Overall shape of text
and how reader/listener
is helped through it
(Discourse Structure, Coherence)

How text is held
together, links between
sentences, turn-taking, etc.
(Cohesion)

Sentence structure,
use of tenses, etc.
(Syntax)

Vocabulary
and meaningful bits
of words
(Lexis and
Morphology)

Sounds, intonation,
punctuation, typeface,
etc.
(Phonology,
Graphology)

Language variation in terms of who you are
e.g. geographical/class identity, gender,
ethnicity, age, etc.

Language variation in terms of where you
are and what you're doing, e.g. purpose, topic,
audience, setting

Some Issues highlighted in Programmes of Study

Accent, dialect and Standard English

Literary language

Purposes of speech

Purposes of writing

Language change

Differences between speech and writing

and 'Little KAL' (Little Knowledge about Language). 'Big KAL' explores broad themes of Language Variation, Language Change, Attitudes to Language etc. 'Little KAL' explores precisely how the language is organised and patterned in such a range of contexts. From this point of view, we could look again at our 'knowledge about language' themes and represent them in the way shown on page 191.

Where pupils are reflecting upon their competence as language users, they are likely to be drawn into debate about systematic properties of language listed down the lefthand side. Their terminology may lack technical precision, but the teacher can judge the appropriateness of intervention in this area by using such terms at his or her discretion once the underlying concepts they reflect have been grasped by the students themselves.

MODEL 3 – IS THIS ENOUGH?

So far we have described the minimal knowledge about language requirements within the National Curriculum and ways of trying to give them some shape which we can understand. However, many teachers would want to go beyond these requirements to include important issues relating to language in society and the relationship between language and power. Similarly, most of us would want to acknowledge that 70% of the world's population speaks more than one language, a condition which naturally disposes language users to greater analytical curiosity concerning words, grammars and meanings. This implies close links between English and Modern Languages departments and, above all, a positive approach to multilingualism within and beyond the multi-ethnic classroom.

With these considerations in mind we might produce a list of topics such as the following, developed by the North London LINC consortium. This list is consistent with the National Curriculum, but transcends it:

Five linked areas for knowledge about language

Whether in the course of other activities within the language and English curriculum or, in some cases, as specific investigations, we might look explicitly at language in ways which pay attention, variously or simultaneously, to aspects of:

Language variety: between speech and writing; of accents and dialects; of functions, registers and genres, in speech and writing, including those of literature; variety as differences between the connections between languages.

Language and society: speaker/listener, reader/writer relationships, for both interpersonal and mass uses of language, with a particular concern for the ways in which social power is constructed and challenged through language.

Language acquisition and development: babies learning to talk; children learning to read and write; a lifelong story of new encounters.

History of languages: historical change in English and in some of the world's other languages, ancient and contemporary; ephemeral as well as long-term change.

Language as system: vocabulary – connotations, definitions and origins of words; grammar – the functions and forms of words in groups; phonology; graphology (including spelling patterns and scripts); organisation and conventions of layout in texts.

IN PRACTICE

The primary and secondary case studies which follow focus on the problem of planning a language curriculum which provides progression and continuity as an entitlement for all pupils. Inevitably, differences of emphasis emerge between primary and secondary planning; however, when reading all of the case studies the similarity of conclusions drawn far outweighs the differences.

PRIMARY SCHOOL'S LANGUAGE POLICIES

The case studies which follow reflect the diversity of possible approaches to appraising a primary school's language policy. The first account describes a language policy that developed from what teachers were already doing in the classroom; the second account shows a language policy emerging from an observation of children's needs; and the third account presents an attempt to formulate a policy which incorporates recent theory in knowledge about language with the National Curriculum requirements. They are offered as springboards for discussion, not as blueprints – for schools plan from different starting points.

PRIMARY PLANNING I

MARILYN CAIN

When I came to Benton Park Primary School (Newcastle-upon-Tyne) two years ago, I was full of plans and ideas, but I felt that there needed to be a time of calm until the teachers knew me. They needed to be confident that I had done whatever I was suggesting myself and had used it in my own teaching. I spent the first year demonstrating ideas through my own practice, talking to people and working with them. Only after the first year was a policy written, drawing together ideas that were known and familiar; we plan to change and update this policy as we learn and develop.

We started by looking at the programmes of study to consider the possibilities that might be there, but we found this of only limited help. One problem that we have met with the National Curriculum is that we are wanting to introduce features like dialect in our own teaching long before they are introduced in the programmes of study. At present, therefore, we are trying to integrate knowledge about language into the kind of work that is already going on in our classrooms, without specific reference to the programmes of study.

In staff INSET sessions we explore where knowledge about language fits into our system of record keeping, and where we have the resources that will stimulate interesting work. Beyond this, a lot of staff development in knowledge about language takes place in the form of casual conversation – meeting people at lunchtimes and mentioning ideas. I talk about my own practice a lot and try to influence people with my personal enthusiasm. I plan work with other teachers and encourage people to work in teams of twos and threes to share ideas. I always consult staff about buying books, and I bring lots of books from libraries and the teacher's centre for teachers to consider. I pick up ideas from other teachers' classes to show that I am learning from them. I keep my antennae out, so I know what other teachers are doing: I can suggest ideas and resources that would give a language slant to their work. For example, in order to widen the language repertoire that they present to their children, I talk to teachers about holiday brochures, railway timetables and other materials that would be useful to them, or I suggest ways of looking at the language of shops in a topic on shopping.

A lot of knowledge about language occurs incidentally from the way in which children work. For example, there is a strong emphasis throughout the school on the children knowing who their writing is for: is it to read in assembly, to go up on the wall, to read out to the class, or is it to be typed up on the laptop or the big computer? If it's for assembly, we will talk about that: the audience will include both four year olds and 11 year olds; will they hear it at the back? Children now expect to think about audience and purpose and they will ask, 'Who is this writing for?', 'Where is it going to go?' When children have written a piece of writing, they take it to a corner and read it to a partner: does it sound all right? Is there anything that needs to be added, changed or corrected? I never expect children to bring the first draft to me; they always read it to a friend first. A great deal of collaborative writing is also done in our classes.

We often explore the way that people talk together and listen together. When you are with a partner, how do you speak? When are you quiet? How do you encourage somebody to talk who's shy? What happens if someone different joins your group? This includes gender awareness: reflecting on roles in group discussion, helping girls to put themselves forward as well as helping boys to be more considerate.

The infants are very aware of different ways of speaking. They know that you don't talk to brothers and sisters in the same way as you talk to your teacher. They are aware of eight or nine different ways of speaking which they can demonstrate in role play and on which they can reflect back. They can explore the language of shops, labels, notices, signs, posters and safety warnings. They can also talk about the language used in rhymes and nursery rhymes, and you can see these ideas picked up in their own writing.

A recent topic that we tried in year 3 was the development of books. We looked at scrolls and examples of early books, and compared them with writing today. Children made scrolls and burnt them at the edges and they looked at old bibles, photocopies of old texts and nursery rhymes with archaic language; they used these as a resource to write their own scrolls and letters.

Other work on knowledge about language arises from topic work in History and Geography and, as these topics are planned through the school, we use this framework to provide progression. This runs alongside the exploration of language in literature, for example exploring words only found in fairy stories. We might develop the history of the language through poetry, looking especially at someone like Robert Louis Stevenson, savouring archaic words like 'nanny' and 'lighting children to bed'. We try to show that knowledge about language can be developed fruitfully in work both on fiction and non-fiction.

Further up the school children look at dialects, different grammar structures, the styles of different authors and poets, different forms and purposes and how they relate to audiences. We use quite a lot of terminology, but not in a formalised way. From the start we use terms like 'word', 'letter', 'sentence'. We also use terminology like 'persuasive language', 'advertising', 'dialect'. Teachers are increasingly aware of the importance of terminology; as for the children, once they have understood the concepts, they are keen to use them and always like the sound of these words.

Our next stage of development will be to prepare a grid to show knowledge about language within children's speaking and listening, reading and writing. This will suggest how threads can be drawn out at each level and in each year group. There will be lists of appropriate resources, and there will be a section in the planning sheets which will refer specifically to knowledge about language; teachers will complete this each term, and I will be able to use it to monitor and guide teachers' planning.

When a new area like knowledge about language is emerging, you think about what you might do and you try it out. It's only when you've tried it and are more aware of the possibilites that you can plan it in as a matter of course. We recognise that our current coverage of this area is patchy, but for the moment we are trying to establish an understanding of what knowledge about language consists of. Our planning will become more systematic later.

PRIMARY PLANNING 2

NICK JEFFERSON

As the language coordinator of a large primary school (Norton Primary School, Stockton-on-Tees), my previous attempts at in-service consisted of a series of 'top down' approaches: teachers' decisions about aims, objectives, appropriate strategies within the classroom and organisation of resources, with the occasional guest speaker invited to give 'the wider perspective'. This led to a policy that looked professional and well documented; and yet it was doomed to spend the rest of its life gathering dust on the shelf, only being used for the occasional HMI visit. Such policies never became working documents because they ignored the fundamental questions: 'What do our children know about language?' and 'How can we use this knowledge to help teachers decide upon appropriate action and resourcing?'

A change of direction was required, one that began with the child. As part of this process, the year 1 teachers volunteered to look at children's knowledge about language within the framework of the National Curriculum and to use the observations to determine appropriate strategies that might support the children through the learning continuum. This working group would then report back to the rest of the staff.

The evidence collected through this close observation of pupils was to be stored in individual work profiles. The format of the profile was seen as very important: it had to be durable, flexible and allow ease of access. Ring binders, box files, manila folders, scrap books were all considered; none of them met all the criteria, however, and none felt appropriate. Instead, we decided to use 'flexible display files' which contained 22 clear plastic pockets A4 size bound together. They had two main advantages:

– The evidence collected could be replaced easily, quickly and efficiently and could be rearranged to show phases of development.
– The files gave a 'professional finish' to the child's work that was important when showing this to parents or fellow professionals.

Once the format had been decided we looked at how to collect evidence. We began by looking at the programmes of study and attainment targets for key stage 1, which we used as a framework, when organising space, time and resources within the classroom. We then looked at examples of children's language.

In one example, a child was observed reading the story 'Peace at last'. The child read into a tape recorder and was given no assistance by adult or peer. We felt this was important as we wished to assess the strategies she employed when tackling a book independently. The book was chosen by the child: it was an established favourite that she had taken home on several occasions. She had also been observed sharing this book with friends in the book area. After discussion of the tape, the working group summarised what it had revealed about the child's understanding of language and made a series of suggestions as to how the teacher might be helping her develop. We also prepared a list of questions that a teacher might ask when working with the child.

Although individual profiles are essentially unique, the evidence collected illustrated the types of settings, resources and experiences that characterise the early phases of a successful route through literacy. Such a philosophy, determined through examining children's knowledge about language, raised many crucial questions:

• How do we support children in the classroom?
• How do we create a suitable language environment?

- How can we make the most of parental support?
- What resources are appropriate for this age group?

The next stage will be to discuss such issues with staff using the children's work and the findings of the working party as the central focus. It is hoped a negotiated policy will result that will be an effective aid to the teacher in the classroom.

The teachers involved feel the work we have accomplished so far has raised their own awareness of children's existing knowledge about language and has resulted in a set of well-defined guidelines that encompass stages in learning language, appropriate teaching strategies and suitability of resources. It is designed specifically to meet the needs of the children in our school, and we feel it has had a direct effect on the children's overall performance and motivation within the field of language.

PRIMARY PLANNING 3

JIM CRINSON AND TOM NOBLE

Spring Gardens is an inner-city primary school in North Tyneside serving children from a wide variety of backgrounds. There are 320 pupils. In 1987, a team of teachers from the school took on the task of preparing language guidelines, with the aim of including the best of recent theory, and with detailed guidelines for practice stemming from the theory. The headteacher's aim was to have a document which a new teacher could use and which would work within the school's aims.

This document did contain some detail about knowledge about language, but mostly the information came from the language awareness movement (see Hawkins, E. 1984) and from *Language in Use* (1971), much of which did not appear to concern the primary teacher centrally. Suggested ideas, mainly for key stage 2 children, included projects on accent and dialect, and considering why tongue twisters are difficult to pronounce.

The National Curriculum forced a radical revision of this document. The main thrust of the revision has been to reorder the document in the light of attainment targets and programmes of study, but an important aspect of the rewriting was to review one or two aspects of general language teaching in the light of insights gained on LINC courses.

The first has been a review of reading material in the school. It became the intention of the school's language steering group to improve access to a wider range of reading material, with the aim of having about one third of the texts being not primarily story. This stemmed from a desire to offer a wider range of reading to 'switched-off' readers, but also in response to work on variety of text-type (the 'genre' debate). This went along with a move to read more non-fiction texts to children.

The move towards offering greater variety of text-types has also been carried through into work in writing. Much more often now classes will work on texts other than personal writing, and children are reported to be more at home in handling these genres. This is one area where work on knowledge about language has taken root. This has gone hand in hand with an increased emphasis, in the writing section of the school policy, on ideas of purpose and audience, and a greater awareness of the need to provide explicit support in story structure.

The second area where knowledge about language has made an impact is in the realm of accent and dialect. The language postholder has reported back to staff on sessions concerned with these issues, and teachers have been interested to have them clarified. The implications of this for children's reading and writing (including spelling) are now becoming clearer.

The main areas for development, which the new language policy will help clarify, are as follows:

- to develop teachers' awareness of when they are actually teaching knowledge about language (e.g. when discussing words like 'full stop', 'vowel', 'syllable', 'speech mark'), and to become more adept at spotting these opportunities in meaningful contexts;
- to become more sophisticated in developing progression for individuals with surface features of the language such as sentence punctuation and capital letters, and with spelling;
- to consider the role of knowledge about language in dealing with issues such as phonics, spelling patterns, prefix and suffix: for example, the relationship between word-history and spelling;
- to work towards a more integrated approach to English through projects (for example, on poetry), which would allow more explicit discussion of knowledge about language issues such as language change over time;
- to work with older children on some explicit knowledge about language projects, such as investigations into local dialect, into words connected with specific activities (e.g. sport) and into the differences between their own conversation and written down plays.

The document itself would benefit from greater consultation with other groups, and it will, of course, require regular revision.

In contrast with secondary colleagues, who have been faced with a National Curriculum strand and who have had to integrate this into their programmes, in this primary school teachers have been dealing with the age old primary issues of how best to provide for reading, how to begin and sustain writing with children, and how to organise talk in the classroom. The teachers have taken from the knowledge about language agenda insights which help them to do this job better. Some are now beginning to consider if a more direct focus on knowledge about language might help with these basic questions.

Conclusions

In the primary schools involved in creating knowledge about language contexts in the classroom, it has become evident that children come to school already with an extensive implicit knowledge about language. For example, many will have read signs used for different purposes; will have seen writing used in different contexts; and will have heard talk used for a variety of reasons. A language policy which acknowledges, and makes use of, this implicit awareness can help children in the early stages of their development to become effective language users.

Planning the secondary english curriculum

Planning to meet the knowledge about language strand which appears explicitly at level 5 in the statements of attainment and weaves together the programmes of study from key stage 2 is a high priority for most English departments.

How three English departments embarked on the management of change is outlined in the case studies which follow. They describe what has been achieved, how it was achieved and, with a refreshing honesty, they share what is left to do! These case studies demonstrate that there is no blueprint, no one way of planning for knowledge about language. Issues such as staffing provisions, resources, school and LEA Policy, INSET provision, accommodation, capitation all have a bearing on the effective management of curriculum change. Intended as starting points for departmental discussion, these case studies offer descriptions, not prescriptions; they are examples of various methods of implementing the processes of change, not exemplars of 'the right way'.

Secondary planning I

JIM PORTEOUS

Brislington is an 11–18 Comprehensive School in South Bristol; it has 1800 pupils and an English faculty of 15 teachers.

From 1987, the English faculty worked to develop broader areas of study across the English curriculum, marking a shift away from the 'English through Literature/class readers' tradition of English and English teaching. Though not inherently radical or innovatory in itself, the new work, with its emphasis on, for example, writing in the local community, local autobiographies, TVEE related units, the language of the workplace, representation of employment, class and gender in literature, analyses of narrative structures, etc., required a collaborative approach. This collaboration not only helped us plan work around new texts and topics; it also helped focus attention on our teaching and learning styles. One significant result of this new work was an increased consideration and awareness – for staff and pupils – of language in context.

In the autumn of 1990 a faculty working party drafted a scheme of work for key stage 3 of the National Curriculum. This was based on a key stage 3 curriculum map of our current practice which we had drawn up over 1989–1990 (including the input of new colleagues) and areas from the programmes of study which we agreed required particular attention. In the latter category, knowledge about language featured prominently. The draft outline was then discussed, modified and agreed by the faculty as a whole by Easter 1991. The main focus of debate, for the working party and the faculty as a whole, concentrated around the 'place' of knowledge about language; was it a discrete area of study, or could we assume that the relevant programmes of study could be met within the context of other units; how much prominence did we want to give it; and, fundamentally, what exactly was work on 'knowledge about language' supposed to involve?

In the end it was decided that, initially, knowledge about language would constitute a separate unit of study, in order to raise key issues for colleagues and pupils and to clarify the kinds of work we envisaged it might involve.

To try to ensure continuity and progression, we organised the scheme of work so that pupils in years 7, 8 and 9 covered the same eight 'Focus Units' in each year, whilst obviously using increasingly demanding texts and resources and highlighting different aspects from the relevant programmes of study. A map of the eight key stage 3 'Focus Unit' is given on the next page.

The map shows that, for example, children will be reading independently all year round, but there will also be one specific block of time in each year which is used for an independent reading project.

The knowledge about language unit seemed to call for a slightly different arrangement from the other seven units, for it was felt that, in order to achieve a proper coherence in our work, we would need to detail specific areas of study in each of the three years; this would also help us to confirm that in each three or four week block all relevant programmes of study were covered. From the programmes of study we teased out three main aspects: Standard English and regional variation, the evolution of English and contextual and structural variation. We next considered our existing practice and resources and worked out the following pattern for our work, aware that we would also need to devise new resources together and purchase additional texts, etc.

In year 7 the unit, 'Text and Context', comprises discussing and categorising a wide range of texts and extracts, including Standard and non-Standard English, transcripts (so spoken and written structures can be contrasted) and pre-twentieth century texts. The year 8 unit is on the Evolution of English. In year 9 the pupils work on 'Language in the Community', studying the links between the social and structural features of language (e.g. regional variety, written non-Standard English, varieties of Standard English, specialist languages). The year 9 unit also addresses 'language and power' with reference to race, gender, persuasion, etc. (These three units are probably all

YEAR 7	YEAR 8	YEAR 9
Knowledge about language: Text and Context	Knowledge about language: Evolution of the English language	Knowledge about language: Accent, Dialect, Standard English
Independent reading	Independent reading	Independent reading
Shared reading: Narrative text	Shared reading: Narrative text	Shared reading: Narrative text
Shared reading: Drama	Shared reading: Drama	Shared reading: Drama
Poetry	Poetry	Poetry
Autobiography	Autobiography	Biographical/ Community writing
Genres and structures	Genres and structures	Genres and structures
Creating a community/audience	Creating a community/audience	Biographical/ Community writing

interchangeable in terms of content and year group; for example, a different type of work on 'Text and Context' could be done in year 9. The agreed framework has the advantage of conforming loosely to existing practice, though we are aware that much planning and resourcing is still necessary.) Each pupil also keeps an English glossary in a small notebook, used to record an emerging 'English' terminology, with examples of the word or phrase in use (the entry for 'onomatopoeia' is usually quite fun).

The past two years have involved a considerable amount of training and preparation with specific reference to knowledge about language and its function and place in our teaching. We had the advantage of being closely involved with an Avon LINC working party, and benefited from a presentation at a faculty meeting by our local LINC coordinator. Three faculty-based INSET days have been spent on the scheme of work, with knowledge about language receiving special attention, as it has in numerous faculty meetings. In 1990–1991, a large portion of the faculty's delegated training budget was spent on, first, supply cover for colleagues working on the draft

Scheme of Work and, secondly, sending a Faculty member to LINC workshop sessions at the 1991 NATE conference.

We intend to develop language work increasingly in the context of other units (for example: evolution of English with reference to pre-twentieth century poems and plays; work on accent/dialect in relation to narrative texts, etc.); a process that will inevitably lead to a reappraisal of our initial conceptualisation of knowledge about language in the National Curriculum and our approach in the classroom. I expect that by September 1993 the faculty's knowledge about language work will be formally integrated into the other units in the Scheme (with relevant elements of the programmes of study incorporated into existing Focus Units) and will therefore no longer be included as an isolated unit in its own right.

SECONDARY PLANNING 2

NIGEL KENT

Bournside is an 11-18 comprehensive school in Cheltenham; it has 1, 499 pupils and an English department of 15 teachers.

The English department in Bournside School and Sixth Form Centre in 1990 was an experienced and successful one. Its members had grown used to delivering tried and tested units of work, the majority of which had literary texts at their centre. Not surprisingly then, the department was concerned that the National Curriculum might devalue such schemes and require a different content and process inside the classroom.

The knowledge about language element was deemed particularly threatening. Did its presence imply a totally new philosophy of English teaching? Was literature to be squeezed out in favour of a body of not particularly useful linguistic knowledge? Anyway, was not knowledge about language already being taught? Such concerns were probably echoed in English departments across the country, but they had to be addressed if knowledge about language was to be perceived as an exciting new dimension in the English classroom, rather than an imposition.

Our starting point in preparing for the implementation of the National Curriculum was to look at the units we had been teaching and to see what we could salvage. What were we doing already that answered the demands of the National Curriculum for English? Not surprisingly, we found that there was a great deal. However, there were aspects of the knowledge about language strand that were covered on an ad hoc basis, or not at all. Obviously we would have to include such elements, but how? We were at that time deeply suspicious of the statement in the Cox Report that all our pupils would find language 'intrinsically interesting and worthy of study in its own right'. Therefore, we were unwilling to develop modules of work whose main focus was language study.

Instead, we decided to adopt the principle of embedding knowledge about language elements into existing schemes of work. Instead of studying the nature of language for its own sake, we wanted to ensure that the knowledge pupils acquired would have a beneficial impact upon their own language use. Language study would not be seen as an end in itself, but as a means to an end. For example, if pupils engaged in a unit on instructional writing, they might be asked to spend some time looking at the difference between spoken instructions and written instructions and to consider the reasons for the difference. It would be hoped that in doing so they would come to understand that their own instructional language breaks down when it is too close to the language of spoken instructions, thereby prompting them to experiment with language forms that meet the needs of the distant audience more effectively.

We were fortunate to acquire some in-service time to explore this issue. One member of the department had operated a pilot scheme prior to the meeting in both year 7 and year 10 to generate exemplar material. In the morning session, these materials and the work arising from them were discussed by the department. In the second session in the afternoon, each member of staff spent time reworking one of his or her existing units of work in order to include a knowledge about language focus; each then contracted to deliver that unit in the following half-term and report back. Such an approach reduced anxiety regarding knowledge about language, removed the mythology surrounding it and opened up previously unexplored possibilities for supporting pupils' language development.

Having established the principle of exploring knowledge about language in this way, the debate arose concerning whether there were elements of knowledge about language that could be dealt with on a once and for all basis, or, like so many other elements in our subject, could they be revisited on a regular basis throughout the school career of each child? On the basis of some further pilot work conducted to explore this issue, the department is now in the process of constructing a key stage 3 and 4 curriculum, which aims to set out when and how different knowledge about language elements might be explored productively at certain times through secondary school.

Inevitably modifications will be necessary as we acquire greater experience in delivering this element of the National Curriculum. It is early days still, and no doubt our scheme will take time to bed down. Nevertheless, in the light of the failure of educational publishers and writers to tackle knowledge about language in an imaginative and stimulating way, our experience suggests we have found a route to making the study of language 'interesting', relevant and productive.

SECONDARY PLANNING 3

NICK BATCHELAR

Gordano is an 11–18 comprehensive school in Bristol; it has 1,002 pupils and an English department of eight teachers.

It is strange to think that only five or six years ago the phrase 'knowledge about language' did not exist as an off-the-peg item in the education wardrobe; and strange, too, how easily it has slotted into the repertoire of educational shorthand, alongside key stages, SATs, ATs and the rest. In the department in which I worked five years ago, language held an uncertain place in the English curriculum. Aspects of language such as language acquisition, oral histories and multilingualism were regarded as interesting but marginal. Literature held privileged status, while there was an underlying lack of interest in the language worlds of the children we taught. The *Language In Use* folder lay on the shelf gathering dust, despite being 'a good thing'. Its open-ended, empirical spirit of enquiry somehow seemed at odds with the literary/creative emphasis in the department.

The media hysteria surrounding *Curriculum Matters* and, later, the observations on language in *Responses* made us feel defensive and uneasy. The crude equation of 'language' with 'the basics' and 'traditional lessons on grammar, spelling and punctuation' (*Daily Express*) was, we knew, not our agenda for English, but we weren't in truth too sure what we *did* want to do 'about language'. There seemed, beneath all the cries for a 'return to basics', to be a silence about language in our practice.

Then *The Kingman Report* appeared, reassuringly rebutting the plea for 'a return to old-fashioned grammar teaching and learning by rote'. It proposed a very different model of language, but left uncertain what it thought to be the relation between understanding and performance in language. No sooner had Kingman appeared, though, than it was subsumed by Cox and the National Curriculum in English. The chapters on language in *English 5–16* clearly set out an agenda on language that would require us to revise our work, but 'language' was now by no means the only, or the most prominent, aspect of English calling for our attention. The key issues seemed to be:

- How can we ensure that all children have access to all of the English curriculum?
- What kinds of agreements can we make about what we teach?
- How do we arrive at these agreements?
- How do we reference these to the National Curriculum but still ensure that we 'own' the curriculum that we teach?

Knowledge about language, although it was evidently an area we needed to develop, came within the broader framework of rethinking in which we found ourselves.

The business of sitting down together to try and work out what our English curriculum should look like was surprisingly refreshing. It was exciting to exchange and develop ideas; although the department was strong on sharing ideas informally, it seemed extraordinary that we had operated in the past without clear agreements on the curriculum we offered. As a result, there was much duplication of work, with each of us in a sense reinventing our own version of the English curriculum; the particular version each child experienced depended largely on the teacher with whom he or she happened to be.

Initially we planned too restrictively and ended up writing lesson plans for each other. We confused what we wanted all children to experience (e.g. shared reading of a narrative text) with the particular ways in which each teacher might organise that experience (e.g. read *Beowulf*). Gradually a framework emerged which enabled us to reach agreements at the right kind of level to ensure this 'entitlement', while still leaving individual teachers free to innovate. We distinguished between those elements which we felt ran through all aspects of English as we practised it, and those elements which had to be separately planned for as discrete units.

Through discussion and reflection, we moved towards agreement about the on-going practices (e.g. Is access to word-processing routine in English here, or do we have to plan specifically for it? How do we really provide for independent reading?). We then constructed a set of units which, alongside this continuing practice, would form the basis of our planning across key stage 3. These did not specify particular content but mapped opportunities and experiences which each teacher would have to manage in his or her own way. The same units would continue across the key stage, but with a different emphasis in each year.

The units we agreed on were:

Shared reading: narrative text

Shared reading: Poetry

Shared reading: Drama

By marking out particular types of text in this way we did not, of course, mean that this would be the only time that pupils would encounter them; but their place in the framework did imply that planning around particular texts throughout the entire year would not be possible.

Independent reading

Knowledge about language

Aspects of the media

These would all be both part of on-going practice and the focus of a specific unit at some point each year.

Self and others: aspects of autobiography and biography

Working with non-fiction texts: knowledge, beliefs and values

Storymaking: exploring different types of stories; making and telling stories

Open space: an opportunity for pupils to draw on the work they had done elsewhere and set their own agendas as writers and speakers

We referenced both the description of our on-going practice (e.g. the pupils' access to the writing process) and the separate units to the National Curriculum by photocopying the entire programmes of study for key stages 1–4, cutting it all up, and finding a home for all the 'bits' somewhere in our framework. In addition to being about the only manageable way of 'reading' the programmes of study, it proved to be a useful exercise in getting an overview of what this version of the English curriculum would look like. It also gave us a sense of ownership of 'our' scheme of work; we'd made the programmes of study fit the scheme, rather than the reverse.

Having established this framework, we obtained INSET time for teachers to work in teams of two or three on specific units. One important feature of this framework was that it provided scope for teachers to work in their own way within the agreements we made together, which are described both in our own words and in the statements 'pulled down' from the programmes of study.

Knowledge about language features in two main ways in the scheme:

- There are predominantly language-focused units in each year of key stage 3 and in key stage 4, for example, 'The Craft of Writing' in year 7 or 'Varieties of Language' in year 9.
- Knowledge about language is also incidentally linked with other units to which it contributes, for example, the language of school in the 'Self and Others' unit in year 7, or in a comparison of different versions of folk tales in 'Storymaking'.

There is also a 'thread' of knowledge about language running through the practice of English in the department, which might provide unplanned opportunities for developing pupils' 'knowledge about language': for example, understanding of genre in choosing books from the library, or 'language about language' in talking about and revising a piece of writing.

We certainly don't feel that by having a language-focused unit in each year we have 'done' knowledge about language. It's merely a way of ensuring that at some point there is that kind of direct attention to language we so often avoided before.

Alongside these units we've had to do some re-thinking of the connections between the 'big' bits of the English curriculum – e.g. texts, genres – and the 'smaller' bits – patterns of spelling, new words, punctuation. There is a convergence of approaches to literary and non-literary texts, including media texts; a willingness to engage in exploratory enquiry into language and a renewed interest in the language experiences of the children we teach. We are developing a more holistic English course at key stage 4; post 16 we are still stuck with the split between Literature and Communication Studies at A level.

A lot remains to be done to integrate the different approaches to knowledge about language within a coherent English programme, to draw more fully on the understandings about language that children possess and to develop our own understanding of language. However, at least now when anxious parents ask, 'What do you do about spelling and grammar?', I can feel more confident about replying in a way which both meets their anxieties and doesn't trivialise the curriculum we offer. And what better material for a study of language in society than this story of 'grammar', 'basics' and 'standards' which looks set to run for a while yet?

In the final piece in this chapter, Margaret Cook asks: where in a school which is knowledgeable about language would we find evidence of that knowledge? What does it look like in practice?

A WHOLE SCHOOL ISSUE

MARGARET COOK

Classroom practice does not exist in curricular or institutional isolation. Children move between school and home and between teachers within school. They take messages about language from each situation and add their own. Understanding language is a dynamic process subject to many influences. A school's approach to developing knowledge about language will mean negotiating a general understanding among everyone in the school and its community about how language works, how it supports and develops learning and how attitudes and values affect children's use of it. Developing this understanding and monitoring its effects cannot be left to chance. Headteachers and other senior managers who want knowledge about language to make a difference to their school will need to incorporate their school's thinking about it into the school documentation. They will also need to monitor its effects in classrooms, seeing how children use language, what implicit and explicit knowledge about language they show in using it and how they reflect on it.

School documentation

At the very least, this should consist of:

- school and subject policy documents which had been developed collaboratively by the staff and communicated to the school community;
- a school policy on assessment and its recording and reporting;
- schemes of work with specific curriculum aims.

Knowledge about language makes a different contribution to each of these:

- to the school policy in terms of its aims and values and how it views language in teaching and learning;
- to the language policy in describing the nature of language;
- to the assessment policy by establishing criteria for achievement based on how language works and how attitudes and values affect its use;
- by providing a focus for particular schemes of work.

What happens in classrooms

Learning strategies

Because language use is essentially about making choices within a system, it is important that children have the experience of a range of language uses to choose from and some criteria for making these choices. Good language classrooms will have children who:

- change the forms of their own language according to the needs of the situation;
- choose between alternatives;
- compare different language uses.

Classroom practice

A good knowledge about language classroom will have:

- a range of good models of language use in many media and from a variety of cultures;
- activities which involve making differently structured genres;
- children learning how to 'see through' language to the intentions behind it;
- recognition of literature as a central means of enlarging children's repertoire of language use;
- evidence of systematic investigations of language for a recognisable purpose;
- attention paid to the forms of language as the evidence of meaning.

Common activities in these classrooms will be those where language use is compared or changed. For example:

- Group talk to plan something or solve a problem. Here the members of the group are continually reshaping their own ideas to incorporate, or resist, those of others. There are many opportunities to compare ideas, and the language in which they are described, and also to fine tune language to the very immediate audiences and purposes of the group.
- Looking at differences between spoken and written language involves looking at how the forms of language reflect the different purposes, advantages and constraints of two different forms of language. Comparing the two brings out the systematic nature of the forms of each while throwing their difference into relief.
- Looking at language for bias and opinion and seeing through it to other meanings means comparing one obvious and accepted meaning with another and seeing how one set of forms can serve two different purposes.
- Seeing writing as a process involves comparing this version with another, as well as getting a good fit between the forms of the language and the structure and purpose of the writing.
- Having a view of reading as active and interactive means that no single 'correct' meaning of the text is looked for. Instead, the reader sets up different 'readings', checking them against what is meaningful and using the evidence of the forms of language to confirm or deny a number of hypotheses.
- Comparing genres and especially using different genres in response to the demands of a single purpose, involves seeing how different genres are structured and how each can serve a different purpose.

Classrooms in which these kinds of activities are usual are classrooms set up for change, where the acts of comparison and change are commonplace, and children expect to have to adapt their language to accommodate new demands and new insights. These are classrooms where, on the whole, knowledge about language bubbles to the surface without the need for direct planning, and where reflection on language serves the purpose of developing language use.

These are not, however, unplanned classrooms: the thinking which supports them should be that which informs a school's aims and its practice, its approaches to teaching and learning, and the broad range of its teachers' beliefs about what language is and how it should be taught. Providing the day to day contexts through which children grow in their understanding of how language works is certainly a matter for classroom teachers. Making sure that this understanding supports a child's learning throughout his or her school life is a matter for the whole school community.

MEDIUM AND LONG TERM PLANNING: LINKS WITH OTHER DEPARTMENTS

Pupils use language, learn through and about language across the curriculum. Many English departments are aiming to consolidate their work with colleagues in other departments, planning together opportunities for pupils to reflect on the specialist vocabulary, written and spoken genres and learning processes which they need to use. Equally, learning to understand the language and culture of one or more countries and to communicate in those languages is another dimension of pupils' knowledge about language. In Severn Vale School, Gloucestershire, year 8 pupils used the knowledge they had of:

- books written for very young children;
- the writing process;
- the vocabulary and grammar of French, Spanish and English

to produce simple books in three languages for neighbouring primary children to read. This cross-curricular liaison exploited opportunities for pupils to compare and contrast underlying structures and verbal relationships in three languages. Many pupils come to school already bilingual at least – a rich classroom resource. Cross-curriculum staff working parties may find the following statement in the Kingman Report seminal:

It can only be sensible for all teachers of language in a school – whether they are teaching French or Latin, English or Punjabi – to ensure that they are employing the same framework of description for talking about language and employing the same descriptive vocabulary. It can only be sensible to make overt comparisons between languages which the pupils know, so that they can be led to see the general principles of language structure and use, through a coherent and consistent approach.

(*The Kingman Report*, Chapter 4, para: 50)

That chapter goes on to advocate '…the co-ordination of all language teaching within a school….' as 'There can be little doubt that a school which has developed…a co-ordinated language teaching policy will also offer support for the teaching of English, in particular teaching about English language. Such a policy will be of value to teachers both of English and of foreign languages, as well as to those dealing with the language used in the teaching of other subjects' (ibid., Chapter 4, para 51).

REPLICABLE PROCESSES

Despite the diversity of local circumstances, the primary and secondary case studies in this chapter reveal shared discoveries, approaches, beliefs and methodologies. Their approaches to the knowledge about language curriculum, as summarised below, may be helpfully considered by other secondary English departments and primary schools:

- The starting point for staff discussion about the language curriculum is an audit of the school's existing documentation and practice.
- Effective change is most effectively brought about gradually, over time and with the active participation of all members of the team. Curriculum change is created by the team – it is not something which is done to them!
- The language policy or English scheme of work is a dynamic, working document, evolving gradually. The process of drafting it is ongoing, never ending.
- The documentation is a description of what actually happens in classrooms.
- The entitlement of all pupils to a knowledge about language strand in their English curriculum has to be planned for systematically. No longer can a language curriculum be so loosely planned, so ad hoc that its delivery is almost entirely dependent on the enthusiasm of the teacher to whom a pupil happens to be allocated for a year – or longer!

Pupil-centred

All planning is based on the conviction that pupils know a lot about language and on the expectation that some of the most stimulating language study will continue to arise from pupils' chance comments or questions. The teacher's timely, sensitive, well-informed intervention at such magic moments will develop pupils' knowledge about language and further excite their engagement with language.

Differentiation and progression

Language development is recursive rather than linear. Therefore, a language scheme will have built-in opportunities for pupils to revisit language areas (e.g. differences between spoken and written language) each time being able to consolidate their existing knowledge and be taken forward in their thinking and developing their knowledge about language. (See the article 'Differentiation in the Knowledge about Language Curriculum'.)

Primary-secondary-FE partnership

Such systematic planning will help to provide a coherent English curriculum which pays due attention to progression and continuity between years and key stages. This has implications for record keeping and planning for curriculum links between primary schools, secondary schools and, in some areas, FE or sixth form colleges.

Knowledge about language – incidentally

Inherent in a staff's management of teaching and learning styles are opportunities for pupils to use, develop and reflect on their knowledge about language. For example, the process approach to writing involves pupils discussing drafts with peers and/or teacher. Such collaboration could include pupils in discussing: the organisation of a whole text and of individual sentences within a text; vocabulary choice; use of verb tense and mood; spelling and punctuation; the use of language to create a desired effect on the reader; appropriateness of a form of writing for a particular audience and purposes....

Knowledge about language – we're already doing it!

Many aspects of language study are already built into and contribute to existing topics and units of work. For example, a shared reading and discussion of Barry Hines's *Kes* provides meaningful contexts for pupils' observations on: regional and social variations in English; accents and dialects and attitudes to such variations; the forms and functions of Standard English; some of the main characteristics of literary language and how they convey meaning; some of the main differences between speech and writing...

A class enjoying the Ahlbergs' *The Jolly Postman* will have the opportunity to discuss most of the above as well as rhyme, rhythm, features of a range of chronological and non-chronological texts, styles of handwriting, the relationship between text and pictures, and between this text and other texts which they have read.

Terminology

Much of the above discussion can take place without using metalanguage. However, in the context of discussing a pupil's piece of writing or making observations on a piece of language data generated by a pupil, a shared, precise technical language can prove economical and precise.

A shared terminology is also helpful when pupils engage in the continuous self-assessment process, for example, when writing their critical reflections on unit top sheets; when writing entries in reading or talk diaries or learning journals; when making an informed selection, assisted by a teacher, of their most successful pieces of writing during a year across a range of genres, for inclusion in a continuous assessment, GCSE or Records of Achievement portfolio.

Resource implications

Creating new explicit language units or topics and/or providing a sharper linguistic focus for some existing ones prompts a survey of current resource provision and use. As a result, teams may set about supplementing existing resources and collating data (e.g. adverts which span 100 years, collections of boys' and girls' birthday cards) which could be used flexibly. All agree that no one 'course' book can meet a school's requirements, nor could it be expected to do so, for knowledge about language is integral to work in English and to all language learning: it cannot be reduced to nor effectively learned via bolt-on sets of decontextualised grammar exercises.

INSET

'A' level and GCSE moderations, TVEE and cluster group INSET sessions and local NATE/UKRA meetings can provide the opportunity for departments to share their good ideas and resources for knowledge about language units of work.

POSTSCRIPT

In classrooms all around England and Wales, pupils and teachers are investigating language. The case studies in this collection are the tip of the iceberg. Just as the pupils, teachers and advisory teachers whose work is represented here have shared their endeavours with a wider audience, so we hope that others will in the future share theirs through: local newsletters and publications; regional NATE groups; contact with advisors and HMI. This book marks the beginning of that journey.

References

Ahlberg, A. and Ahlberg, J. (1986) *The Jolly Postman* (Heinemann)

Avery, V. (1969) *London Morning* (Arnold-Wheaton)

Browne, A. (1986) *Piggybook* (Magnet)

Burningham, J. (1982) *Avocado Baby* (Jonathan Cape; Armada Books, 1986)

Carle (1970) *The Very Hungry Caterpillar* (Hamish Hamilton; Penguin, 1974)

Carter, R. (ed.) (1990) *Knowledge About Language and the Curriculum: the LINC Reader* (Hodder & Stoughton)

Central Advisory Council for Education (CACE) (1967) *Children and their Primary Schools* (the Plowden Report) (HMSO)

Cooke, T. (1989) *Mammy, Sugar Falling Down* (Hutchinson; Beaver Books, 1990)

Cox, B. (1991) *Cox on Cox* (Hodder & Stoughton)

Crystal, D. (1987) *The Cambridge Encyclopedia of Language* (Cambridge University Press)

Dahl, R. (1981) *George's Marvellous Medicine* (Jonathan Cape; Penguin, 1982)

Dahl, R. (1982) *Revolting Rhymes* (Jonathan Cape; Penguin, 1984)

Derewianka, B. (1990) 'Rocks in the Head' in Carter, R. (ed.) (1990) *Knowledge About Language and the Curriculum: the LINC Reader* (Hodder & Stoughton)

DES (1978) *Primary Education in England: a Survey by HM Inspectors of Schools* (HMSO)

DES (1986) *Curriculum Matters 1: English from 5–16* (HMSO)

DES (1986) *English from 5 to 16: the Responses to Curriculum Matters 1* (HMSO)

DES (1988) *Report of the Committee of Inquiry into the Teaching of the English Language* (HMSO)

DES (1989) *Report of the English Working Party 5–16* (HMSO)

Dixon, J. and Stratta, L. (1986) 'Argument in the Teaching of English: a Critical Analysis' in Wilkinson, A. (ed.) *The Writing of Writing* (Open University)

Doughty, P., Pearce, J. and Thornton G. (1971) *Language in Use: Schools Council Programme in Linguistics and English Teaching* (Edward Arnold)

Freeborn, D. (1986) *Varieties in English* (Macmillan)

Freeborn, D. (1987) *A Course Book in English Grammar* (Macmillan)

Fuller, S. (1990) *Language File* (BBC/Longman)

Goodman, Y. (1985) 'Kidwatching: observing children in the classroom' in Jaggar, A. and Smith-Burke, M. T. (eds.) *Observing the Language Learner* (International Reading Association)

Graham, R. (1990) *Crusher is coming!* (Collins)

Hawkins, E. (1984) *Awareness of Language: an introduction* (Cambridge University Press)

Hines, B. (1968) *Kes* (Michael Joseph; Penguin, 1969)

Hoffman and Burrows (1990) *My Grandmother is coming* (Beaver Books)

Hughes, T. (1968) *The Iron Man* (Faber & Faber)

ILEA English Centre (1981) *The Languages Book* (ILEA English and Media Centre)

Jones, T. (1990) *Fairy Tales* (Penguin)

Magorian, M. (1983) *Goodnight, Mr Tom* (Penguin)

Mahy, M. (1986) *Non-Stop Nonsense* (Magnet; Mammoth, 1990)

Marsh, G. (1988) *Teaching Through Poetry* (Hodder & Stoughton)

Martin, J. R. (1984) 'Language Register and Genre' in *Children's Writing Course: A Reader* (Deakin University Press)

Martin, J. R. and Rothery, J. (1989) 'Exploring and Explaining Factual Writing in Primary School' (Paper delivered at ARA Conference, Perth, mimeo)

Naipaul, V. S. (1971) *Miguel Street* (Penguin)

Nathan, A. and Hedly, S. (1989) *The Cat With Two Tales* (Macdonald)

Robinson, R. (1984) *Frankly Frankie* (Macmillan)

Rodgers, M. (1976) *Freaky Friday* (Penguin)

Schools Council (1985) *World Studies 8–13* (Oliver & Boyd)

Seely, J. (1991) *Language Live* (Heinemann)

Thompson and Fairclough (1988) *Making a Book* (Franklin Watts)

White, J. (1986) 'The Writing on the Wall: Beginning or End of a Girl's Career?' in *Women's Studies International Forum*, Volume 5, Number 5 (Pergamon Press)

Willis, J. (1988) *Dr Xargle's Book of Earthlets* (Andersen Press)

Willis, J. (1990) *Dr Xargle's Book of Earth Tiggers* (Andersen Press)

Wilson, B. (1988) *Ging, Gang Goolie, It's an Alien* (Young Lions)